DISAPPEARING

DISAPPEARING

THE STORY OF A MODERN WOULD-BE NOMAD, THE PEOPLE HE UPSET AND THE MANY WHO DIED

CHRIS HEAL

Published by Chattaway and Spottiswood
Milverton Taunton, Somerset

www.disappearing.candspublishing.org.uk
disappearing@candspublishing.org.uk

A catalogue record for this book is available from
the British Library

5 4 3 2 1

ISBN 978-1-9161944-0-3

Design by Vivian@Bookscribe

Printed and bound by T J International, Padstow, Cornwall, UK

For

Sam

and

Ismail, Mariam and Sara

and

Juliet Samuel, columnist,
who called for the corrective of a modern Don Quixote,
a bolshy pensioner with a mission

Old men ought to be explorers
Here and there does not matter
We must be still and still moving
Into another intensity

T S Eliot, 'East Coker', *Four Quartets*

He is by nature led
To peace so perfect that the young behold
With envy, what the old man hardly feels

William Wordsworth, *Animal Tranquillity and Decay, A Sketch*

The publisher of *Disappearing* acknowledges the permission of Faber and Faber Limited to quote extracts from the works of T S Eliot.

CONTENTS

LETTER FROM THE AUTHOR, MAY 2019

Thank you for picking up this book. I need to explain to you, and to myself I suppose, why I've written it. My story is mostly about today and the near today. I have had my share of tilting at decrepit windmills and battling against armies of cloudy sheep with about as much success as Don Quixote. Cervantes borrowed the guts of his tale from an old Moorish author but, for you, I have had to lean on my own creaking memory.

People who don't know each other and, actually, don't know who I am, are looking for me. These are people who use their power casually and don't like to be embarrassed. They are amoral and righteous; freedom is not a word they recognise as suitable for ordinary souls.

What's set these people against me? I can count more than a score of things I've done that they may not like, some of them not even morally wrong or illegal. This book, then, is my attempt to lay the chase bare in front of anyone I can interest. My truth will be in print. Whoever wants to do me harm might not like the exposure and decide to call it off. That's what this book is about.

Fantasy? Could my exposures instead prick some secret best left mouldering in a memory? The last thing I want is to re-energise a manhunt. I still hope that I can slip away for the rest of my years.

Book-readers, like you and me, are the most thoughtful, educated and generally sensitive people. Of course, we try to believe in the rule of law, but it often isn't a fair or sensible world. I've had my fill of play-safe bureaucracies and uncaring police forces. None of them fight for the individual. I want to share with you my struggle to build an alternative that suited me. The book is also about that journey.

I endorse Quixote's conceit that individuals can be right while society is quite wrong. Quixote searched for long-lost chivalry; I hankered after a teenage concept of freedom – both reasonable objectives, don't you think? Were the Don and I equally insane and useless when facing choices between reality and adventure?

Some of my targets were poorly chosen, I admit, often based on indignation rather than common-sense. But, other times, I know I was spot on. I'm not putting my hand up for everything that happened, but I'm not pushing round a wheelbarrow of guilt.

Whatever, there was no poorly-brained Sancho Pança to dissuade me with pragmatic arguments or an exhausted horse to carry me home. I bruised important egos and in doing so saw too much sudden violence.

I don't have sleepless nights about yesterday; my sleepless nights are about tomorrow.

Nowadays, anyone can assume the cloak of the offended and demand dire retribution. The internet is the 'largest and most abundantly stocked pantry of grievance in the history of mankind'. Weak souls, the perpetually upset, political opportunists and the plain nasty scan the electronic horizons for chances to make a fuss, to introduce hurt and chaos, and to claim their moment in the sun. A couple of times I was dragged into this unreasonable media mire. Unkind and wilful criticism had a souring effect.

I tell you frankly that if you recognise yourself in the previous paragraph, if you wallow in social correctness, don't read this book. I promise you that if you go ahead anyway, you will be offended, hopefully many times. And, what is worse for you, you won't be able to vent your ire on me because you won't be able to find me. I will never see what you write.

Where to start?

I was a battered and mentally abused child. If what happened to me in the 1950s were to happen today, a posse of social workers and counsellors would be at the door. I survived and I certainly don't want any retrospective pity. While not inured to damaged minds and ruined bodies, I now have a tougher skin than most, but I can still be disturbed. I am a loner with a slow fuse that will spark when some bully or faceless official interferes. Then I prefer direct action and enjoy my revenge taken with ice. An extreme example, I know, but if I ever found Qaddura Mohammed Abd Al-Hamid, I would kill him and watch him die.

I have a deep disgust of the ubiquitous surveillance of people like you and me by the big corporations and the modern state. When the irritation got too much, I wondered whether it was possible to just get up and go. Could I disengage from all records – government, business and financial

– to evade scrutiny and to escape personal history? As a hobby, I built a library of covert identities. I had no police or conventional military record, no declared DNA, no fingerprints on file, no close family and nobody with whom I maintained contact. Planning for my disappearance became a way of life: nationality, accreditations, internet, mobile phone, bank account, credit cards, house and property were all rejected.

I am possibly the last person to attempt what I have tried to do. As technology takes its grip, it will soon not be possible or permitted. As a consequence of my freedom, I believed I could not be found. I could commit any act as long as I was not caught in its commission. In minutes, I could always become someone else. But the truth is not always a good friend. Somewhere, somehow, I made a mistake. My persona, my mask shall we say, slipped.

I have a love of painting and architecture, not by me I might add for I can hardly draw a wiggly line. Perhaps, as you'll find, this determination to engage with great art has in a roundabout way brought me to my current state. I don't know who is being chased, one of my old selves or one or all of the people I became. Adept at losing my identity, there seems no way to regain it. Now, I'm 'nobody' and I am alone and on the run.

I have sent almost thirteen chapters of my story to a publisher in the UK and paid them to print and publicise it in a few months with or without any final words that I might live to write.

Foremost, I just want to be left alone. I don't think I have wronged a free society; I think that a corrupt society has wronged me.

I sign myself Chris Heal, but that is not who I am as I will explain. There's a risk, I know, that I might lose your empathy. Promise me, you won't decide without knowing all of the facts?

Chris Heal
Marrakech
May 2019

NOTES FROM THE PUBLISHER, MAY 2019

This book represents an unusual project for us in that we have never met the author whom we identify as Dr Chris Heal, a man in his seventies. Last year, we agreed a contract with him by email which left us considerable freedom of action on a part-seen manuscript. Earlier this year, after hearing nothing for two consecutive months, under the terms of the Agreement, we accessed his cloud storage. We found what we thought to be a remarkable, unconventional, but unfinished, narrative which begins with Heal's childhood and explains how he became the man he was. There are also detailed chapters on the decisions and mechanics of how he quit society. The closing chapters detail his struggles as he lived 'off grid'. We believe the whole catches the mood of the moral apocalypse facing the United Kingdom.

We have conducted some limited research and have established that an author called Chris Heal, a doctor of philosophy from Bristol University, wrote an extensive social history about the Gerth brothers, u-boat commanders, before, during and after the First World War. It was called *Sound of Hunger* and published by Unicorn in June 2018. After moderate sales, Heal was interviewed by the BBC and his comments on Brexit and Germany provoked international controversy. We have also established that the events of which he writes, in the UK, notably in Hampshire; in Biafra in Nigeria; and in Kenya, Morocco, Portugal and Sri Lanka are, as far as we can see, historically correct and we have no reason to doubt their veracity or his involvement. Overall, his story rings true to us with the great single exception of the metaphor of the assassinations in Brussels last year.

We would like to make these points:

- Opinions, predictions, unanswered questions and occasional inaccuracies are as per Heal's manuscript. We accept no responsibility.

- Heal admitted to us that he had altered the names of some of the protagonists, and of a few of the places where events occurred, on the basis that these changes may protect us and him from litigation and innocent individuals from unpleasant intrusions. As a further device to these ends, Heal made the timeline of his story deliberately inaccurate at some points. This explains, for instance, why the book will be published in July 2019 whereas Heal's story concludes a few months later.

- Heal indicated that he sometimes read apposite descriptions of places and activities that he did not believe he could better in the time he had. Those descriptions that were specified by him, or he asked us to trace for him, are indicated by simple endnotes so that due credit can be given. A short reading list of these publications is also included.

- During our investigations, we gathered supporting illustrations and made four maps, none of which Heal specified, but which we have included for the reader's interest.

- Finally, Heal begins each chapter with a quote from the works of T S Eliot, mostly from *The Waste Land*. He gave no explanation of this, but we decided to follow his wishes as, clearly, he saw these extracts as pertinent. His selection may be no more than homage, but we suspect there is a deeper point. The relevance of several of these quotations are immediately apparent, others only after reflection, while some remain opaque. We believe there is a clue in the title, *The Waste Land*, and in Eliot's other poetry up to 1930, and his view of the awful traps facing humanity. At first sight, *Disappearing* (*Tilting at Windmills* was Heal's suggested title), as with much of Eliot's work, may seem disconnected. However, there is an underlying form which, we believe, brings most things into place.

Chattaway & Spottiswood
Taunton
May 2019

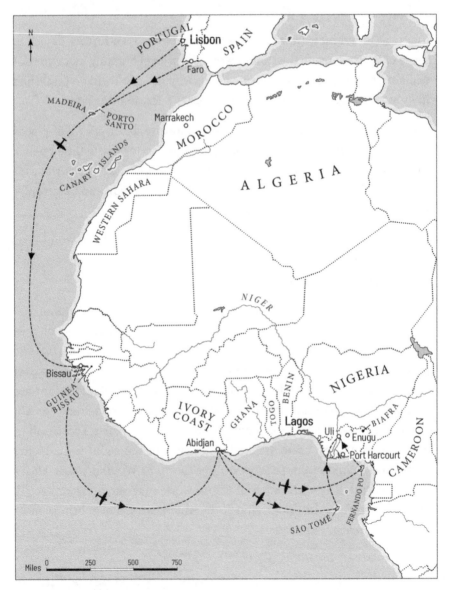

Map 1. European nations sided with Biafra, directly or tacitly, against the Nigerian, British and Russian sea and air blockade. They facilitated well over 7,000 mercy and armament relief flights in the three years of war. The greatest help was provided by the Portuguese, Britain's oldest ally. Aircraft from Lisbon and Faro refuelled at Porto Santo, Bissau and São Tomé, all Portuguese territory; at Abidjan in the Ivory Coast, independent, but with a strong French influence; and at the Spanish island of Fernando Po. Aircraft flying to and from Biafra took wide sweeps out to sea after each staging-post to avoid embarrassing neutral African countries and to stay clear of British and Nigerian-controlled radar and fighters.

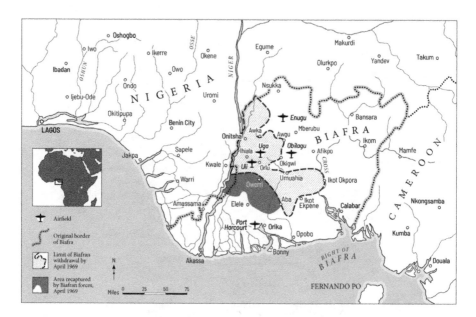

Map 2. The sea and air blockade and the ever-tightening squeeze on Biafran territory meant that, by 1969, it was impossible to feed the indigenous population and the flood of refugees from federal massacres. The Nigerians held the coast and the oil refineries. The loss of the airports at Enugu, Obilagu and Port Harcourt forced almost complete reliance on large air freighters landing at night on the converted road strip at Uli. The dawn trap against a marauding Nigerian MiG 17F by two DC-3 Dakotas was launched simultaneously from the Uga and Uli airstrips.

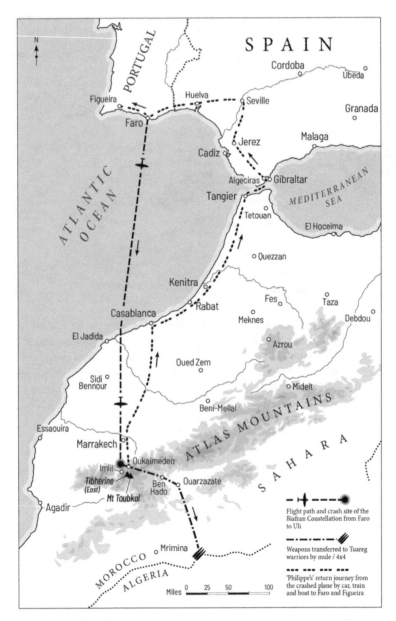

Map 3. The flight path of the Lockheed Constellation airliner in December 1969 flying armaments from Faro to the Portuguese island of São Tomé for transfer to the airstrip at Uli in Biafra. After losing three engines within five minutes, the aircraft crashed into an upper slope of Mount Tibherine next door to Morocco's highest peak, Toubkal, in the Atlas Mountains. Its remains are visible today. Berber tribesmen acquired the small arms and, over New Year, transferred the heavier weapons south and bartered them with their Tuareg cousins from Mali.

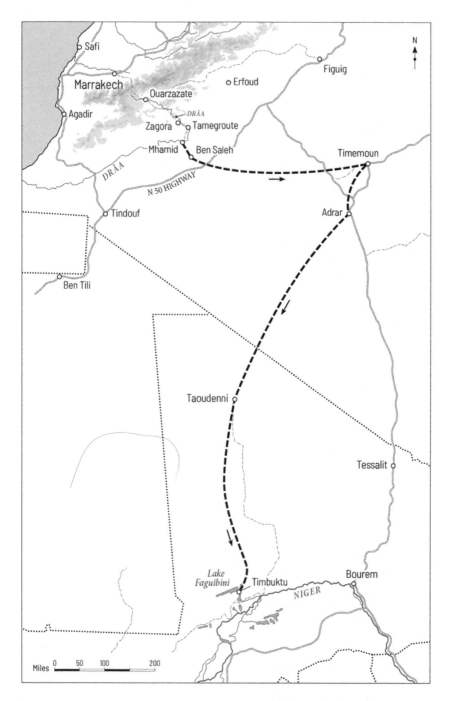

Map 4. The route of Heal's ill-fated attempt in 2019, assisted by Berber tribesmen, to cross the Sahara unobserved from Mhamid in southern Morocco by camel to Timbuktu.

ILLUSTRATIONS

Section 1, following page 36:

European viper
Advertisement for airline pilots for BEA / BOAC, mid-1960s
Pete Crew, Clogwyn du'r Arddu, 1960s
'Solo' de Havilland Chipmunk, Hamble
Hamble airfield, 2005
The Victory Inn, Hamble, 2019
Spectator attack on Harold Wilson, 1968
Emeka Odumegwu Ojukwu
Kwashiorkor, Biafran war, about 1969
BUA DC-3
BUA Handley Page Dart Herald
Frederick Forsyth
Harold Wilson
Heal's written-off DC-3, 1969
Offloading British armoured cars, Nigeria, after 1967
Heal's ex-Lufthansa DC-3, Abidjan, 1969
Nigerian MiG-17, about 1968
Last flight of Heal's Flughjalp DC-6, São Tomé, 1969
Heal's Lockheed L-749A Constellation before lease to Biafra, 1967
Constellation payload: M1 Rifle and M1 Carbine
Berber cave enclosure
Aza and *Hand of Fatima* pendants

Section 2, following page 96:

Associated Press Telex, 1970
Crash site, Mount Tibhirine, Marrakech, 2015
St Mary the Virgin, Old Alresford
Ray Tindle, retirement, 2017
Bomb damage, Norfolk Hotel, Nairobi, 1980
Mark Zuckerberg, 2018
The Snake Goddess, Heraklion Archaeological Museum, about 1500 BC
Moonstone, Polonnaruwa, about 1150
Michelangelo Merisi da Caravaggio, *St Jerome Writing*, Valetta, 1607-8
William of Rubruk, *Mongol nomads*, 1243
Heleen Levano, *Gypsy Memorial*, Amsterdam, 1978
Women of Ravensbrück, Amsterdam, 1975

Vincent Van Gogh, *Landscape at Twilight*, 1890
Martin Selmayr and Jean-Claude Juncker
Assassination, L'aube sur Aÿ, Brussels, 2018
Makarov 9 mm pistol

Section 3, following page 192:

James Rouse, *La Belle Alliance*, Waterloo, 1815
Claude Monet, *Water Lilies*, after 1916
Reina Sofia Museum, Madrid, 2018
Alexander Calder, *Carmen*, 1974
Marc Pataut exhibition, 2018
Pablo Picasso, *Guernica*, 1937
Sandro Botticelli, *Boccaccio's Decameron*, 1487
Atocha Train Station, Madrid, 2019
Grand Café de la Poste, Marrakech, 2019
Marrakech apartment, 2019
Street of home of Al-Hamid, Marrakech, 2019
52 days to Timbuktu, Zagora, 2018
Saharan horned viper
Resurrection plant
Asso's silver Southern Star, 2019
Black Beauty meteorite, 2.1 billion years old
Amkssa, 2019

1. FREEDOM TO GROW

A current under sea
Picked his bones in whispers. As he rose and fell
He passed the stages of his age and youth
Entering the whirlpool.[1]

These days I can barely remember my parents nor do I believe that I ever missed them when they had gone. I was alone apart from a distant cousin who, it was said, looked a bit like me. There were no close relatives on either side; certainly none interested enough to swap Christmas cards, let alone visit.

My mother, my father claimed, was handsome in her younger days; this I can believe. She was young when she married my father who was her senior by many years and she was middle-aged when I was born. She came from a family of French Protestants, natives of La Rochelle on the Atlantic coast. Her family, named Jomas, fled with perhaps a million others when bad King Louis, egged on by the Pope, revoked the Edict of Nantes and set about wholesale religious persecution. They escaped the massacres by a few months. With little money, just a few louis d'ors in their purse, they knew the vital skill of felt hat-makers, a trade which was little practised in England but much valued. They carried a bible and a couple of old swords which had seen service for their religion and drifted with other craft families to Bristol where the city fathers provided a church, Gaunt's Chapel, and the freedom to worship in their own language.

I recall only two stories. The first was a pleasant irony. When the felt-makers left France there was no one left to make stylish creations for the French nobility or the red skullcaps for the cardinals in Rome. As a result, both ordered their hats from a celebrated manufactory in Protestant Wandsworth in south London. The demand was high, so part of the work was contracted to Bristol where my forebears agreed to make hats for their recent persecutors often with traces of human excrement worked into the fabric. The second was the skill of fluent French which my mother passed on to me. She would often sing Huguenot hymns while moving about the house. One still sticks in my mind for I worked at its translation:

Thou hast provided for us a goodly earth;
And made us free of bad and intrusive Governance;
Thou waterest her furrows,
Thou sendest rain into the little valleys thereof,
Thou makest it soft with the drops of rain, and blessest the increase of it.

As for my father, I think he hated me from before we ever met. He was jealous of my mother's attention and would shriek with rage whenever he thought he was short-changed of affection. Human beings are born too soon and I had a lengthy stay at my mother's breast. Like all babies, I came to rely on my mother against a universe of physical and psychological dangers. My father intruded violently into this attachment and, therefore, became the enemy. I was never jealous of him for I coveted nothing he stood for: a simmering neurosis, possibly, but my feelings soon grew into independence and outward antipathy. I was curious about Oedipus and Hamlet when I came to read their stories, but I never saw myself in their place.

My father's tempers were legendary and feared within our little family. Three Christmas lunches in a row were snatched from the table and thrown into the dustbin as punishments; my mother then having to make him a sandwich while the rest of us did without. He would lash out; my mother was often bruised in places which could be hidden; my brother was feared dead one time; and several times after a perceived slight I came to with a singing head after crashing into a table or skirting board.

There were many small cruelties, a list too long to recount, bar just this one. From before I can remember I loved two constant companions, teddy bears, one blue and one yellow, named Adolphus and Theophilus. When I was four, my mother horrified me by deciding they needed a wash. My father came into the kitchen during the debate, took the bears in one hand, my ear in the other, and marched all of us to the back garden. I was made to stand and watch while he lit a small fire of sticks and burned my best friends.

It was time I 'grew up, time to be a man', he said, and hit me across the head for crying. I remember being angry with my mother for not intervening. From then on, I plotted to kill my father and would spend hours drawing torture machines into which his begging body would be fed to be stripped of skin, blinded and boiled alive in acid.

I had just one sibling, my brother, four years older; a beautiful child with an angelic face, blue eyes to my black, and light chestnut hair. His face was the mirror of his mind. I knew of no more amiable a person and he was loved. He learned his alphabet, I was often told, in a few hours. In a day or two he could decipher the names of people, places and businesses on doors, on houses and over shop windows. He grew to stand in the centre of company. I became a lover of quiet corners, delighted to leave the room and to sit for hours with a book in hand.

Perhaps no two brothers were more unlike than we two: 'as light is opposed to darkness, he was a happy, brilliant and cheerful child to my sad and melancholy being.'[2] Once, in North Wales, I saw, far below, a stream with rapid waters sparkling in the sunshine. Nearby, in a granite basin with steep sides, slumbered a deep, dark lagoon, shaded by black pines and yews. It was a wild spot with white-necked ravens hovering and croaking, magpies chattering, and I heard the distant mews of circling buzzards. I looked down on the gay river and then at the dark lake close by and I thought of my brother and myself.

During a coastal holiday in France, in the early evening, we brothers were playing near the dunes. Mother was looking at wild flowers and father was fretting for a glass of wine. A bright yellow and, to my eye, beautiful object appeared at the top of the bank and gliding down began to move across the sandy lane, like a golden line of light. I sprang forward and seized it near the middle. It lay inert as I looked intently.

My brother began to shriek, 'Mummy, he's holding a viper.'

He tried to knock the snake from my hand. The viper raised its large triangular head menacing my brother. I glimpsed my mother running and my father looking away. Standing for a moment almost erect, the reptile launched and its fangs closed between my brother's eyes. Wrenched from my grasp and hissing furiously, it disappeared. My brother fell to his knees, screaming, and within seconds slumped to the ground in a coma.

My mother and I carried him to our rented apartment while I watched as my brother's head swelled, turning black and yellow. My father retired to another room saying to call him if needed. No one called.

By the time the ambulance arrived, my brother's skin was ice cold and clammy. He was still unconscious, but vomiting and his short trousers were stained with diarrhoea. The crew declared his pulse feeble, his breathing shallow and all the while he tossed and spasmed and moaned. The discolouration was etched across his whole head and neck as if he were an alien. I never saw him again; I was not allowed to. I was told nothing could have been done because of the amount of venom injected and its placement. The body was incinerated within hours on medical instruction, perhaps to guard the family against the sight.

I was just ten years old. No one discussed the incident with me in any detail, except for a brief examination by the coroner back in England. I was unperturbed and people remarked within my hearing that I was in a strange state.

'Did you know what it was when you saw it?'

'I saw it was a snake, sir'.

'Why did you pick it up? Weren't you frightened?'

'I picked it up, sir, because it was beautiful. I didn't know I was supposed to be frightened.'

'Have you ever heard of a viper? Did you know they could kill people?'

'I've read about them and seen pictures, but I never thought it was dangerous like that. It did not seem bothered by me and I showed it to my brother who was upset. After it bit him, it just slithered away. I was sorry to see it go. I'm sorry that my brother is dead. It was horrible.'

There was no choice but to declare an accidental death although I still experienced my father's blame. Over time, his wrath grew as he told of the importance of his role, the terrible sights he had to bear and the uselessness of my mother which brought her to tears. I never saw her happy again. My parents' conflicts became part of our daily life. I caught both of them, in their own way, looking at me with a bewildered look. It wasn't until much later that I realised what my mother was thinking, but not saying. Often, I slipped out through the back door because I had nothing to offer and did not want to be trapped in the cross-fire.

I spent all the hours I could taking long walks; there was little interest in my absences. I made myself sandwiches and ate out. I suspected that home was quieter, at least less tense, without me. I was happier alone with my thoughts about far away countries where I knew I belonged. I dreamed of the day when I did not need to return, but could always go on, ever curious. My stories in class had nothing to do with England. I was from the Urals. My parents were not my parents at all. I was an orphan of a nomadic chieftain. My family tried to escape across the river frontier in the dead of winter: boat slewing through the ice, rifle fire from the black trees, blood in the snow, sole survivor. One girl burst into tears. The headmistress suggested to my mother that I might see a psychiatrist.[3] I didn't go, of course; my father would never have allowed mental illness in the family.

I was star-struck by the simplicity of people who lived without permanent homes and carried little with them, their separation from the rules of foreigners and their timeless vitality. When a family of gypsies parked their caravan in a common field a couple of miles away, I often visited them and was welcomed. There were three boys near my own age with whom I played football.

One school morning as we sat around the open fire waiting for water to boil for tea, I told the story of my brother's death. I was asked to recount what happened in detail. At first, I took this interest as a part of the everyday gypsy closeness with animals and the ways of the natural world. There was much nodding of heads and short comments in their strange language. My handling of the viper was dissected and the grandmother who sat listening entered the conversation. On her instruction, I was taken to a black pony, bought as an eventual trade for a replacement for one of their two draught animals. It was renowned for its quick temper and we boys were warned to keep our football away from its hooves. I was led to the pony's neck and my hosts withdrew. I stroked the dark hair and the animal nuzzled me. I felt a great peace and confidence.

'See if you can mount him, boy.'

I did with a rope rein, but without saddle or blanket, and walked him around for a few minutes.

'See if you can get him to trot.'

And away we went. As he reached a canter and I started to slide about because of a lack of strength in my knees, the pony reacted and altered his gait and posture, and I was righted. When I got back, nothing was said for a while.

Then the grandmother spoke. 'Had you not noticed that the dogs never bark when the boy is coming, but run to him and welcome him?'

After the Second World War, my father began his career as a detective in the Post Office. Into the sixties, he gained increasingly senior positions in general management and we three moved from town to town. There were several new schools, but I was always faced with established cliques whose pupils had known each other for almost as long as they could remember. They had fought their personal battles and accepted their social ranking. I made a few friends after many a taunt and bloody fight, but recognised that my closest mates were the playground misfits and solitary characters. Since those days, although I sometimes looked for company, especially with women, I do not think I ever understood loneliness.

My father's investigative skills were never far away; he was always keen to uncover some lie or misdemeanour within his own domain. Once, head deep in a book, I asked the meaning of the 'Hippocratic Oath'. A few days later on a Friday, I proudly brought home a copy of a general knowledge test from school. My father glanced through it and pounced on the question that asked the meaning of the 'Hippocratic Oath'. It was proof positive that I had cheated and had prior knowledge of the test in which I had come a clear top. I was badly smacked about the head and confined to my room without food for the weekend. I got out down the drainpipe and visited the gypsy family in the hope of getting something for the pain and cuts, but they had gone leaving only flattened grass and a circle of stones enclosing a wooden arrow and some stick letters which I could not decipher. I knew it was gypsy women who keep their men on the move. I all but followed.

I never understood why my father believed himself popular with his men at work. He seemed respected as a manager, but I sensed an ambivalence that suggested more to it than I could fathom. Without his knowledge, for he would never have agreed, I arranged a meeting with the trade union shop steward in his office in West Bromwich to give me background for a school project. The man could not speak more highly of my father and congratulated me, winking all the while, on my choice of parent. The essay did not fare well, being deemed too political.

It was about this time that my father received a hint that his position warranted him buying a car. He was an appalling driver; the rumour was that an arrangement had to be made with a retired postman who had become an examiner. My father had no understanding of the simplest machinery, let alone the complexities of a petrol engine. He had been told that, if unused each day, the car, a black Hillman Minx, should be started once a week and run for at least five minutes. Each Sunday, my mother and I were marched to sit in the car in the garage while the car was started after pre-flight checks:

'Doors all shut? Don't just say "Yes", check each one, idiot. Indicators flashing? Answer me. Are they flashing? All the right lights on?'

And here we stayed while the carbon monoxide billowed around us and my father counted the time on his watch. Once I had German measles, confined to bed, but was still called out for the ritual ceremony otherwise the car could not have enjoyed its weekend exercise and therefore an expensive mechanic would be needed.

With my father a little more confident, he began our Sunday morning drives, not for pleasure, of course, but so the car could have a run and that he might be seen out with his family. These were times of high tension when all my hatred of my father welled up. I was deputed to sit in the back and to navigate. My job was to give a running commentary on turnings, road signs, other traffic's intentions, our route, and to anticipate hazards. My mother and I were not allowed to speak about ordinary matters because this would distract the driver.

Any error was a navigational problem; fortunately or unfortunately, I was at home with maps and road signage. My father had no understanding or empathy for other road users. He concentrated on what he was doing inside the car and when he felt the time was right for some manoeuvre he executed it as of right. One outing, we were crossing a river bridge in a West Midlands town after which we were supposed to turn left. In front of us was an open lorry carrying scaffolding poles which hung over the back and had a few pieces of red cloth attached as warnings. I gave the instruction to turn, but my father was so stressed by the bridge and some traffic lights that it was too late for him.

He wrenched around to scream at me. My lapse meant he would have to drive 'for another hour' to get back on the agreed route. Diversions were not allowed. I was a 'complete and absolute failure'. It was the last thing he ever said to me.

The lorry stopped in traffic and my father, concentrating on me with spittle drooling from his mouth, did not notice and kept driving. I think my mother just froze in the passenger seat. I saw what was going to happen in a long second before it did. The scaffolding extended far enough to reach over our bonnet and through our windscreen. My mother took a blow to the side of her head, caving in part of her skull and I hope she died instantly without pain. Another pole caught my father mid-chest, lifting him from his seat. It pierced him far enough for some red rag to show through his back and he dangled there. He was still looking at me in the rear seat when he died and I had just enough time to tell him how pleased I was. I remembered and missed my teddies.

I sat for a while, then got out of the car and walked to the side of the road. For a full minute nobody realised the seriousness of the accident. I might as well have not been there. A woman began screaming. I walked over the bridge and hitchhiked home without incident. There was the luxury of four lamb chops and two bottles of beer as I watched our tiny television. I wondered if I might have nightmares that night, but such is the whimsicality, the illogic of dreams and the subconscious, that my sleep was untroubled. Next morning, I felt refreshed and cheerful. The police called, but I was at school. We met during my lunch break. I was a little shocked by their news and accepted comfort from two teachers.

'No, Sergeant, I was not surprised when my parents didn't come home because they sometimes stayed away when they went out on a Sunday. My father didn't like driving in the dark.'

After much discussion, it was decided I did not need to attend the inquests, the details being too gruesome and I was not a witness. The funny thing was that that was the end of it. Nobody visited to check up on me. I told the police and school that I would stay the other side of town with relatives, but there were no relatives. I was just seventeen and alone.

I went through my father's papers which he kept in a locked oak bureau that I forced. The house cost £3,500 and there was a £1,200 mortgage which was rescinded on death. A joint will left everything 'to my dearest spouse' and in the event of their proximate death it all fell to me when I reached twenty-one.

Everything had been handled by a local solicitor chosen when we moved to West Bromwich and who therefore did not know my father or mother well, nor of any other family. He introduced me with studied arrogance to the arcane laws of probate. His venality was evident and we agreed, after some heated discussion during which I threatened to take the business elsewhere, that he could raise his fee and become a sole trustee providing he smoothed my path. The Post Office paid out life insurance of three times my father's annual salary of £1,750. We agreed £50 a month to me – and that was a struggle – if the estate dealt with house taxes and utilities. The car was a write-off which was a pity, but there was a further death benefit to add to its replacement value. The trust would be shut down when I reached twenty-one and the solicitor and I would say goodbye. I would pay him a gratuity based on a percentage of remaining funds, but only if he met my personal requirements and stayed out of my daily life. If I died before, then he got twenty-five per cent with the rest going to a cats' charity. I chose cats because it was apparent that he hated them. Our arrangement was recorded as much as it needed to be, but was not to be shared. The police never asked.

The accident was dealt with in a small way, only one representative of the Post Office and the shop steward attended the funeral. I was away that day. Life went on.

There was one surprise in my father's papers. Alongside my out-of-date passport, unused since my brother's death, were my birth certificate and a newspaper cutting. I was at once twice orphaned. I was pleased to discover I had been adopted. Perhaps I was no Huguenot descendant, but I could speak French and, among her own background, my mother might have had a further reason for her love. My natural mother had been killed soon after I was born in, irony of ironies, a car crash in Rouen. She was in her early twenties, French, and unmarried. I wondered if there was some family connection between the two women.

Reading between the lines, I was a convenient replacement for a child who had been stillborn. This was no bombshell, but a harmless unexploded device. I decided to keep the information secret, especially from the solicitor.

A second-sense made me pause while I held my 'first' birth certificate and I began what became a long-term interest, not obsession, well, perhaps, but certainly the start of a determined collection. With my adoption certificate attached and uninterested staff at school verifying my photographs, I wrote to the French service and received a passport. I now had two identities and nobody knew of the first nor had any inkling of my alternate name or, I thought, its association to me.

I was a grammar schoolboy, reportedly just scraping the entrance examination which I took aged eleven. I slumbered through half a dozen Ordinary level GCSEs and was in my last year for Advanced levels. I chose a curriculum-challenging English and Maths.

'Are you going to study arts or science? You can't do both. You must make up your mind.'

And, of course, I added French, which I could speak better than any of my clutch of modern language teachers. The school was in new buildings in Clarkes Lane within walking distance of my West Bromwich home. I decided to stay on because I had a life-plan.

As soon as I could wield a tube of plastic glue, my bedroom ceiling was stringed with model aircraft of all vintages and countries, carefully identified with transfers and special paints. Books of test flying, war-time exploits and famous flyers crammed my shelves. I wanted to be a pilot and some simple research showed there were two routes: the RAF and the University College of Air Training at Hamble near the river at Southampton. This second option was supported by a generous grant from the local town council as was the way in those days. I applied to both and, over the next months, with various forged documents from my father sent ahead, attended a stream of selection courses.

I had two other priorities: finding more money to fund my social life and rock climbing. I improved my income by setting up a window cleaning round. I enlisted a schoolfriend, bought a set of extending ladders, two buckets, shammy leathers, and was persuaded to get some insurance against accidental glass breakages which, I remember, cost £3 for the year. A short bus ride took us to some of the dingier parts of the Black Country where window cleaners were never seen because of the industrial grime. We were welcomed with open arms, but less open purses, visited most houses monthly, and within a short time I was employing casual labour. My interest was to find new clients, collect the money and deal with complaints. Occasionally, some of my lads decided to go it alone and tried to steal sections of my rounds. I learned an early lesson: strike quickly, strike hard and cause enough personal damage to strike fear. Soon, a forcible warning with a new lad before 'employment' was enough to protect my interests. I hired a couple of silky schoolboy publicists who would mix in the classrooms with my young cleaners and scare them with stories of horrible retribution.

My untaxed income became impressive; my trust's monthly £50 stayed untouched in my bank account. I held court, paid out wages, and arbitrated disputes on Tuesday and Wednesday lunchtimes in the *Coach and Horses* pub in Kesteven Road just out of sight of the school. The pie and a pint special was celebrated and was our preferred fare and also that of the younger maths and science teachers who were always short of money. The pub became a useful place for sorting out educational difficulties. I was able to make opportunistic short-term loans at low interest in useful and deserving cases.

Most of my difficulties at school stemmed from my rock climbing for which weekends in North Wales, specifically the Llanberis Pass, were essential. It was something over a hundred miles and took four hours of determined hitchhiking when I couldn't organise a lift. In those days, hitchhiking was a friendly and expected way of travel for the young and a rucksack with a prominent dirty-white nylon climbing rope often eased the way. I was seldom left standing for more than an hour. Many drivers expected an intelligent conversation and the subjects covered, and the education and shared experience received, were part and parcel of growing up.

It was also normal for me to beg lifts in and around town on the way to the shops or to school. The sixties were a carefree and uncomplicated time to be a teenager, before drugs and political correctness. Dating was more formal, light sex more hesitant and, to be honest, infrequent. There was less to buy, television was largely irrelevant, no mobile phones, in fact no electronic devices at all. I am sure we were happier than the teenagers of today. There were few regulations, minimal bureaucracy, basic healthy food, good manners were expected and usually given, and there was a lot of walking. There must have been bad people about, but they were not fed to the population by the media every minute of the day. Crime was a mostly simple affair, recognised when it was seen, perpetrated against body and property. There were no imagined or sought after offences which demanded counselling and the setting up of instant support groups. Individuals were expected to get on with things, stand up for themselves. If there was debris, I never saw it.

To reach the rock cliffs as the afternoon darkened, it was better to leave school at mid-day so I wore as much of my climbing clothes as was permitted on Friday mornings. I collected my gear from the maths study at the lunch break and headed west. Only one lesson was missed – maths again – and that could be sorted at the *Coach and Horses*. The trouble was the return trip because two full days' climbing meant striking tent early on Monday. Lifts were seldom easy in the hills at first light, often short hops shared in the back of aged, spring-damaged Landrovers with a couple of panting Collie sheepdogs.

Some days I was lucky and back in lessons by mid-morning. I soon found that to clump in half-way through a discussion on Molière was seen as disruptive and disrespectful. I learned to make my entrance between lessons, but matters started to get out of hand as my classmates began to bet on my arrival time. The weeks' results were posted on a school noticeboard with the winners identified. I tried hard to work my way through this, but the best way, I found, was to drop French as a subject so as to curtail the embarrassment. In retaliation, the school declined to enter me for public examination, but a sympathetic and loan-heavy teacher did that for me, even paying the registration fee against a written-off personal debt. The last morning lesson was maths and I was regularly given a firm, loud and public dressing down and told to, 'See me afterwards'. However, this recent graduate was also a devoted climber and 'afterwards' meant our disciplinary talks were held in the *Coach and Horses* where he quizzed me in great detail on my latest ascents.

When in Llanberis Pass, I camped because from a tent it was simple to get to the foot of the crags. These routes, with the standards rising each year, were and still are legendary across the UK and round the world. I went back many years later and was struck by the difference. The road had turned into a car park with small parties waiting in line for their allotted time to take on a beginner's slot.

My skills and strength were limited by my above-average height. The legend of the fifties, Joe Brown, was the man to follow and soon became the man to beat. Pete Crew and Martin Boysen led the challengers. I watched Crew many times and have never seen anyone climb so quickly while on the edge and in whatever the weather. He had a clear eye for the shortest, most direct route. He made liberal use of nuts and bolts jammed into crevices to protect himself against falls. He redefined 'impossible'. It was Crew who introduced me to the intricacies of hand-jamming, which he said he had picked up from Brown. Anyone can jam a hand into a small crack and flex it so that the fist provides a wedge to hang from. It's the wide ones, he said, that took the skill.

'Look at the crack once, shove your arm in and look away. Feel until it is right, then, just pull up to the next move. Never look into it, you'll keep fiddling about until your strength ebbs away.'

That lesson led to my one climb with him. He had arrived early at a new pitch to be named *Yellow Wall* from the tiny flowers in the ledges and found he was without a partner. The weather was set for heavy rain. He knew I could hold him if needed – I was needed twice. The climb took him just over the hour as he ferreted his way and me twice the time.

It was the only occasion that I got my name into the climbing hall of fame and that brief burst of publicity led to a letter from my distant cousin, a few years older than me. We agreed to meet in two weeks in the Pass; he lived in Bolton. It is time to give the first name in this book because it had repercussions for the rest of my life. He was called Chris Heal.

We became inseparable that summer as I squeezed managing the window cleaners around my A' levels and both of them into climbing trips. Chris and I had long talks as we lay in our tent planning the next day. He had lost his parents in an air crash when his father worked in the United States, and we shared and relished our independence. Chris was a keen, if novice, follower of Freud and Jung. He was much attracted to a cult book by Joseph Campbell, *The Hero With A Thousand Faces*, which delved into modern psychology and its interweaving with universal myths and symbols, and read W. B. Yeats and Robert Graves with a passion. Chris agreed with Campbell that life was a rite of passage of three principal parts each with its own initiation. The first we had both achieved by luck through the forced losing of our parents. Because this happened when we were young, we thought ourselves saved from many of the neuroses that stem from the more gradual separation struggled with by most children. As young unencumbered men, we had the chance to enjoy the second phase to the full, the quest for knowledge and adventure, the 'lure of love', the constant drive to satisfy our heady curiosity. Freud emphasised the passages and difficulties of this search for independence and identity. Jung, on the other hand, emphasised the crisis of the last phase, that of growing old, the 'descent and disappearance into the grave'; death became the challenge when 'life-weariness seized the heart and death not love held the promise of bliss'.

Chris spent two years in America immediately before his parents' accident. He was much interested in how Americans sought to deny any acceptance of ageing and this forced positivity became a vital attribute for career and social acceptance. He believed that this personal struggle caused Americans great unhappiness. The inverted emphasis became pathetic: the goal was not to enjoy the benefits of growing old, but to live as Peter Pan, to remain young and to emit a relentless and optimistic attitude whatever the circumstance. As Chris put it as the Welsh rain lashed the tent, not to 'mature away from a loving mother, but to cleave to her'. While husbands worshipped at their personal boyhood shrines of photographs and trophies in masculine 'dens', wives searched for love and eternal youth. Age was the enemy and, when it began to win, as it must, some could not withstand the shock and self-disgust.

We laid our plans. I would not know the results of my school examinations for many weeks. I had no inkling either from the RAF or from the air college. Chris was restless and wanted to follow his personal journey into the unknown. We decided to hitchhike to Kashmir and then to reassess. In those days of a failing and protected sterling currency, there was a small problem. Individual travellers were allowed to take only £50 in notes out of the United Kingdom and could not access sterling funds until they reached another piece of the British financial area, which in our case would be Pakistan. How much money might we need? How could we eke it out? Could we subvert the restrictions?

We talked into a number of late nights. Why should we with more than enough to live on in comfort feel drawn to a long journey to France, Italy, Yugoslavia, Greece, Turkey, Persia, Afghanistan, Pakistan, and into India. Was there a natural melancholy in our settled condition that needed a change of air?[4] Did we need to hunt, perhaps, for happiness? For confrontation? Or did we seek a unicorn? After all, there are only two kinds of men in the world, those that stay at home and those that do not.[5]

Our climbs were never at the level of the greats: Brown, Crew, Hugh Banner, Chris Bonington, Lew Brown, Don Whillans, Rowdy Yates, all of whom I met or stood near, and more than a dozen more. As a climbing pair, Chris and I were seen as more accessible, less aloof, and, for that reason, we had our own occasional acolytes who begged to join us on routes where serious injury was not a close companion. One such, a loner, was a Frenchman with a thin beard from Brittany called Philippe who turned up from time to time without warning. One weekend, he made two successful climbs with us. On the third route he died.

It was late on a Sunday evening and the crags had cleared as other part-time hill worshippers went home. We were alone. Chris led and was ensconced on a narrow ledge thirty feet above a tricky overhang. I held Philippe's support line as he peeled off after giving clear warning. One of Chris's safety nuts slipped free, wrenched another after it, and Philippe fell head first onto a small rock pinnacle. It was a matter of inches either way between a ruined shoulder and his skull. There was a single report like the cracking of a walnut. He made no sound. There could be only one outcome. A drawn-out, 'Shit', drifted down from above. It was followed by a much-repeated stronger expletive.

Philippe was twenty feet across from me, moving in a slow pendulum. I had a good view. Memories of the final moments of my mother and father swayed though my mind. I tied the body still. There followed a strange shouted conversation with Chris in which priorities got adjusted and self-preservation became our priority. We could have been heard a quarter of a mile away if there had been anyone there.

'I can get across to him.'

'And do what?'

'Well, if I take the spare rope across I can attach it to him and lower him.'

'And then what?'

'Well, I could release your rope. Could you pull it up and abseil down?'

'Yes. Easy enough. Is there any chance . . . ?'

'None at all. I can see what's left of the side of his head.'

'And what do we do then?'

'Let me think. The obvious thing is to lay him out, one of us to stay guard and the other walk, what . . . four miles, to the village.'

'And what's the less obvious thing?'

'Well, we both wish it had never happened, but it was our nuts that slipped out. Now he's dead and there's nothing we can do about that.'

'So what?'

'Well, so, nobody knows he is here. No one knows he was climbing with us. He never talked about his family. He was always alone. We don't know where he lived. Might have a job in London to improve his English. We have no idea.'

'Where are you going with this?'

'Well, we are going to go to Kashmir, right?'

'Right.'

'We don't need this. I don't want any hiccups to my flying applications. We could just pretend it never happened.'

'Like we lose the body?'

'Yes. Down one of those lower fissures where nobody climbs. It'll be years, if ever.'

And that is what we did. A suitable place was easy to find. We emptied his pockets and placed him well out of sight. Within forty minutes of his death he had disappeared; it was dark and it was done. For all I know, Philippe is still there.

As Chris put it, 'We can't change our minds now. Can't reach him. We'd never get him out, poor sod.'

Chris cooked some sausages and mash and we had a whisky from the small bottle we allowed ourselves. I pulled down Philippe's one-man tent, packed it, and went through his belongings. He had £30 in cash and his passport. He was from Brittany, born in Ploërmel, and there was a French ID card giving an address in Rennes. I looked at Chris who was carefully not watching me. I pocketed the passport and card.

'Some English cash, but nothing at all to identify him. I suggest we split the money, there's three fivers for you on your rucksack. I'll take all his stuff and dump it well away from here. Agreed?'

'Sausages are almost ready. We're leaving early tomorrow morning. Let's eat and get some kip.'

In our sleeping bags we talked again about our trip. We parted company somewhere near Shrewsbury where I dumped Philippe's rucksack and its contents in several bins. I didn't see Chris again for more than a year. When I got home there were two letters waiting for me. The first was from the RAF instructing me to an aircrew officer's course next month at South Cerney near Cirencester for basic flying training. The second was from the civil flying college giving me till January when I was to begin training under the joint auspices of the two nationalised airlines, BEA and BOAC.[6] I was part of the response to the explosion in air travel with the arrival of profitable passenger jets. I wrote back accepting both to give me time to decide which I wanted most and set about sorting my affairs. I contacted Chris. I think he understood and accepted my decision to forego Kashmir. Within a month he was gone on his own. I got just one postcard from Dover telling me what I was going to miss and that was that.

There was no need to pretend, no lies to tell. Chris's farewell card called Philippe briefly to mind, but the memory of the accident didn't linger. I felt no remorse and that interested me. No guilt. Just distance. I began to forget the details. I sensed the seriousness with which people might view what Chris and I had done. But that would never happen.

South Cerney was a disaster. I decided to follow my boyhood yearning for the RAF, planning that, if I didn't feel comfortable, I had a more than acceptable back-up.

Perhaps, in my heart, I suspected it might not work. I lasted just three weeks, but got away without signing too many official papers or, more accurately, left when I could no longer prevaricate. It was an unpleasant time. I was the only grammar schoolboy among twenty cadets, surrounded by monied accents, people who had known each other or at least each other's schools. What made it worse was that I had come top in all but one of the preliminary flying tests and, when these were posted in the classroom, it didn't meet with the respect that might have been expected.

European viper

ABOVE: Pete Crew leads on the Great Wall of Clogwyn du'r Arddu on the north flank of Snowdon, Wales, one the best climbing cliffs in Britain. *John Cleare*

LEFT: One of the adverts that attracted Heal to the College of Air Training at Hamble

Heal's 'solo' Chipmunk under maintenance at Hamble just before conversion to College of Air Training Day-Glo colours. *Brian Doherty*

Hamble airfield, the large green expanse at centre, from about 1500 feet, flying roughly south, looking west. The River Hamble is in the foreground with Southampton Water in the distance and Southampton Waterside area beyond. *Derek Haselden.*

The Victory Inn, Hamble

When the time comes for a dispassionate history of the Wilson administration to be written, it is quite likely that the historian will select the Government's policy on Biafra as its wickedest and most disgraceful act of all. For the first time in our history this country has become an active accomplice in the deliberate slaughter of hundreds of thousands of men, women and children whose only crime is that of belonging to a proscribed nation: in short, an accomplice in genocide. And the British people, together with a supine Opposition, have averted their eyes and let the Government pursue its shameful way without hindrance.

Exactly one year ago, on 30 May 1967, the former Eastern Region of Nigeria, in-

Front page editorial in *The Spectator, 31 May 1968*, on prime minister Harold Wilson's 'wickedest and most disgraceful act'

Emeka Odumegwu Ojukwu, President of Biafra

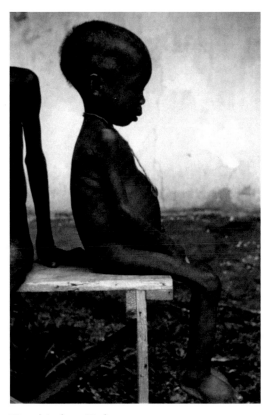

Kwashiorkor: Biafran war

BUA DC-3

BUA Handley Page Dart Herald 211 G-ASKK, in the airline's final livery, at Manchester Airport in 1967. *RuthAS*

Frederick Forsyth

Harold Wilson

LEFT: A poor picture, but excusable given the circumstances. In 1969, Heal's DC-3 was welcomed back to Uli after its successful mission by Biafran anti-aircraft fire which attracted two strafing attacks by a Nigerian MIG-17. The plane was a write off. *John Trent*

British armoured cars offloaded in Apapa Harbour, Nigeria, shortly after the Biafran coup in 1967. *Al J Ventner*

The first ex-Lufthansa DC-3 pictured at Abidjan in 1969 on its transfer flight from Faro to Uli with Heal in the right-hand seat. *Roger Caratini*

An early photograph of a MiG-17 that Moscow insisted Eqypt give to Nigeria. *Ares Klootwyk*

Vernon Polley's Flughjalp DC-6, TF-AAE, after its return from Uli to São Tomé with a cargo of injured children in 1969 and with Heal illegally in the right-hand seat. The plane was too damaged to fly again and was stripped of useful components by Heal's flight engineer. *Jokob Ringler*

Lockheed L-749A Constellation N86524, one of two ex-Western Airlines aircraft leased to the Biafran gun-running fleet. It was brought down by sabotage of three of its engines on Mount Tibhirine, Morocco in 1969 while in flight to São Tomé. *Western Airlines publicity postcard*

The M1 Rifle (top) and M1 Carbine (below), which made up a large part of the Constellation's payload, share only a buttplate screw. They also use different sized .30 caliber ammunition

Berber cave enclosure in the Atlas with mountain goats

Aza and *Hand of Fatim*a pendants similar to those gifted to Heal in Marrakech

We were introduced into the care of a flight sergeant, Pope, who made caricatures of the army drill sergeant majors seem tame. Pope was universally loathed. I can still hear his voice when I slouch; it took me many months to learn how to walk naturally again. If I was shocked by my disenchantment, the RAF personnel officer was horrified. Nobody had ever left in the first month. What would my parents say? Had I no pride? Didn't I realise how much money had already been wasted on my miserable person? The sooner I left the better, only please do it under cover of darkness. There would be no lift to the railway station.

One fellow student did come to see me off. He had his own car, of course, as they all did. He ran me to the train, but only after I agreed to meet him covertly half a mile down the road, standing in a lay-by with my suitcases. It was an interesting happenstance when I met him by chance fifteen years later. He was stuck as a Flight Lieutenant, had failed his pilot's course and been turned into a navigator, a job he had come to despise, made worse by his good pay and no affordable way to escape the burden of three children and a mortgage. Two others from our entry were still in the RAF with only one flying a front-line American-built Phantom on reconnaissance and tactical strike missions. Of the rest, four had failed within a year, three had left after five-year contracts to try for non-service flying jobs, and the other nine were dead, either in air accidents or car crashes.

2. FREEDOM TO FLY

Son of man,
You cannot say, or guess, for you know only
A heap of broken images, where the sun beats,
And the dead tree gives no shelter, the cricket no relief,
And the dry stone no sound of water.[7]

I arrived with all my possessions at the College of Air Training early in January 1967. There was much of the RAF about Hamble: the rail warrant to get to Southampton, the lorry to pick up the recruits sheltering from the rain, the old air station still with defensive gun emplacements, rusting rail-tracks, peeling accommodation blocks, a 3,000-foot all-grass runway and run-off, ageing but robust single-engine de Havilland Chipmunk 22 trainers built just after the war, and, even more aged, the ex-forces instructors who fronted the classrooms or sat in tandem behind the tyros for flying training.

At least it was a touch more relaxed. We had our own rooms, more than acceptable, mine in Dorado House. No one saw an aircraft close to for the first six months. I often despaired in the classroom as my lack of a science background shone through. What was second-nature to others was a foreign land to me. I struggled and it showed, but I scraped along. Several of my fellow students already had a Private Pilot's Licence (PPL), paid for by their parents. Spare time was spent tinkering with cars, playing football and 'popping' home, but with every free moment head down in a training manual. I was taking a break from rock climbing which was made easier because apart from the crumbling sea cliffs on the Isle of Wight there was little local choice nearby. I started each day with a five-mile run twice around the airfield perimeter. I often spent the evening alone in a local pub, the preferred spit-and-sawdust *Victory Inn*, with a novel or history book, rather than with the yachties at the up-market waterside *Bugle*.

Letters from my past arrived during my first month. One from Cambridge awarded a distinction in my privately-funded French examination; a certificate was enclosed. The only comment was from my oral where it was suggested that I should be careful with the amount of slang that I used in everyday speech. That was all the good news.

The headmaster of the grammar school announced that I had been expelled because I had wilfully absented myself from lessons; failed to reply to invitations, as a house captain, to mandatory school-leaving ceremonies; and had not presented myself before an internal investigation concerning money-lending, an activity which was against the school code. This last was a surprise admonishment. It was noted that my relations who had been acting in *loco parentis* had not been available for comment having moved away, but it could be anticipated that they would be ashamed of my behaviour. This all sounded like a badge of commendation.

The RAF described how I had left my course at South Cerney as a cadet officer without permission or explanation. My service file had been black marked as 'unsuitable for service in any of Her Majesty's Forces at any time'. I never took any oath as an officer and had been instructed to leave after a, shall we say, fulsome discussion. Truth was an early casualty in the officer class.

That winter, I developed a friendship with the only black person at the college. Okigbo Biggar was Nigerian, known to all as 'Chuck' because he would sound off at length to anyone who would listen about his relative through marriage, Chukwuemeka Odumegwu-Ojukwu, the leader of the province of Biafra which seceded from Nigeria in May 1967.

I finally got my hands on a Chipmunk with its *Day-Glo* orange outer wings and rear fuselage, went solo in ten hours, and passed my PPL in November. Chuck was the other trainee to pass on the same day and he took great delight in my aircraft registration number – G-AMUG. He also deemed it significant that this plane was an older Type 21 and my solo was its last flight at the college; it was sold within days with its three sisters. I read that in 1974 this plane failed to pull out from an aerobatic spin and crashed in a field in Malton in Yorkshire killing the experienced pilot. Chuck and I celebrated our licences with a memorable pub crawl along Hamble High Street. Chuck was retaking his first year because, while he was a natural pilot, he hadn't put in the study hours. He had private money behind him, but his world had changed. He received firm instructions after his disappointing first year: 'Get qualified or the money will stop. Pilots are needed in Biafra for the war.'

The relationship cemented because we both knew Pete well, at least on drinking terms, a fellow trainee, who had died two weeks before. We drank a number of toasts to his honour. What we remembered most, apart from his long pockets, was Pete's imagination and subsequent story-telling skill, an art much admired by Chuck, brought up in West African oral traditions.

Pete's death was a strange case. He came to prominence because while practising solo over the Isle of Wight he started playing mind games and was transported to a Battle of Britain Spitfire. The push radio button on a Chipmunk was where a fighter pilot would fire his machine guns. Every time Pete took on a Messerschmidt 109, using an endless supply of .303 ammunition, he activated his microphone and broadcast to the control tower at Hamble. Some unkind soul switched the excited commentary to external loudspeakers. Within minutes, the whole station was sliding down the walls of the two hangars as Pete warned his luckless mates of wicked Huns on their tails. The immediate fun was strangled when a senior instructor cut into the manic traffic with a curt, 'Red two, red two, this is red leader. Return to base. Fuel low.' There was a pause, then a desperate and lonely, 'Oh . . . shit'.

I have never seen an aircraft land in such a sheepish manner, almost hiding behind clumps of grass as it crawled to dispersal. Pete got out, but there was no one there. All was quiet; the first hangar was deserted. He made his way to report to the control tower when, from around the corner of the second hangar, almost a hundred men charged him firing imaginary Sten guns.

Ten days later, Pete was over Sandown on the Isle of Wight again practising stall turns. The court of enquiry did not work out the background; Pete's imaginary dogfights over Kent were kept quiet. What was clear was that his Chipmunk pancaked from a serious height, a failed recovery after a deliberate stall. His coccyx received such an impact that his backbone was pushed through the top of his head. Later, all the trainee pilots were shown a photograph of the corpse in the cockpit. More images I thought long forgotten, today drift back into view.

It seems strange today how little coverage there was in Britain of the first year of that nasty little war in Nigeria. It wasn't until later that I found this was deliberate policy encouraged by the government of Harold Wilson and supported with enthusiasm by the old boys of the BBC and their chums in the Commonwealth and Foreign Offices. The British press was invited to concentrate on Vietnam, the other war of that era, which was portrayed as an American embarrassment, rather than to investigate Britain's shameful secrets closer to home.

At heart, Biafra was an oil war, of course, with most of the trade controlled by Shell and BP inside Biafran territory, but all the time working hand-in-glove with the Nigerian government. On the ground, it was a tribal and religious conflict with northern Moslem Hausa set against eastern Christian Igbo; a great simplification I now know.

Chuck's rage grew as the year went on. Prime Minister Wilson and Foreign Secretary Michael Stewart could no longer keep the lid on the atrocities they allowed; Chuck would argue 'encouraged'. As a young man without a cause, I was easy fodder for Chuck's arguments and emotions. Within days of Biafra's secession from the Nigerian Federation, the government in Lagos instigated a sea blockade cutting off food supplies. The new country was given little chance of a future when food shortages were added to the central government's overwhelming strength in land and air forces.

What stuck in Chuck's craw was that mercenary former officers of the Royal and Indian Navies were contracted to operate the Nigerian blockade. One of the British officers directed the team and also assisted with the planning and execution of sea-borne assaults. The Biafrans were convinced that these men acted with the full support of the British government which had done nothing to stop them enlisting with the Nigerians for £1,000 a month paid into Swiss bank accounts. All living expenses in Nigeria, including drinks and girls, were covered by the Federal government.

Famine was Britain's forte; blockade the strategy on which she won many of her overseas wars from Napoleonic times. In 1899, the British declared food destined for the Boers in the Transvaal and the Orange Free State as contraband at the neutral port of Lourenço Marquès. Starvation followed on the farms of the high veldt. Many viewed Britain's blockade against Germany during World War 1 as a war crime and, especially afterwards, when it was continued as a vital part of the pressure brought to bear in the

Versailles peace negotiations. The consequences of that blockade in human terms were long-lasting and devastating. It was not a 'starvation policy' for a town or localised area, but a preparedness to embrace 'untargeted mayhem'. According to the old warmonger, Winston Churchill, the intent was to treat 'the whole of Germany as if it were a beleaguered fortress', and avowedly sought to 'starve the whole population – men, women and children, old and young, wounded and sound – into submission'.

On 19 May, the Biafrans lost Port Harcourt, a potential lifeline, and on 25 July the Nigerians launched an unexpected and spectacular sea-borne attack of the island of Bonny, the last piece of land before the open sea to the south of the port. Bonny was the oil terminal of the Shell-BP pipeline from Port Harcourt. It was also well-known to any historian of the English slave trade as one of its centres on the Guinea Coast, 'located in mangrove swamps, infested by mosquitoes and other disease-carrying insects, and frequently oppressively hot and humid'.[8] On 9 August, the Biafrans struck back in earnest with a coup that shook observers everywhere. Starting at dawn, a mobile brigade of 3,000 men swept into the Nigerian Midwest and changed the balance of the war, putting the whole of the country's oil resources under Biafran control.

Chuck and I transferred to training on Piper Apaches, less than ten years old, a potent step up. These were much more powerful machines with six seats, two abreast, and a range of well over 1,000 miles. We began the introduction to night journeys, flying blind on instruments, and landings and take-offs at large airports, away from our grassy comfort blanket. Hurn at Bournemouth and Southampton were local favourites and far less busy in those days. We also spent many hours flying in and out of the recently-opened Gatwick during times of low traffic. We gained our Commercial Pilot's Licences (CPL) on the same day in March 1968 which, after many detailed exams, meant for us a 350-mile, same-day, round trip in Apaches from Hamble flying in opposite directions with stops at Bristol and Torquay. Now, at least, we could be paid to fly passengers.

We then began training on an early-version Handley Page Herald, a two-engined high-wing airliner, flown by British United Airways (BUA) after they acquired Jersey Airlines. The college rented the co-pilot's seat by the flight on scheduled services. The Herald was a loss-making aircraft coming to the end its days; a financial failure because British and German opposition produced more attractive aircraft with better engines more quickly. This was a great pity from a pilot's perspective because the Herald was a dream to fly. It had two characteristics which later stood Chuck and I in good stead: first it was designed as a replacement for the iconic Douglas DC-3 (Dakota in the UK, C-47 in the military) and was built with considerable input from its operators and, second, its large flaps meant it could take off and land in less than 500 yards. I loved flying it and often sat in the right-hand seat taking around fifty passengers to British regional airports including the Isle of Man and Jersey and, on one happy day, to Paris Orly.

It took the British public a full year from the outbreak of the Biafran war to acquire even a hazy and largely uninformed outline of what was going on. Chuck explained that Eastern Nigerians had always lived on the edge of protein sufficiency. Their normal food, cassavas and yams flavoured with peppered gravy, contained little protein, but was supplemented by dried cod, called stockfish, imported from Scandinavia, by salt, and by 2,000 head of cattle a month from the north. The fish represented the protein part of the diet along with home-grown goats and chickens. British journalists like Frederick Forsyth and John de St Jorre were adamant that the starvation of the Biafrans was 'not an accident, or a mischance, or even a necessary but regrettable by-product of the war'. It was a deliberate and integral part of the Nigerian war policy and Nigeria's leaders made few bones about it. With the British-advised blockade and the war, the supply of imported foodstuffs was cut off. While adults can stay in good health for a long time without adequate protein, children require a constant supply. The Biafrans set up intensive chicken and egg-rearing farms to boost production and might even have beaten the problem had it not been for the shrinking of their territorial area and the influx of up to five million refugees.

By mid-April, experts noticed an increasing incidence of kwashiorkor, a disease which stems from protein deficiency and which mainly affects children. The symptoms are a reddening of the hair, paling of the skin, swelling of the joints and bloating of the flesh as it distends with water. The results were damage to the brain tissue, lethargy, coma and, finally, death. Besides kwashiorkor there was anaemia, pellagra, and just plain starvation, as children wasted away to skin and bone.

Children began to die – publicly. Chuck showed me an editorial in *The Spectator* which said:

> *For the first time in our history, Britain has become an active accomplice in the deliberate slaughter of hundreds of thousands of men, women and children, whose only crime is that of belonging to a proscribed nation: in short, an accomplice to genocide. And the British people, together with a supine Opposition, have averted their eyes and let the Government pursue its shameful way without hindrance.*[9]

In the last days of June, the first pictures of small children reduced to living skeletons hit the pages of two London newspapers – *The Sun* and the *Daily Sketch*. Four hundred deaths a day spiralled to 10,000. The Red Cross called it unequivocally 'the gravest emergency' it had handled since World War ll. The relief agencies all agreed in July, after a tour of Biafra, that unless massive help came one million people would be dead by the end of August and another six million would perish in the next six months. As Forsyth put it, his personal disgust growing by the day, 'The most scabrous act of all was the British Government plus the American State Department during August and September attempting to interfere with relief by pressuring the Red Cross not to send any supplies at all.' In September, Richard Nixon called it genocide.

The pictures of starving Biafran children reached into every corner of British life. Seeing them through the press and television every day, the British public reacted. 'In the next six months, people did everything they could within constitutional limits to change the Government's policy over arms to Nigeria and to donate assistance to Biafra,' recalled Forsyth later. 'There were committees, protests, demonstrations, riots, lobbies, sit-ins, fasts, vigils, collections, banners, public meetings, marches, letters sent to everyone in public life capable of influencing opinion, sermons, lectures, films and donations. Young people volunteered to go out and try to help, doctors and nurses did go in an attempt to relieve the suffering. Others offered to take Biafran babies in their homes for the duration of the war; some volunteered to fly or fight for Biafra. They were all snubbed by the government.'

In the midst of the daily horror, Chuck called an open meeting to discuss Biafra which the college management banned from its premises. It was diverted to the village hall, made public, and over one hundred people crowded in with a liberal sprinkling of cadets and staff.

One lunchtime, I was slipped a note written by Chuck asking me to meet him within the half hour at the *Victory*. He was spitting tacks and, at the same time, deflated. Grim-faced and unsympathetic police from London had interviewed him that morning. It had been a brief, but aggressive thirty minutes. BOAC and BEA were government-owned businesses, so was the college. Using public property to attack the government of the day with inflammatory and false propaganda was not appropriate. Chuck had broken the terms of his student visa. He was to leave the country within twenty-fours and a seat had been booked for him on a BOAC flight to Lagos. There was no appeal.

We were both shocked. In the first place, Chuck and I were about to sit a dozen examinations for our Airline Transport Pilot's Licences (ATPL) and his chance was lost. Second, a trip to Lagos, the headquarters of the murderous Nigerian generals, was tantamount to a death sentence for an Igbo pilot and relative of the Biafran leader. Chuck decided he had to disappear and had arranged a covert seat on a BUA freighter leaving that evening for Switzerland. He just wanted to say goodbye. I was near tears. All I could do was to borrow a car and drive him to Gatwick. We embraced in the freight hangar and he was gone.

That summer saw the most action-filled months of the war. I scoured the daily papers. Biafra seemed to hover on the point of death as the Federal noose tightened. It was also the wet season and this intensified tenfold the suffering of those trapped inside the Biafran enclave. As the rain poured down and thousands starved to death, three major towns – Aba, Owerri and Okigwi – fell. One airport – Obilagu, was overrun, and another – the vital Uli – came within Federal shelling range, closed temporarily, reopened and, finally, after a desperate struggle, was made secure.

I passed my ATPL that November. While I had over a thousand hours logged, I was restricted from full captaincy until I was twenty-three and had built up 500 hours as a co-pilot on multi-engined aircraft. I also needed separate accreditation for each aircraft type heavier than 12,500 pounds which, so far, I had only gained for the increasingly rare Herald weighing in at near 25,000 pounds.

I was unhappy and jaded and knew in my heart that being a well-paid bus driver flying to repetitive city airports and fleshpot destinations was not the career for me. The new large jets held no lure. I think, perhaps, I became a little unstable. My close relationship with Chuck had been noted and, I was told, there was a whiff of suspicion that I had been involved in his disappearance. I knew background enquiries had been made because my solicitor in West Bromwich told me so, with care protecting his imminent share out from my Trust fund. He assured me that he had withheld the information about the death of my parents two years before but, as he said, perhaps with a little humour, that he couldn't be sure that the cat was not out of the bag.

Pressure mounts in surprising ways at a place like Hamble: relationships with fellow cadets suddenly cool, sharper marking of essays, less flying time, formal criticism of small technical errors that might otherwise have been mentioned only in passing.

It came to a head early in December. I was in West Drayton in the far west of London to be introduced by proud engineers to BOAC's newly installed Boeing 707-420 flight simulator. It had been bought to ready pilots to fly the fifteen Boeings which were delivered from 1960 to replace ageing Bristol Britannias and suspect de Haviland Comet 4s. It would be a prestigious posting for a new co-pilot, a jet with over 200 passengers.

The simulator was a big white container in which you were isolated and flew on your own with voice commands coming through earphones. It was quite primitive, for instance it didn't move and had no engine sound, but the visuals on the cockpit screens were realistic. I flew the simulator in half-hour bursts for four days straight. On the fifth day, I sensed something was different, even hostile. I strapped in and took off for Cairo. Safely at cruising altitude, I began to relax. Then I lost an engine and there was a brief burst of flame, I was told. The procedure was straightforward and I controlled the engine shutdown, put the supposed fire out, and asked for alternative airfields for an emergency landing. That was when a sudden thunderstorm hit everywhere in my path and I had to divert away from safety to evade lightning strikes. Despite fifteen per cent spare fuel for Cairo, matters were looking bleak. Then, of course, one of the passengers began to give birth and this meant a rapid descent below 8,000 feet so that air cabin pressure could be made more sympathetic for the delivery. A lower altitude dramatically reduced the range of the aircraft.

I was beginning to get fed up. I found I was talking to an Italian air traffic controller with limited English at a military airfield with an impossibly short runway. I tried French, but I think that was seen as impertinent. On the edge of the possible, I was informed that there was a terrorist on board who was barricaded in the toilet and claimed to have a hand grenade. It was likely he did because his partner had been overpowered and his grenade confiscated. Whether the plane would withstand a blast in the toilet and a hole punched in its side was a moot question.

'What is it he wants,' I asked? 'There's not a lot I can do for him sat up here alone.'

'What are you going to do?' demanded the voice in my ear.

I had had enough. I was thinking about Chuck and the British government as a future employer and made an instant decision to change career. I brought the engines up to full power to the sound of admonishing shrieks for which it seemed earphones were unnecessary and flew the aircraft straight into the ground. Modern simulators can bring sound effects to accidents. In those days, I was met by a stunned silence from the technical crew as I opened the door.

The lead instructor broke the ice. 'You've just killed over 200 people. Are you mad?'

The best that I could manage was, 'Possibly, but the world is short two terrorists and we won't get other aircraft hijacked to try to force a prisoner exchange.'

No forms, no debrief, just a frosty departure.

Back at Hamble I was called to an urgent Saturday morning meeting with the Principal, an unheard of time for a dressing-down. I had already packed my bags. He was an older man, short and skinny, bald but with a sad grey moustache that had seen better days; rumour had it that he had flown biplane fighters in the last year of World War l. Like many in the forces, especially among flyers, he had no comprehension that someone given the chance would not want to follow his chosen career.

'There's no good appealing,' he shouted at me as I opened his door. 'You're out. You're unstable. We've had our eye on you. You'll never fly for a British airline.'

This was good news as it meant they had no plans to revoke my licences, but, of course, I hadn't had a flying accident.

He hadn't finished. There were worse charges to follow. He began to dribble down his chin in his exasperation and disgust.

'You're politically suspect,' he charged. 'And,' he said, glaring up at me, 'I hear you write poetry.'

My friendship with Chuck, a black-skinned deserter, was remembered to no great surprise, but the last crime did surprise me. A year before, I entered a national competition with a verse about flying, cringeworthy today. I came third and won £5, long drunk and forgotten. My effort had been posted on a college noticeboard and much ridiculed. It seemed the Principal was among my detractors. There was one more barb to come.

'You realise that you were an experiment, don't you?'

I was trying to keep a straight face.

'I was against it from the start, letting arty-farty people into an engineer's world. I suppose you think that we are not good enough for you with your English literature and fancy foreign languages. Too much imagination! Get out!'

'Thank you, sir,' I said. 'I'm sorry for both of us, but at least I'm leaving.' And, I turned, and left.

I went straight to Gatwick airport to see my pals at British United. I was honest about what had happened and they were disapproving, but privately delighted with the story. I was lucky, because I was a timely answer to one of their problems and I wasn't yet on any industry blacklist. Within three days, I was signed up and making my first flight under training on a Douglas Dakota freighter. Fifty hours later, all squeezed illegally into two weeks, I was qualified and my captain was off to jet training school. BUA's DC-3s were taken out of service in 1965 after a fatal accident at Jersey on a flight from Orly. Lacking modern instrumentation and in bad weather, the pilot at his second attempt to land in the driving rain hit runway lights and twenty-six people died. Public confidence in the old planes as a passenger aircraft fell through the floor. However, BUA kept one DC-3 in service off the main fleet, no paying passengers, and used it for odd jobs at all hours, often at weekends: flying freight, emergency spare parts and lost baggage, and ferrying executives and engineers at short notice. It was a cheap and cheerful option; the plane wasn't kept in pristine condition, but it took me everywhere. Against all the rules, my co-pilot had no licence. Stan was a flight engineer in his fifties, a heavy drinker, not long divorced, and the only person left in the airline who had experience of patching up a DC-3. No-one seem bothered that I was not yet twenty-three.

Who knows where it would all have ended? Stan and I were stashed in a bar at Manchester airport in February waiting for the snow to be cleared. We had to get to Gatwick to pick up some VC10 replacement electrics and take them to Madrid to put on a connecting flight to Sierra Leone. We wore donkey jackets to cover up our flight crew stripes. I got a Tannoy to report to flight operations and suspected our drinking had been spotted. However, it was a message asking me to confirm by telephone as soon as possible a personal meeting at an address in Lisbon. Stan was happy that we should have an engine problem when we left Madrid and thought Lisbon was the best place to get it fixed. It all went to plan. After checking in and making sure that Stan was happy and settled in a bar that I could find again, I went off for the meeting. It was in a hotel in a dingy part of town. In the lobby, Chuck was grinning from ear to ear. We hugged for a long time, for my part with relief that he was still alive.

Then he made me an offer that I accepted with little thought.

3. BIAFRA'S FREEDOM

What is that sound high in the air
Murmur of maternal lamentation
Who are those hooded hordes swarming
Over endless plains, stumbling in cracked earth
Ringed by the flat horizon only ...[10]

On my next visit to Lisbon, I was recognised at Heathrow by the second officer on my flight as he walked past the waiting passengers. Although he was a casual acquaintance from Hamble, there was no acknowledgement. He spoke into his captain's ear, who stopped and looked straight at me. I was the man who had crashed a Boeing 707 and embarrassed the fraternity. Could I be a danger to his aircraft? All would appear normal in the passenger manifest, but my departure would be tagged on a file in London as my destination had a special security significance for a pilot. For me, it was an early lesson learned.

Flight over without incident, I cleared customs and left the international area. Chuck advised that a *nom de guerre* would be useful as the British had become obstructive to mercenaries, especially pilots, heading for Biafra; four ex-RAF men were turned back at Dover and another arrested in Malta for supposedly using forged papers. Those who preferred Nigerian dollars were given a much easier passage.

I emerged from the men's room, clothes changed, as Philippe whose actual body was decaying deep in a Welsh hillside. I had renewed his passport using his ID card and my photograph with rearranged hair and a French beard. I trialled it a few times on my BUA Dakota flights to France with Stan so as to collect some recent stamps. My new identity was almost ideal. I could likely fool any Frenchman except a native Breton for whom my accent and lack of dialect would be evident. The other difficulty was I was two inches taller than Philippe, but who checks?

I was on my way to an odd war with strange bedfellows. Britain refused to withdraw its support for the Federal Government whatever atrocity it committed, and she was aided by the United States and by Russia. France meanwhile took the Biafran side and at a recent cabinet meeting had given the fledgling state virtual recognition. Within political limits, France went so far as to supply arms to Biafra. It was an open secret that its efforts were directed by Jacques Foccart, President de Gaulle's right-hand man in links between the establishment and the upper reaches of arcane cloak-and-dagger operations. Foccart worked from a suite of elegant offices at 138, rue de Grenelle, in Paris's elegant seventh arrondissement. As usual, De Gaulle's strategy countenanced only French interests. He preferred a weak Nigeria comprising a patchwork of economically-linked smaller states which would be less threatening to the surrounding francophone countries. Biafra also appealed to the French as a nation struggling for self-determination and equated it with Quebec's desire for freedom from British Canada. In any case, de Gaulle rarely missed an opportunity to have a go at the British and the Americans.

The Portuguese, although Britain's oldest ally, turned a blind eye to Biafran support and allowed the use of their airports at Lisbon, Faro, Guinea and their Atlantic islands for relief flights of food and medicine and, more quietly, armaments. In one of the greatest humanitarian gestures of the war, Portugal opened its military airfields on the staging island of Santo Porto, off Madeira, and on São Tomé to mercy flights run by a consortium of church groups. São Tomé was a short 400 miles from the main Biafran airports at Port Harcourt and Enugu before they both fell to the Nigerians and, only a little further, to the last-ditch lifeline at Uli. The International Red Cross also organised a most efficient airlift from the Spanish island of Fernando Po off the Cameroon coast. Together, it was a convincing if confusing assembly of European nations disturbed by Britain's inflexibility in the face of starvation.

I caught a bus to an hotel near Lisbon airport which I was told had been booked for me. There was no booking so I moved into the centre of the city to find something cheaper which I could fund myself. The next day, I went back to the airport to check on my flight to Biafra scheduled for that evening. There was nothing as sophisticated as a check-in desk. I soon found Hank Wharton, the soft-spoken American mercenary pilot who held the franchise for the Biafra run. Chuck had described him as a diffident and morose figure, nothing like a dashing operator of clandestine airlines. Hank was surprised to see me.

'You're on the original list,' he said, 'but you were taken off. Don't worry. It happens all the time. Usual cock-up. There's some room for you and a suitcase. If you still want to go, that's OK with me.'

He started on his apologies: the aircraft was being repaired; the navigator couldn't be found and, anyway, he was often drunk; the Biafrans hadn't paid the 25,000 US dollars for the round trip; and, finally, the British were trying to sabotage the run. He was a little wary of me because he guessed I would be flying within Biafra, not for him, and not on his big four-engined machines, and he didn't know what I would be doing or who was paying me. Neither, to be honest, did I.

He looked up at me, hopefully. 'Do you have any hours on Connies?'

'No, just Darts and Daks.'

'Funny. Nobody's got any Darts down there. There are a couple of wrecks of Zambian DC-3s but, I tell you, don't go within a mile of them.'

Then, as an afterthought, 'If I were you, I'd go back to your hotel and check out. When we go, we go, but it won't be before nine in the evening. No waiting for passengers to pack their bags in some swanky hotel and then find a taxi in the early hours. You need to be around. Make sure you have some sandwiches and a bottle of what you fancy. The other passengers are over there. Go introduce yourself. Bye.'

At the hotel, I had a slow lunch in the sunshine and watched the seedy men in dirty linen suits and the painted girls strut to and fro. I re-arranged my bag so that no one could see my tins of corned beef and soup, bottles of vitamin pills, packets of salt, some half-bottles of whisky, and the rest of my Biafran survival kit.

Except for us few, the lounge was empty without night flights in early March, off-season for tourists in those days. In 'our' corner of the waiting lounge there were four hard men, more than twice my age, who I took for mercenaries, three Irish priests in white soutanes, and a couple of solitary individuals who kept to themselves in various degrees of unhappiness. The mercenaries don't bother to respond as they sipped beer after beer. The priests were approachable, but were in their own deep conversation. From the window, I could see two blacked-out Connies, Super-Constellations, on the other side of the field glistening in the sun.

'Infinitely patient and elderly, like a pair of graceful swans,' said one of the priests, and crossed himself.

I understood the comment, but dignified though the planes may have been, they were well past their prime. Twenty years ago the Connie was dubbed 'Queen of the Atlantic', troublesome to fly and with a record of oil leaks and engine failures. I wondered where this pair was serviced. I took out my copy of *Ulysses* and continued to struggle with it through the rest of the afternoon and evening. I bought some sandwiches and a couple of cans of beer and waited. At two in the morning, I tried to sleep on a bench and dozed till dawn when Wharton announced that we would not go till that evening. Drained and worn, I caught the bus back to the hotel and tossed and turned till dusk. It was the same story the next night, and the next.

Just after three in the morning, slack bodies were nudged one by one to join a half-world of officialdom: departure forms, but 'destination' left bank; luggage placed by grinning porters on a conveyor belt, but unlabelled; a small bus and trailer ready, but no public announcement. In a lonely corner of the airfield, we scrambled up a ladder.[11] The main cabin had boxes of ammunition lashed to the floor in neat rows in place of the seats. The plane was overloaded, about ten tons deadweight, and I knew about these things. It took us the length of the runway to unstick and I was pleased to hear the pilot say that he was going to dump some of the arms at São Tomé. All day long we lumbered around the West Coast of Africa, well clear of anyone's airspace.

There were refuelling stops at Porto Santo and Guinea, also gripped by an independence war. Coming in to land at Bissau, low and slow over the jungle, someone fired up at our Constellation. One bullet came through the floor, missed a crate of mortars by two inches, went between my parted thighs and out through the ceiling. On the tarmac, the crew examined the holes, decided that no harm was done; we could refuel and fly on. I drifted up to talk to the pilots and the flight engineer, but it was a lacklustre conversation. I was young and inexperienced; they were neither. My place was right at the back, a single tail seat by a toilet that might not have been cleaned in months. The other passengers took turns sleeping on dirty mattresses thrown over the ammunition boxes.

We came down heavily at São Tomé in the late afternoon. There was a grey haze over the airport, the air hot and dripping, smelling like an old wet dog drying in the sun. We were in the Bight of Biafra, the armpit of Africa, the home of slavery, tribal wars, ivory and palm oil, the lubricant for the first steam locomotives, the original blessing of *savon blanc de Provence* and the foundation of the Lever family's fortunes. A few Irish missionaries from Biafra were busy with relief cargoes while we passengers were corralled in the stale and sweaty airport lounge which buzzed with flies as geckos waited patiently on the walls. The drinks machine was broken and the *Coca Cola* warm and sticky.

The last leg into Biafra was flown at night. Our lightened Connie glided into the air, the priests gone to their island mission and a quarter of the deadly freight unloaded under arc lights to await another aircraft. The pilot took a long, twisty route doubling the flight time, but avoiding Nigerian jet fighters and flak. About an hour before landing, the cabin and navigation lights snapped off without warning. It took a lot of judgement to fly like this with no reference to a visual horizon and I felt a serious drain in confidence. I knew there was no radar, no instrument landing system; pilots depended on beacons, some of them mobile, and a primitive radio.

A neat pattern of tiny landing lights appeared below for less than thirty seconds: Uli, part of the main road from Owerri to Ihiala, turned into a busy international runway. Uli was never used during the day. Its disguise was simple, but effective. The widened road verges, loading bays and airport buildings were camouflaged with palm fronds while the runway was left uncovered. From the air, it was a long, boring stretch of open highway only twenty-one metres compared with a normal runway more than twice as wide and heavily defended by anti-aircraft guns. Landing at night was dangerous enough, but it was made worse by the steady, closely stacked line of aged relief and supply planes that waited out of sight. The skills and experience of their crews were variable. Timing was crucial. A Russian bomber or a converted DC-4 or DC-3 mooched about taunting with its broadcast warnings. When the tell-tale lights came on, the Nigerian mercenary pilot attempted to join the queue of incoming planes, dropping bombs onto the runway and firing at the momentarily highlighted laden freighters. Early most mornings, Russian-supplied MiG jet fighters, flown by Egyptians and

Brits, rocketed and machine-gunned any planes visible on the ground. If fighting was nearby, the Nigerian shells came from British-donated guns and armoured vehicles.

Our Connie stayed high, a security precaution. Then, the pilot spiralled tightly downwards as on a helter-skelter funfair ride. I saw lights, palm trees and two church spires flash past through gusts of rain and blotches of heavy cloud.

'Put your heads down and hold your knees.' That instruction was seldom good news.

The pilot circled once more to get his bearings and, I thought, overshot, but gently made contact, hit a badly filled crater, lurched, lifted a little, and then ran smoothly in. I settled further into my seat and eyed the ammunition as the dowager 'Queen of the Atlantic' pulled sharply off the road into the trees. I was impressed and shaking. The door opened. Someone screamed into the fuselage, 'Out, out'. In charge of unloading was a legend, a priest whom everyone called Glade. He was about fifty, walked with a limp, and shook hands with his left, guarding his badly injured right. He claimed, and proved time and again, that any plane could be unloaded in twenty minutes. I was in the way.

Sheltering under the wing, I watched soldiers in tattered uniforms dart inside and man-handle crates and boxes down a make-shift ramp. Others, like a termite swarm, shouldered or hauled them onto an unlit truck that was driven off into the darkness and immediately replaced. The next plane in was a four-engined DC-4, big brother to my BUA DC-3, that had seen better days and sported an American military registration that no one had found time to paint over. It swung next to my Connie just as a bomb fell onto the road a hundred yards away. A truck ready-laden with crushed rubble raced out to fill the hole. Two pilots climbed down from the DC-4 already unloading its stockfish and grain. I recognised one of the voices.

'Chuck? Is that you?

'Bloody hell, is that you. What are you doing here? You're supposed to be in Faro.'

'What do you mean? You asked me to come.'

'But didn't you get my message in Lisbon?'

We had a hug and he walked me over to a hut that was a makeshift bar and canteen. It turned out I had been too smart too early by changing my name to Philippe. There had been a booking for me at the hotel, but through what seemed was a straight misunderstanding the receptionist had not heard my name but used the one on my French passport. And there was also an envelope with a ticket for the train to Faro and instructions to report to the highly secret Phoenix Company at the airport. I had a job ferrying one of some newly acquired DC-3s.

'Well,' said Chuck, as we clinked bottles, 'at least you've had experience of landing at Uli. We want you to bring the bird here without making a fuss. I've been told there is a special job for them, but I don't know what it is.'

That news, especially about landing at Uli in darkness, made my night and I had another lukewarm palm wine. Chuck went off to report my arrival and make some arrangements. I sat on an empty mortar crate in the rain and heat as the mosquitoes found me, watching all shapes of planes landing minutes apart without incident. The bomber seemed to have gone home for dinner.

Chuck came back looking pleased, accompanied by a corporal who smirked as he dangled some car keys in my face. Behind him came a priest in a soaked and filthy soutane leading a wretched line of wounded soldiers, some walking, some on stretchers, and began loading them onto Chuck's plane.

'All sorted. First, I've got to get my beast back to Fernando Po tonight with these poor sods. Get them to hospital there, a good one run by the priests. I need to take off in twenty minutes; I can't afford to miss my slot. Second, this is Corporal John, a number one driver, and he's got a clapped-out Peugeot 403 that'll take you to a government rest house where you've got a room for at least three nights. Third, there'll be a Connie coming by in a day or so that will take you back to Faro. When you get there you can do what I wanted you to do in the first place and check in with our co-ordinator at the airport. His name's João, so he won't be difficult to spot. Find your crew, meet the guys from the other plane, check yours out, and you need to be back here first week in April.

'We'll have another bottle when you get back.' He waved from the ramp of his plane. 'See you in a few weeks.'

John found my bags, loaded the car and off we went. He was no number one driver and the road was not a lot better. All the government rest houses were named Progress Hotel. It pays to be positive. I unpacked by candlelight: torches, pills to make poisonous water drinkable, mosquito repellent, and gadgets to remove boy scouts from horses' hooves. I left the tins in my bag and inched into an old-fashioned bed with steel sides, a lumpy, odorous mattress and sagging springs. The net gave poor protection from mosquitoes and other flying creatures that slipped through its many holes. Bats squeaked and clawed up the outside. Perspiration saturated my pyjamas, sheets and pillow. The night seemed endless as I listened to the unfamiliar sounds: insects hummed, frogs croaked with gusto, small lizards scuttled, black beetles crackled. After the cicadas, the geckos began, calling to each other from opposite walls. By three, everything had stopped except one small bird with a cry of one pure unwavering note. As the light started to reach the room, there was a sound 'like a silver coin falling against a rock' followed by a growling moan. I was told later it was a cobra singing.

In the morning, at a pleasant late breakfast of fruit and strange coffee, I was given the hotel rumours and rules. The house was haunted, there was leprosy nearby, always check my boots before putting them on, snakes were in every clump of grass and the water was contaminated. And, oh yes, I was to hand over my tins if I wanted to eat. I was assured that all the main services functioned after a fashion.

Driver John and I had a day to kill and he took me into Uli. I set about trying to understand more about the famine that filled British newspapers and was, to my mind, why I was there. A stream of refugees trudged through the town carrying all they had, but there were no beggars. Help was given where it could be in a spirit of tribal togetherness. There was no doubt that the average person was suffering from the rise in prices and shortages imposed by the blockade. Yet, there was no demand for the war to end, to give in to Nigerian brutality.

'Better to light a candle than curse in darkness.'

Nigerian coins were still legal tender alongside Biafran currency. Beef had risen from three to sixty shillings a pound, but was seldom obtainable; eggs, once four shillings a dozen were thirty-eight; a chicken at perhaps fifteen shillings before the war rose first to £5, then £15; stockfish, the mainstay of the airlift, had gone from five shillings a pound to sixty; and, most dramatically, salt, once a penny a cup, was now twenty shillings. Rats, snails and mice all fetched a good price. Soap, cosmetics, most items of clothing and, of course, medicines were in short supply. Cigarettes and beer were unobtainable. I gave John my cigarettes and never smoked again.

As a thank you, John tried to find an ex-pat clubhouse for an afternoon palm wine. I was given a section of the sky to watch for enemy aircraft that strafed and bombed anything that moved on the roads. One MiG fighter appeared low from behind us and John slammed on the brakes and we threw ourselves into the jungle, but there was no firing.

There were a dozen desultory drinkers at the club, which, with stained walls and half-eaten rush mats, had seen happier times. The Europeans I talked to seemed inured to the daily air strikes, monotonous food and suspect drinking water, malaria and occasional typhoid. In the corner, a fresh-faced young man was tapping with zest at a typewriter. I recognised Freddie Forsyth from occasional appearances on the BBC while I was at Hamble. What better source than a journalist?

I plonked my last bottle of whisky on the table in front of him and asked him in my French-accented English for information. He poured a large slug and answered in French which he spoke even better than me, or at least with more swear words. That's what French mothers do for you. Forsyth talked almost non-stop for the next two hours, a bitter and angry young man. Disgusted by the anti-Biafran bias of the BBC, he resigned just before he was fired and last year returned on his own as a freelance. It was obvious that he was close to the Biafran leader, Chukwuemeka Odumegwu-Ojukwu.[12] I mentioned I was here to fly in Biafra because of Chuck, one of Colonel Ojukwu's relatives.

'Don't know him,' he said. 'But it's all one big happy family.'

Forsyth had his arguments ready. There were two stances, in particular, which interested me.

Britain's misguided policy, Forsyth declared, began with a biased and flawed analysis by Sir David Hunt, Britain's High Commissioner in Lagos, for whom Forsyth had few good words. The policy had been adopted by the Commonwealth Relations Office, taken over and intensified by the Foreign Office, and 'cravenly endorsed' by Harold Wilson and Michael Stewart. Hunt's second wife, the dynamic and glamorous Iro Myrianthousis, whose family had large trading interests in West Africa, was a journalist in her own right as editor of the *Lagos Weekly*.

Forsyth wasn't alone in his views. Walter Schwartz in his later book said:

For years, Whitehall's political thinking on Nigeria had been based on a resolute refusal to face the realities, an obstinate conviction that with enough pulling and shoving the facts could be made to fit the theory, and a determination to brush under the carpet all those manifestations which tend to discredit the dream. It is an attitude which continues to this day.[13]

But why? Forsyth cited a conversation he had with American Consul, James Barnard, who explained that the 'single immutable political reality' of Nigeria was that in any 'race for the material benefits of life, starting from the same point and on the basis of equal opportunity', the easterners [the Igbos, pronounced *ee,bo*] are 'going to win by a mile'. This was intolerable to the North [the Hausa]. The only way to prevent it happening was to impose unacceptable and artificial shackles to progress on the East. In every sense, claimed Forsyth, Biafra was the most developed country in Africa with more industry, the highest per capita income, the highest purchasing power and the greatest density of roads, schools, hospitals, business houses and factories.

Forsyth moved with enthusiastic distaste to Britain's covert involvement in the war. For twelve months, he said, every possible effort was made by parliament, press and public to ask the Wilson government what was going on. In parliamentary answer after answer, the questioners and the House were 'misled, deceived, rebuffed and frustrated'. Government spokesmen deliberately told the House that the British government was neutral, only to admit ten months later that they were not and never had been. In 1968, Wilson told the Commons, arms were supplied exactly on the basis that they had been in the past and no special provision was made for the needs of the war – despite the growth of the Nigerian army ten-fold from 8,000 to 80,000 men. In the face of government denial, lorryloads of shells and bullets sped through the night in covered trucks to Gatwick where they were given permission to ride around the taxi-track in order to load up at a secret bay on the far side of the field. Arms went to Nigeria out of the British Rhine Army stocks at Antwerp: notably mortars, artillery shells and fresh supplies of Saladin and Ferret armoured cars that not only made up losses, but expanded armoured contingents considerably. The government was even reduced to arguing that if the British didn't supply the weapons then someone else would.

With relish, Forsyth quoted word perfect, for I checked later, a speech in the Lords by The Earl of Cork and Orrery:

> *It is the same as saying that if somebody is going to supply the arms in any case, then why not we? But unless you are going to insist that the purpose for which they are going to be used contains no evil – and I do not see how you can say that – then this is an argument that no honourable government can use, for it is the classic self-justification of the black marketeer, the looter, the drug pedlar … a burst of 9mm bullets in an African stomach is an evil thing any way you reckon it, and if we send those bullets from England knowing that they may so be used, then that particular share in the general evil is ours, and that share is neither diminished nor magnified by a hair's breadth by the likelihood that if we did not send these bullets they would be sent by someone else.*

To add to the British involvement in the blockade, the armoured cars and ammunition, the 'approved' pilots and the odd mercenary, British NCOs arrived to help with communications. Biafran forces noted a phase of distinct and costly improvement on the front line. Rumours long persisted that part of London's extensive help to Lagos had been the presence of British special forces.

'Political denial has always been a bit too shrill,' announced Forsyth and helped finish the bottle.

'Well, you did ask,' he concluded. 'The main question is how many children will die before it is all over?'

I was tipsy and exhausted after the torrent and shuffled off to find John and reach the rest house before sun-down and curfew. There was a message waiting for me. My Connie would leave Uli that night for Faro. I was to be at the airport well before midnight. All went surprisingly easily. As one of the loaders said, 'Europeans have watches, Nigerians have time.' It was even my 'old' Connie. I was the only passenger in an empty plane with no food or drink supplied. I made my way to my seat near the toilet, which still hadn't been cleaned. However, the bullet holes in the floor and ceiling had been patched. We made good time and I was able to have a late solo lunch in Faro with a bottle of *vinho verde*. About half-way through, I had a quiet few minutes gazing into the distance. What I had ordered without thought was *bacalau*, the classic Portuguese dish made with dried cod – stockfish.

After lunch, I found three Luftwaffe C-47 Dakotas sitting forgotten on the tarmac alongside some RAF-surplus Meteor jets. The Daks' papers showed they had first been sold through the West German government's Frankfurt-based surplus disposal agency, VEBEG, to Luxembourg Aero Service where their owner was Tom Fuller. He was a former Seaboard World Airlines flight engineer with dual American-Luxembourg nationality, working on US military charters into Vietnam. Fuller registered the C-47s in the US, but kept them at the German border airfield of Trier where they were fitted with a crude bomb-release system and additional fuel tanks before their delivery to Faro. There was a small irony here for I knew of Trier and included it in my later World War l history. It was the town where John Maynard Keynes had twice negotiated in 1919 with German representatives in an attempt to find a financial route to feed the starving German civilian population after the devastating success of Britain's five-year food blockade. This blockade from 1914 killed, perhaps, 750,000 people, a forerunner of the current Biafran genocide.[14] Trier was also where the first mass survey was conducted to assess the effects of severe malnutrition on young children caused by the blockade. The conclusion was that those from poorer stock suffered a 'general and sometimes permanent lowering of the whole intelligence level from even a moderate degree of malnutrition and that the change would be permanent'.[15] I hoped, in some way, my efforts could stem a repeat of that British success.

The papers also suggested that VEBEG sold the DC-3s for $5,000 each; then a middleman called Ernest Koenig paid $11,000, while the Biafrans agreed on $45,000 on receipt in Biafra. Two planes were to make the long transfer to the war zone with a third kept in Faro in reserve. When I checked my plane over I realised another irony: it had played a central role in the Berlin Airlift in 1948–49, making dozens of flights for the United States Air

Force flying food and medicine into the city to beat the Russian blockade. It had cargo doors and was configured to take ramps for rapid unloading of pallets. Later, the plane had been handed over to the West Germans as part of a plan to bolster the new Luftwaffe.

I left Faro at the beginning of April with a sixty-five-year-old American pilot and 6,000 pounds of tinned food, dried stockfish and medicines. In later reports, the co-pilot was named Grimwood, but, in fact, I was called Grinward. I did almost all the flying as it turned out my captain had limited experience of C-47s and, anyway, he needed his sleep. We crawled around West Africa: Porto Santo, Bissau and Abidjan where we were caught in a severe rainstorm. The unpressurised C-47 was built for bad weather, but showed it was true to type with constant leaks around the windshield. I spent an hour wearing an improvised leather apron to try to keep dry and warm. On the final sector to Uli from São Tomé another standard fault developed, well-remembered from BUA, when the port oil cooler sprang a leak, the pressure dropped, and I had to shut down. Flying on one engine restricted our height to 6,000 feet, which, in itself, was no problem. The fix after landing, of which Stan had been a master, was to get a long rod threaded at both ends onto which were screwed little rubber gaskets over large washers. The whole was bolted to make a seal.

It was a quiet night at Uli from both Nigerian bombers and relief flights. I was third in. To be honest, with all my experience with this type of plane at airports all over Europe, including grass, it was a straightforward landing even with just one engine. However, I couldn't perform a fast and tight spiral descent so I went in low from a distance out, yawing almost sideways at times in the wind, dropped smoothly onto the road and swung easily into the jungle cover which, luckily, was on the left. You really could put a DC-3 down anywhere. Glade and his ants swarmed through the cargo door as soon as I switched off.

'Out, out,' he yelled.

The worst part of the trip was the aircraft's general condition. The faulty oil cooler could be temporarily repaired, but would need a replacement at some time, the landing gear needed several attempts to get it down and locked, the windscreen leaked, a side window was cracked, and the flaps were sticky. A couple of secondary instruments didn't work. I was already thinking about how to arrange some basic maintenance so I wasn't at all surprised to hear that when the second DC-3 from Faro reached Bissau its commander, Australian 'Bunny' Sommerville, quit. He had complained on the radio throughout the flight of the appalling state and general serviceability of his aircraft.

After a little thought, I placed a telephone call to Stan at Bournemouth and asked him how he was doing. He was beyond morose. The BUA Dakota had given up the ghost and was gathering cobwebs and rust while waiting for an unlikely sale for spare parts. BUA was going all jet which meant that Stan, a committed, old-fashioned petrolhead, would have to requalify which was something he didn't want to do and, considering Stan's age, was something with which BUA agreed.

What did Stan think about a little foreign holiday with some rough and ready Dakota work thrown in? I suggested $800 a month. He bit my hand off. I asked him to get to Bissau or Abidjan yesterday with a good supply of whisky and a large bag of tools because he'd be making do.

I got a message three days later asking me to pick him up at Abidjan. His manager at BUA heard what Stan was up to and thoroughly approved. The pictures of emaciated Biafran children had done their work. Stan told me later that BUA were only too pleased to release him and gave him a good pay-off. He got a free seat on a Super VC-10 on a scheduled route. What's more, he was encouraged to take what he wanted from the unwanted BUA DC-3. I don't imagine they meant an engine, most of the electrics, two oil coolers, a new flap, some side-window Perspex, and a complete landing gear with spare tyres, but by working through two nights with some enthusiastic ground crews, that's what Stan borrowed. Stan always boasted that he held the world record of one hour forty-seven minutes for replacing a Dakota engine; that his replacement didn't match the existing engines in Biafra didn't faze him. He had even come up with some new type of plastic glue in a tube that might fix the windshield. Everyone seemed delighted to help.

I sought out Chuck's commander at Uli with some trepidation and told him what I had done and that I needed $800 a month to cover Stan's costs. I did point out that he was getting the world's most experienced Dakota engineer in return, plus some spares. He stared at me for a full minute, left the room for ten, came back, and told me to get on with it.

As I reached the door, he shouted that I would never make a good Nigerian. 'Come-back tomorrow' was the by-word for Lagos bureaucracy.

At Bissau, the co-pilot John Mitchell-Smith, formerly with Mercy Missions for the UK, had taken over the aircraft discarded by Sommerville and I was despatched via São Tomé, under the name Archer, to take his co-pilot's seat from Abidjan. On 11 April, Stan was sitting at a table at a tired café just off the tarmac with a cold bottle in hand. He proudly introduced John and I to a tarpaulin-covered pile. He had already organised loading and dodged customs because the spares never left the flight area. The locals knew where we were going and didn't want to know. At São Tomé, a grateful Mitchell-Smith left the plane. I took the night flight into Uli alone. A beaming Stan sat in the right seat as, on the flight down, he was squeezed in the back between his engine, a roof-high pile of spares and several crates of whisky. We were instructed to change to the Uli Tower frequency before gaining clearance for a direct approach to what was euphemistically known as 'Runway 16'. I gave thanks once again for the automatic variable propeller pitch which eased the engines' performance during take-off, climb, cruise, descent and, especially, landing. As I came down between the trees, the pitch, in combination with hydraulically operated trailing edge wing tips, meant that I could bleed airspeed for a safer, slower landing. A gentle bump, a quick turn into a ready gap beneath the palms and I was home.

We needed the whisky at Uli when we were told of our mission. It was a madcap idea with little chance of success or survival. We were to convert both Dakotas into gunships based on a successful adaptation used by the Americans in Vietnam. The big difference was that the fast-firing 9mm guns at the rear and along the inside of the fuselage would fire upwards, not downwards. Our target was one of the Nigerian MiG 17Fs that attacked Uli most dawns. The attack profile of the MiG was almost always the same. The first pass was at altitude before losing height quickly to make a low run across the airstrip from the north. The armed C-47s were to be airborne just before first light, making for Uli above the palm tops, one aircraft from the north and one from the south. Each aircraft was to fly low and to the right of a centre line so as not to be on a collision course. The crew would be advised by a ground controller when the MiG-17 began its run. Then, all of the guns aboard the two C-47s would be fired upwards in such a manner that the Nigerian bomber would literally fly through a shower of bullets. Stan thought he knew where the idea came from: a couple of years before some C-47s were converted into the USAF's first operational gunship, the AC-47, and had flown several hundred missions in Vietnam. During the current year, the Americans started using them for 'Spooky' missions, flying from near Saigon to drop propaganda leaflets onto Southeast Asia. The crews named the airplane 'Puff the Magic Dragon', based on its propensity to surround itself with the smoke of gunfire. Of course, there may also have been a few reefers aboard to help the crews through long flights.

I took my plane the fifteen miles to Uga, north-east of Uli, an airstrip on the road from Orlu to Awka. The surface was fine for Dakotas and light aircraft, but crumbly and dangerous for four-engined freighters. The plane was pushed back into the bush and camouflaged with leaves and branches and Stan and I set to work on our maintenance and conversion with the help of some bright local trainee engineers. It took two months, mostly while waiting for our guns. The building blocks of the Dakota's construction facilitated work on the airframe; there were few expensive or specialised parts. Mechanics could create as much of the aluminium work as was required when they found spare metal.

We shared the strip with one of the air legends of the war, Carl Gustaf von Rosen, with his initial fleet of five Swedish 'Minicon' Malmö planes, the 'Babies of Biafra' in honour of the starved children. We mixed over a drink from time to time, but kept our operations apart, both missions deemed secret. Rosen took his tiny planes into Nigeria in highly successful treetop-hugging surprise bombing and rocket raids that caught Russian MiGs and Ilyushins on the ground and put oil and command installations out of commission. His Minicons were painted green above and blue below to aid camouflage.

Stan and I were given a good house in the town, a chef, a liaison officer, and John turned up with his Peugeot. Our house was well camouflaged and we had access to an underground bunker. Almost immediately, Nigerian Air Force MiGs began making dawn attacks on Uga as well as continuing raids against Uli. It was, the Biafrans felt, almost as if the Nigerians had been tipped off. Stan suspected British special forces; not such a wild claim as things turned out. Although our aircraft was not hit the suspicions remained. The Biafrans vented their distrust of all British crew and arrested John Mitchell-Smith who was expelled and flown back to Faro. Our small team was left well alone as we worked all hours and drove back and forth to Uli. We listened to Biafra Radio while we tinkered and, sometimes, Radio Kaduna, controlled by the Nigerian government. The station's theme tune was a chant in Hausa, which we had translated:

Let us go and crush them. We will pillage their property, rape their womenfolk, kill off their menfolk and leave them uselessly weeping.

There was little variety in the food we got, chicken, cassava and sweet potatoes, but it was much better than that scavenged by the passing tide of humanity. From time to time, we swam at the large natural spring at Obizi. One day, a Biafran pilot we called Zac turned up, a gift from Chuck. He claimed a hundred hours on twin-engined Cessnas. Perhaps it was Chuck's idea of a joke, but Zac was enthusiastic and I could make use of him in the right-hand seat pulling levers, reading instruments, turning on switches and handling the radio when Stan was working on the ground. What freaked Zac and our engineer gunners was the flexibility in the Dakota's wing tips. These could 'flap' five degrees in flight and caused serious initial consternation to our workforce.

The effects of the blockade were becoming more evident each day. The total shut-off of protein-rich foodstuffs was having its effect. No one had foreseen this because no one had thought the war would last this long. The priests and nuns knew what they were looking at: kwashiorkor, extreme protein deficiency, which transformed an incompetent bush war into a massive humanitarian tragedy the like of which neither Africa, nor Europe, nor North America had ever seen. The children died in the villages, by the roadsides and, alongside those who survived on the relief food, in the feeding centres and, sad to say, there were two near us at Uga. They were built around the local missions, church, school, dispensary and a field the size of a football pitch where the wasted children lay on the grass, on rush mats or the laps of their mothers, who held them close, watching them wither and slip away. As the effects of kwashiorkor intensified, the dark brown curly hair diminished to a ginger fizz. The eyes lost focus, but appeared immense in the wizened face. The weakness of departed muscle made them listless until, unable to move at all, they died and a figure in a cassock came to intone a last blessing and take them to the pit.

The day of the trap was set for the third of June. The evening before saw a long argument between Stan and I. He was determined to come; I was against it, but that was based on emotion. Two worn-out thirty-year-old piston-engined military transports were to take on a Russian jet fighter that was the American's primary adversary in Vietnam. In its lower nose, the MiG carried some of the largest guns ever used for air-to-air combat, one 37mm and two 23mm cannons. It could make 30,000 feet in three minutes, while the Dakota was so old it could just make 20,000 feet. The MiG's top speed was over 700 mph, twice what we could manage after we had warmed up for thirty minutes. The MiG was renowned for its nimbleness; steady might best describe the Dakota. I didn't expect to come back. Stan said he hadn't come all this way to be left in the jungle without a friend. Besides, he had directed most of the engineering and part-building to fit the 9mm guns. He had earned the right and if anything went wrong he needed to be at hand to fix it. And if that wasn't enough, he was more than twice my age so I should do what I was told.

We had had three days of practice runs and co-ordination with our partner plane. We both took off twenty minutes before dawn and mooched about out of sight of Uli fifty feet above the palm tops. We each had pre-decided landmarks that we had to cross at the same time in order to catch the MiG on the line of the road after it came out of its strafing run. The three aircraft had to meet at the same time when we had to fire for three seconds and then the target-hunting MiG would be gone.

Ground control sent the alert. The MiG had been spotted. Then, 'Go . . . go!' We went.

I saw the MiG above and behind the other Dakota. Its pilot appeared more than surprised; no one flew at Uli in the early dawn. He was too close and too high to fire and he pulled his nose to go round again for his easy prey. For that reason, he didn't see me as both C-47s opened up as he flashed over. My plane seemed about to fall apart as Stan let rip and the wall of bullets leapt upwards. It was over almost as it began and I dived left for cover.

Stan had a good view and saw the jet soar upwards and, then, a trickle of smoke which became a steady plume. The MiG, still under control, fell out of a stall turn, spotted our sister plane and raked it before heading west back to Nigerian territory. It was an impulse and stupid, but I banked and followed at a respectful distance. The MiG's speed was well down. Stan joined me and our two Biafran gunners crowded us from behind, whooping as if the war was won. Crossing the Niger River, we were more vulnerable, but the smoke from the MiG got thicker, then flames, and the engine cut. The pilot ejected and the MiG came down nose first and exploded in thick bush east of Kwale. It made quite a fire.

Stan noted the position and I turned abruptly and headed for Uli before the sky filled with vengeful Nigerians. We swaggered past the pilot as he dangled downwards. I thought about flying straight into him as a hate burned inside me. Before I could decide, he stuck up two fingers, suggesting he might have been British. There was a burst of gunfire from the back of my plane. No one said anything.

The other C-47 had landed safely on one engine, a riddled mid-fuselage, one Igbo gunner with a flesh wound in the arm. The aircraft was irreparable and was run deep into the bush. The pilot had seen nothing and reported the mission a failure. The assumption was that we had been shot down and that explains why, instead of a hero's welcome, Biafran anti-aircraft fire welcomed us as we approached. We were too low to be inconvenienced, but the black flak clouds attracted a MiG-17. I made it down and lost no time in turning into cover. The manoeuvre was slow enough for the jet to see where I had gone. The four of us ran deep into the palms and dived into the insect infested and rotting foliage as the MiG ripped open our valiant plane. The smoke guided the pilot back for a second go. When all was clear, Stan was near tears as he realised that not even he would ever fix that pile of wreckage.

We debriefed the flight commander, gave him the position of the downed MiG, and were promised medals.

The cover up had already started. Reports came in of a Nigerian fighter that had made it home with engine trouble. No mention was made of a loss and, somehow, despite local jubilation, the affair died away. I was told later that the Biafrans kept quiet because they wished to repeat the surprise and wanted no details leaked on how it had been done. There was another

MiG strafing the Uli runway the following dawn, but with a modification: a second fighter now stood guard high in front of the rising sun. With both C-47s lost beyond repair, unhappy events on the ground took control.

That night, as Stan and I sat under the stars with our third palm wine, our meagre bags collected from Uga by Corporal John, one of Flughjalp's DC-6Bs was trying to land at Uli with a full load of stockfish. Flughjalp was a good example of the topsy-turvy world of European regulation applied to aircraft and pilots operating in a war zone. Transavia, from whom half the aircraft used in Biafran relief were chartered, was applying pressure over the number of hours crews could legally work. The demands of operating into Biafra meant that legal limits were always being broken and, under Dutch civil aviation regulations, Transavia could no longer continue its charter agreement. The solution to both problems was found by establishing a new and non-profit-making company specifically for humanitarian relief work, called Flughjalp, *Aid By Air*, and registered in Reykjavik. Flughjalp was owned by three partners: Nordchurchaid, the protestant Evangelical Lutheran Church of Iceland, and the Icelandic airline, Loftleidir. The only differences to the aircraft on the airlift were their colours and a simple change in registration letters. Aircraft were repainted in a standard scheme with the characteristic 'double-fi h' badge and the new company name.

The DC-6 made its first approach to Uli and, as usual, called for the runway lights to be turned on at the last moment. The pilot, finding himself too low and off the centre line, decided to overshoot and try again. We recognised the plane as TF-AAE and knew the pilot was Australian Verdun Polley, well-known for repeating this error since joining the relief airlift eight months earlier. We stood with mounting apprehension as Polley made two deadly mistakes. Instead of climbing to re-connect with Uli's beacon he decided to turn a full circle to port in order to make a second approach. The runway lights turned on and again he was off the right line, but this time a long way out and only at 200 feet. Polley switched on the DC-6's landing lights, corrected his approach, but left his lights on. Two MiG-17Fs were patrolling, no doubt angry at what had happened to their colleague that morning. With landing lights blazing, Polley's plane was a perfect target for a head-on attack. I heard at least two rockets. As Polley touched-down, he switched the engines to reverse pitch while cannon fire hit the runway and exploded upwards, either side of the cockpit. Despite sustaining direct hits, there were no injuries among the crew and Polley managed to taxi the DC-6 clear of the landing area and into a parking bay. Following close behind Polley, a second Flughjalp aircraft continued its approach and landed, without lights, further along the road.

The damage sustained by TF-AAE was seen as light enough to allow the aircraft to be flown out of Uli. The main fuel tanks had been ruptured, but the auxiliary tanks in the outer wing sections were undamaged and contained enough fuel to make São Tomé. The major problems involved broken hydraulic cables and two flat mainwheel tyres. There was also some cannon damage to the fin but the rudder hinges were untouched. By now, Stan was a local engineering legend and here was his forte. At each attempt to jack up the wing to replace the tyres, the thin bitumen surface of Uli's tarmac collapsed. Stan decided, as there was one shattered tyre on each side, it was easier to remove the torn tyres and leave bare rims; the hydraulics he repaired with pipes and fencing wire.

In the early hours, Polley decided to fly back to base, but his co-pilot was in fever and destined to spend the flight slumped and shivering in a bucket seat. His incapacity was covered up because the only available co-pilot was a young Frenchman – me – experienced on DC-3s, but with no hours on any four-engined plane, let alone a DC-6, built as competition for the mighty Constellation. For that reason, but mainly because of the condition of the aircraft and what I had seen of Polley's skills, I was reluctant to make the flight.

My mind was made up for me when an Irish missionary arrived shepherding seventy newly orphaned children onto the airstrip, many sick and dying. He demanded they be flown to his hospital at São Tomé. Did I have any option? The hospital had been built by Caritas Austria and was run by Caritas Germany and its Protestant counterpart, Das Diakonische Werk. Irish missionary sisters came from Biafra to assist local staff. The children were wrapped in blankets, placed on inflated mattresses and strapped to the floor of the aircraft.

The plan was to fly at low altitude to the coast and then climb. The smells from damaged children mixed with the stench of dried cod and damaged fuel pipes haunted our air on the flight deck. Polley did most of the flying during the thirty-minute transit while I followed instructions, monitoring instruments and adjusting controls. Stan sat alongside the flight engineer, Hordur Eiriksson. As we approached São Tomé, the first thing that struck me were the lights. Nothing special in themselves, but they were switched on, in stark contrast to Uli. The approach was made with hydraulic pressures reading zero, no brakes and little fuel. Polley landed at just above stalling speed and then allowed the aircraft to gently turn to a halt. Ambulances, doctors and nurses were waiting to rush the children to treatment.

Daylight showed extensive structural damage, too serious for repair. God had been with the children. Stan organised stripping the engines and useable components, including the complete nosewheel assembly.

At São Tomé, I fell sick with fever and was hospitalised on the island for a month, too ill to move with typhoid. From my hospital bed, then a chair in the garden, and later from the beach I watched the skies. 'Paradise Island' was beautiful with long, golden sands under stunning wooded mountains. It could have been thronged by tourists, but most of its 60,000 Africans and Portuguese survived by growing coffee and cocoa. This was a prison island and a military base. Visitors were not welcome. It was hard to believe that the idyllic island's jail was feared for its torture. I witnessed the astonishing number of aid flights organised from São Tomé by Joint Church Aid (JCA). By the end of April, the month when I arrived, JCA had completed 2,279 flights from the island; the 2,500th flight was recorded at the end of May. There were 7,350 relief flights into Biafra in the three years of war, perhaps seven flights a day taking in almost a million tonnes of supplies.

The pilots were an extraordinary bunch of people, most of whom worked for passenger or cargo airlines. They felt they were 'doing something useful' when they spent their annual holidays on the airlift. Many stayed on, arranging leave of absence, some quitting their regular jobs. Most of them had never flown in a war before. They also broke the international rules, which limited aircrew to a legal maximum of 120 flying hours within any twenty-eight-day period. Some pilots achieved more by having themselves rostered under false names, sometimes with the name of a captain who had long left the airlift. It became quite normal for pilots to average 180 and, sometimes, over 200 hours a month.

I told the authorities that I had lost all my papers in making the emergency flight with Polley, and a Red Cross passport with a new name was added to my collection. Stan left for Europe with my blessing. Later, we tried to meet several times. I heard that he had bought a pub, become an alcoholic as he dealt with his Biafran nightmares, and died a few years later.

With leave due, money still coming in, and weak from malaria that still returns, I was ordered into a passenger seat aboard a Constellation to Faro where I continued treatment and spent the late summer recuperating and reading on the beaches. I decided to stay on the payroll to await my next assignment, the sight of the emaciated Biafra babies and the orphaned children aboard Polley's DC-6 visiting me every night.

The position in Biafra near the end of November 1969 had shafts of hope, but, in truth, was desperate. The Faro staff got regular updates of the real situation as the flights came through. By the end of September, Biafra had been reduced to roughly half the size of Ireland, a quarter of its original area. All the non-Igbo and most of the oil-producing areas had been overrun. Biafra had copious supplies of low-sulphur fuel, an essential and coveted component in the search for alternative green sources. Forsyth wrote that people were 'packed like pilchards in this tormented fragment of the land of the Rising Sun'. An estimated eight million people – a third of them refugees – were, according to the relief agencies, dying at the rate of 3,000, 5,000 and finally an astronomical 10,000 a day. The archetypical starving Biafran baby with its pathetic pot belly, matchstick legs, fleshless rib-cage and soulful eyes which had been appearing in comfortable European living-rooms with the frequency of soap adverts, stirred people's consciences … The lines between genuine humanitarians, guilt-ridden do-gooders, religious crusaders, romantic adventurers and plain nut-cases grew blurred. The world did, after all, care.' The answer to Forsyth's rhetorical question to me of about six months before of how many children had to die became clearer. About a million, it seemed.

Writing this chapter some fifty years later, history repeats itself. The British love of a good blockade continues in the Yemen where Saudi Arabian ground forces, aircraft and warships established a land, sea and air lock when they invaded in 2015. The stranglehold was tightened two years later when the United States, with thinly veiled support from the United Kingdom, provided additional resources. Publicly, the UK called on

Saudi Arabia to ease the siege and allocated £4 million to meet emergency requirements. Less publicly, Saudi Arabia remains one of the UK's biggest arms purchasers. The blockade has resulted in widespread starvation with the United Nations anticipating the world's deadliest famine in decades with eight million people 'on the brink'. The World Health Organization says that the number of persons with suspected cholera has reached almost 500,000.

In further shades of Biafra, the Cameroon, with a five million Anglophone minority, is sliding into a vicious and largely unreported civil war. 'Ambazonia', with the same population as Scotland and with greater oil reserves, is campaigning for independence, fed up with the indifference and lack of investment from the French-speaking majority government. Britain is doing nothing to stop the genocide as men and machetes take on US-trained military forces. In fact, the British helped bring it all about when the English-speaking Cameroons were dragged to a referendum in 1961 in which they were forced to choose between joining either the French Cameroonian state or Nigeria.

4. FREEDOM OF THE GUN

To Carthage then I came
Burning burning burning
O Lord Thou pluckest me out
O Lord Thou pluckest
burning[16]

I had all but given up on a return to Biafra when a cable arrived late November at the Phoenix Company offices in Faro. Chuck wanted me to fly to Uli where he would give me more information. There was also a medal to collect. Arms flights from Europe had dwindled to less than one a week. Ordinary Biafrans contributed most of what they had to buy weapons to continue the fight; poor villages took collections, rich men emptied their foreign accounts. As the funds dried up, it was the French and Jacques Foccart who came to Biafra's support with a motley and covert supply of World War ll-era rifles and field guns, affordable if not bargain basement.

In retaliation, sabotage by the CIA and by the British, often using Nigerians as front men, became common. I knew of two incidences. The previous June at Lisbon, a bomb was found inside a Constellation's engine hood during pre-flight checks. The plane was unloaded, but no more explosives were discovered. The flight engineer slept in the plane to be sure no further attempt was made before take-off the next morning. In Bissalanca in Guinea Bissau, now Osvaldo Vieira International Airport, mechanics working on a Connie saw yellow smoke emerge from the cargo. They leapt off and ran as a huge explosion blew out every window in the terminal building. When the dust and smoke cleared, clouds of Biafran money floated in the sky. Portuguese soldiers ran around grabbing fistfuls of banknotes, stuffing them into their tunics only to find later that the currency was worthless. The bomb was planted by an American captain who had been nobbled by Nigerian security; the device was timed to explode over the ocean between Bissau and São Tomé.

I was to hitch a lift aboard another Connie to Uli.

In the autumn of 1969, under a complex leasing arrangement, two former US Western Airlines L-749A Constellations, acquired in a merger with Pacific Northern Airlines, joined the Biafran government fleet. Repairs were conducted at Lisbon by German mechanics who did little preventative maintenance. They only fixed things that were broken. These Constellations had a strengthened floor, fuselage and landing gear, which increased dead weight by over 4,000 pounds. Initially, they operated with full US-marks and retained their former airline scheme, including the large head of a native American on the nose. They also had a tub-shaped object under the belly, a 'Speedpak', an external container used to increase the aircraft's cargo capacity. Our plane was 5N85H, the hyphen forgotten, formerly US-registered N86524.

I made sure I was on the tarmac to lend a hand with security, but nobody checked me.

The plane was loaded with the latest French offerings, mostly personal weapons, but included anti-tank bazookas and a few field guns. Nobody seemed too sure. There were three crew and six passengers of which I was one, an extra mercenary joining at the last moment. We took off in the cool of late evening. I sat close to the flight engineer, a German-American, who said his name was Nuber.

The Connie was a flight engineer's aircraft and only as reliable as the technician in charge allowed it to be. Pilots demanded fully qualified flight engineers in whom they had absolute trust. Early versions of the Constellation could present a mess of problems to somebody who hadn't done his time with these machines and understood their many idiosyncrasies. Sitting directly behind the captain, the engineer was able to operate any of the levers and buttons within reach except, of course, the flight controls. The pilots did not even have a propeller-feathering button up front. Their only engine controls were the magneto switches, one master propeller lever and four throttle levers. Everything else was in the hands of the flight technician. The engineer was also in charge of the throttle power levers during take-off, climb, cruise and landing.

After crossing the Moroccan coast, Nuber sprang to life as the outer port turbine stuttered. He feathered the large Wright engine to guard against an oil leak and the chance of fire. In itself, this was no great deal; a Connie on three engines was almost normal. The experienced captain was taking no chances and decided to squeeze down at Marrakech to check the cause. He began a wide sweep holding the aircraft at its cruising altitude of 20,000 feet rather than face another problem over the Atlas mountains. Flying on into the Sahara was a risk as there were few places, all a long way away, that had an operational runway of over 5,000 feet.

There were two loud simultaneous bangs. I saw the cowling leap from the inner port engine and the Connie yawed wildly as tendrils of flame showed in the dark. The starboard inner stopped with a shriek as metal gouged into metal. This was no accident. Not even a Connie loses three engines within five minutes. A 'mayday' went out with identification, position and condition. Nuber was shutting down power demands and firing extinguishers. We fell into a backward dive with the remaining engine fighting the thin air. Nuber turned to me, ashen, but calm.

'We're going in,' he said. 'One engine, no way out. Go find a seat near the tail. Best chance.'

The captain continued his useless battle with a heavy plane already beyond control, its tanks brimming with fuel.

'Got to get away from the mountains,' he gasped. 'Got to find some flat. We've got 13,000 feet on the clock, losing it fast. What have we got in front?'

The co-pilot was ready with the answer, 'Highest point, Mount Toubkal, over 13,000 feet. We've got to turn to starboard. Continue the turn. Tighter. Continue the turn, dammit.'

As I went to the back, Nuber gave up. There was nothing more he could do, but hope. I clutched the crates of munitions for support and fought my way downhill to my old seat by the toilet. Two of the passengers had lost it, yelling obscenities; another was deep in prayer; someone grabbed my leg, for what benefit, I didn't know, but I shrugged him off. Through the portholes I could see snow reflected in the moonlight pierced by black … black rock … and it all seemed close enough to touch. I made the seat but hadn't strapped in when we hit almost parallel to a slope and the pressurised fuselage ruptured. The last engine screamed as its fifteen-feet propeller tried to claw its solitary way up the mountain. There was a long tearing sound as of something dying. I saw a world of inky blue, the moon, thousands of stars, and I was flying.

I came to mid-morning with just scrapes, bruises, and a sore back, parts of an engine lying in the same deep snow pit, its pipes two feet above my face. Early snow had collected on the wreckage and made me a snow cave. The stench of fuel was pervasive and I felt dizzy from the fumes. There had been no fire or I would have burned to a crisp. I slithered my way out into the cold. Most of the plane was in six large pieces and in plain sight, gripped by the incline. Birds of prey, vultures, ravens and kites, wove slow and intricate patterns upon the hard grey sky. There was no sound but their calling.

Everyone was dead. The pilots had gone head first through the windscreen into rock and their faces were unrecognisable. Nuber remained strapped in his seat, but with a set of throttle levers in his gut. The cargo was intact with no sound, no ticking from the mortar rounds. The only damage was to a crate of refurbished M1 carbines which had spilled its contents. I found food, which I ate unheated, and blankets which I wrapped around myself. It began to snow hard and visibility dropped to almost zero. I settled into the tail fuselage, the most complete section, as I started to shake with shock. The Connie had ripped and separated two feet forward from my seat. I waited out the storm and spent the night in bitter cold until I fell asleep.

The morning was bright with far views and a sharp sun which began to restore some warmth. I thought I could see Marrakech, a smudge on the horizon and, to the right, the flat of the desert and in several places below wisps of village fires. Having found the bags and gathered my papers and collected everyone's money, I took the passports, one German, one American, from the people closest to my age and who most looked like me. I put on the thickest collection of clothes that allowed movement. Looking like Michelin Man, I found and emptied a rucksack and filled it with the rest of what food I could uncover, chocolate and sandwiches and a few tins of soup. I added the mercenary's large fighting knife, tied a rope on top, picked up an M1 carbine with its short barrel, several magazines, left the bodies where they lay, and started the descent.

The first 500 feet involved troublesome climbing, which I found technically interesting. Several times, I lowered my supplies and carbine by rope and then climbed to where they waited. Then gaps appeared in the snow and cracks in the rock slabs and it became a steady scramble. Late afternoon, after some hours of stumbling, slipping and several falls, I heard the bells of goats and then their bleating, the black Berber goats that blend with the rocks of the Atlas Mountains. I was seen by a nomad who raised his hand in greeting and I worked towards him along a thin trail scratched through the gorse.

We examined each other for a full minute.

'Anaruz,' he said, pointing at his chest.

'Philippe,' I replied, with my finger to mine.

Anaruz gestured for me to follow and led down another thousand feet to his caves. Every five minutes, he turned and welcomed me, '*Yallah marhaba, marhaba*'.

We passed through a drystone-wall enclosure. Anaruz stopped at one entrance, bowed, and said with no trace of irony, '*Maha babicum*', Welcome to our door.

Painted in white on the wall of the living and cooking quarters was a Berber script, 'ⴰⵣ', and I saw the confident central motif repeated in several carpets which covered the floor near to a small bracken and log fire. The cave, perhaps ten feet high, was warm. Anaruz's wife saw my slight injuries and the blood and her face became serious and she kept repeating, '*Labas, labas*.'[17] The three young children had broad smiles and demanded, '*Ammi trit atay*?'[18] Hot mint tea appeared. The family spoke no English, but used hand gestures to supplement their Amazigh dialect as they asked what had happened. I mimicked the plane crashing and they became animated; I surmised that they had heard the engine pass close overhead and might even have heard the impact. I was bandaged with herbs picked nearby and given a fatty goat stew of unknown body parts with dried vegetables and warm unleavened bread. Manna.

I offered my tins, sandwiches and chocolate and gave Anaruz's wife some of my clothes, which were all snatched with gratitude. However, it was my carbine that caused the greatest interest and it was taken outside to test its effective range. Anaruz fired five times at a stone pile and decided 200 metres. That was enough for me. I mimed sleep and was taken to the next-door cave where I lay down and was out for over twenty hours.

Two days later, Anaruz was visited by his son, Idir, who often guided tourists in the mountains and spoke a little French. I told him all that had happened and gave him the mercenary's knife. The M1 was no longer of any use to me and I asked Idir if his father would accept it as a gift in thanks for looking after me. Thus this stolen weapon became the most successful present I ever gave. Anaruz took it in both hands, talked to it, stroked it, checked the firing mechanism, emptied the magazine, and cradled the gun to his shoulder. I passed the spare ammunition to Idir. Tears fell and then Anaruz leapt up and hugged me and kissed me as a son and as a brother.

It was agreed, with little discussion, that I was ready to lead the two men to the wreckage. Idir left early one morning and by dinner returned with two mules and a good supply of old rope. He was confident that they would be able to follow my trail as there had been little fresh snow, but was less confident of finding the plane as it was concentrated on the uppermost slopes of Mount Tibherine above steep walls. Another younger son, Aderfi, accompanied us to manage the mules when the climbing started.

At ten o'clock, after the cold had abated and the morning fog lifted, our little party set off. The men barely paused to examine the ground for my path seemed to them as evident as a signposted road. It took two hours to walk what was only three kilometres of snaking trails to the rock face beneath the crash site, so much easier when you know the terrain. At the foot of the crag, the mules could go no further. This was where I could help. I traced the line of my descent and decided there was an easier return route. I fashioned some slings from offcuts and trailing a line began the climb. I managed it in three moves because of intermediate ledges and walkable gullies. My agility pleased me and impressed my companions. After an hour we had ascent ropes secured and Anaruz and Idir joined me at the top. The bodies lay where left, frozen, and in good condition apart from the eyes which had been pecked. The Berbers were like children in a sweet shop as they forced a few more crates to assess the cargo. After an hour of prodding and lifting and sorting, there was a short meeting and Anaruz and Idir reached a decision. They would take everything.

I thought about it briefly. The guns were bought and paid for by the Biafran government. They were not in my charge, but I was the government's employee in a sort of way. Also, I favoured the weapons reaching their intended destination because anything that might stem the deaths of Biafran children was entirely a good thing. However, what could I do? Even if I were able, there was no obvious way to get them across the Sahara, down the Niger River, through Nigeria and into Biafra. The Berbers would not let it happen and neither would the Nigerians. In between, Tuareg brigands and the Mali government would also have a say. The guns had also smoothed my rescue. I kept my concerns to myself and joined in the pleasure at Allah's beneficence.

I showed the best way to make slings in order to slide the containers down in stages to the mules. We began with four crates of carbines and, while I waited on the first ledge, the mules were each loaded with ten loose carbines. Aderfi set off and Anaruz and Idir climbed with me back to the top. We slowly worked four more crates to the mule point and waited for Aderfi. As the light faded we made our final trek of the day, one of the mules loaded with empty containers. The refilled crates fitted snugly in the back of the goats' cave, but not before Idir and Aderfi made their personal selections.

I left them to it and busied myself with pen and paper. During the never-changing goat stew, I made my first suggestion to them and, while chary, they agreed to try it. The inner stub of one wing hung almost two metres over an edge nearly above our mule station. From below it looked like a pinnacle of rock. I showed how, with the addition of a few timbers and some more rope, we could set up a suspended trestle strong enough to take about fifty kilograms. Boxes could be slung ready and then swung out before being lowered straight to the ground. I reckoned twenty minutes a drop with three men on top and two beneath. All of the arms could be moved down regardless of the number of mules and their arrival times.

I then tried to assess the haul. The manifest, still in the cockpit, reported unspecific 'manufactured goods', but it did show the payload at a little under 6,000 kilograms. I did some simple sums: one mule, twenty-five kilograms a trip, equalled 240 trips. Given, say, two trips a day in winter, working six days in a week, twelve trips, we needed about twenty mule weeks. It was mid-December. To be clear by the end of January and before the weather improved and search parties and early, hardy tourists got in the way, we needed at least six mules and preferably more. Then there was the matter of fodder, the extra men, their food, and secrecy. And, of course, the arms had to be stored and distributed. To whom? Given, sold, or bartered? What were my hosts' intentions?

Lastly, I had been making notes at the crash site. I had a good idea of what was there. It was an all-French cargo majoring on early version, light-weight, semi-automatic M1 carbines, much used until a few years before in the Algerian war. There were also a few M1 rifles, some second-hand, pre-war MAS-36 bolt-action rifles and PA MAC 50 (MAS-50) 9mm semi-automatic pistols and a couple of boxes of FR F1 sniper rifles. All of these would be of personal interest to the Berbers, many of whom I later realised still used aged French weapons from the nineteenth-century: the single-shot Fusil Gras and its successor, the bolt-action, eight-round Lebel. Other crates contained French LRAC bazookas, important to deal with British Saladins and Ferrets, then two small artillery pieces, mortars and three heavy machine guns, all with ammunition. I did know that captured Soviet weaponry was of limited use to the Biafrans because Russian ammunition was bigger by one millimetre. When captured ammunition ran out, the Soviet weapons were useless. The Biafrans made a decision to try to use only equipment built to NATO standards.

I laid this all out for Idir and he went into a long huddle with his father. The next day Idir went down to their home village to negotiate and came back three days later with six more mules laden with timber, rope and supplies and six more men. In the morning we climbed back to the mule site. The new men wanted to make the ascent to see the crash and I spent the morning assembling the trestle and pulley system. By mid-afternoon, the first load went down like a dream in under fifteen minutes.

One incident raised my prestige even higher. As the mules began their trips, one was badly spooked. Carbines went flying. Nobody saw what caused it, but a snake was suspected. One of the newcomers started beating the mule with a stick. I slid down the rope and stood in front of the kicking animal, looked it in the eye and held out a flat hand. Within a few seconds it calmed and was nuzzling against me. Influence with animals was a respected and magical skill among the Berbers. The men discussed me and my exploit at great length and with some excitement.

I stayed down as it was clear that I was no longer needed up top. After half an hour, I was invited to join Aderfi leading a mule train down to the caves. The mood had changed, in no way threatening, but I sensed the men were beginning to become nervous about my presence.

Later, Idir took me on one side and explained. I was now kin by honour and invitation, but I was not Berber and I looked foreign. Just four families from the tribe had been let into the secret and they were working together to bring the weapons down and to distribute them. A stranger would bring unwanted attention and gossip. The men did not want any suggestion that there had been a survivor from the crash or any worry that salvage had taken place until the plane was found. They wanted to expedite my departure and that meant getting me out of Morocco. What did I think? What did I want to do?

I thought Idir was right and said so to his great relief. What he didn't know, none of them knew, was that there were eight crew and passengers on the manifest and there were eight bodies, the last-minute mercenary taking my place. A number, certainly, travelled under false identities and some of the passports were missing. It seemed likely that no one would ever know I had been on the plane. I decided to keep this to myself. I also said that now the wreck was found and a system was in place, I had little more to offer. I was healed and ready to go. What I would like to do was to move to Tangier and slip across the Straits of Gibraltar and from there go back to Faro.

All of that brought a huge smile from Idir, a big hug, kisses on both cheeks, and he rushed to tell his tribesmen the good news. I was immediately surrounded and thanked in Amazigh, Arabic and French for all that I had done. I gave all of my pages of workings-out to Idir and went to sleep.

Idir, Aderfi and I travelled down to the road to Oukaimeden village, spending a couple of nights sleeping in rocky crevices in the cold. We took a mule loaded with three goats for trade. The plan was to follow normal practice and for Aderfi to visit the weekly market to get winter supplies to take back to the cave, and for food for the regular move to their next pasture.

Idir announced that he would accompany me to Marrakech where we would stay a few days until arrangements had been made and then he would take me to the station for the night train to Tangier. After a night of soft sheets in Oukaimeden, we left for a one-day drive sitting with two others on the back seat of an old Mercedes van; the driver and three others squeezed on the front bench, one straddling the gear stick. They were all part of the wider family and restrained from questioning me. It was no place for serious conversation anyway amid a non-stop blast of news sharing and gossip, laughter and simulated indignation as the stories unfolded. We paused three times at wayside garages for fuel, tea, toilet and prayer for which Idir proffered me a mat and a jellaba to guard me from suspicious eyes. I was not left alone.

The Mercedes dropped us in a mean back street, dark blank walls on either side, a street sign, Derb El-something in Roman and Arabic characters. Old houses rose up amid the labyrinth, wall to wall, huddled together safe behind the ramparts to give warmth in winter. The monotony of plastered masonry, often crumbling to little heaps revealing poor mud bricks, was broken only by a wooden door within a door, heavy and studded with metal. There was no sign, no number, no bell. Ducking inside, I saw a heart-jolting fountain open to the sky and bathed in candle-light. Water burbled into runnels. Tiled pathways quartered the courtyard into small gardens studded with fruit trees, herbs, hashish shrubs and rose bushes. It represented paradise on earth. The ladies of the houses, flitted, veiled, in the background. I was shown to one of several surrounding bedrooms where I was given two hours of rest before dinner.

Idir introduced me to his uncle, Moha, in his sixties with a brilliant blue headscarf and matching jellaba, far-away brown eyes set in a deeply creased face. Several other men joined us but, while part of the family, conducted themselves with deference. A steaming plate of couscous and mutton with a thick spiced sauce arrived. Moha dipped his lean fingers in the dish and speaking perfect but heavily accented French gestured that I should take the place of honour and follow him in my selection of food.

'I was educated in Paris,' he told me with a twinkle in his eyes. 'I have known many French women. I may even have French sons, but they will be Berber in their hearts.'

Moha asked after my family and I explained I was alone. This occasioned some shock that there was no extended kin to protect me and to look after my interests. I was asked what I was doing on a plane carrying guns to Biafra. I told the group, Idir translating for me, that I was a pilot who had flown for the Biafrans, fell ill, and had been on my way back from Faro to continue the fight. I believed in the Biafran cause, was sickened by the actions of the British government and was scarred by the sight of so many starving children. The men spoke among themselves for several minutes and reached agreement.

'We are at one with the Biafran people,' said Moha. 'As Berbers, we have struggled for over a thousand years against colonial powers. For many years we aided our brothers in Algeria against the French. We seek to maintain our way of life, our independence. We have never suffered like the Biafrans, but we stand with them in our heart, a tribe fighting for its freedom, that which matters most to a man.'

There were grunts and sighs from the intense group. Moha reached inside his clothing and retrieved a silver pendant about two inches, old and long-worn, with simple carvings. He presented it to me.

'This was my grandfather's,' he said. 'He was a great man and head of our family. He would have welcomed you to his tent and be pleased to make this gift. You may know us as Berbers. This is a word that we accept only from foreigners, but it is a word from the Greek conquerors and signifies 'barbarians', people who do not speak Greek. We call ourselves *Amazigh people*, the people who see the sun set.'

Moha reached for paper and wrote, 'ⴰⵎⴰⵣⵉⵖ'. This is *Amazigh*, this is our word for the 'free man'. This freedom has always been a part of us and you can sense it in the character of every Berber. It is our way of life. We are all nomads and keep moving from the Atlas Mountains to desert plateaux looking for forage and water for our animals. We have no choice in our souls; we always go back to the desert.

'This symbol I have given you is the letter "z", the *aza*, ⵣ, taken from our *Tifinagh* script which is older than your prophet Jesus. People say that the *aza* used to be a weapon. It is still a weapon. It is the most important part of our character. You will see it in the heart of our word for *Amazigh*, on our walls and woven into our carpets. I give it to you because you also are a free man. Hopefully, one day this *aza* will be part of our flag and fly over a free country. You have given many *amazigh* new guns and this is another freedom, especially for our brethren in the desert and in the hills. I thank you on behalf of my tribe.'

It was quite a speech and an unworthy and embarrassed tear crept from my eye. Moha paused for a drink and a significant handful of food.

'I have one more personal gift for you,' he announced as his hand slid again into the folds of his costume. He gave me another thin pendant of impressed silver.

'It is the hand of Fatima,' I said. 'Is it for protection against evil?'

Moha was pleased. 'Yes, it is. It is called the *Hamsa*. It is the hand of the daughter of the prophet Muhammad. It protects and brings good luck. Wear it as you travel or place it above your door each night. Because I have given it to you, it also means that your new brothers will protect you as you are one of their family.'

He held up his hand to mean that no words were necessary and stood. I rose and he kissed me on both cheeks and left the room. As he went, he said, 'You may have questions about the guns. Talk with Idir.'

I remember Idir's comments well. A few trusted families had been brought quickly into the organisation. This meant that transporting the weapons was not hard to arrange, but all was kept secret so that the profit could be ensured. It would take another two weeks to get everything down from the wreck to caves spread throughout the valley. Boys were set with goats to keep watch. Men in the main villages were charged to raise the alarm should there be any increase in government troops or a sign of search parties. There were none so far. Each man was allowed his choice of personal gun and a supply of ammunition. This was his price of silence and also allowed others to recognise each conspirator as a party to the arrangement.

In the second phase, the rest of the weapons were to be taken late at night to the market place in Imlil village. The transfer, already under way, was by mule, with scouts walking ahead, each trip finishing well before sunrise. Here, they were to be stored until their sale was arranged. It was understood that mortars and field artillery had little value to the Berbers themselves, but there was a dangerous market nearby across the southern border with their Tuareg brothers.

'You must see the Tuareg, Berbers and Biafrans all fighting the same fight,' said Idir. 'When the French left ten years ago, we expected a new nation to be formed in our desert – our Sahara. Those in the north – Tuareg, Berber and Arab – would come together. We even had a name – '*Azawad*', but instead we got Mali and the new government was corrupt and tried to suppress the old ways.

I bit my tongue. Even I had read enough to know that the romanticised 'Blue Men of the Desert', with their indigo-dyed, traditional flowing garments, claimed a proud heritage. Like many a partly-subdued people, the Tuareg hankered after their heyday, lauding the days when their supremacy allowed them to take what they wanted from their sedentary neighbours. Their rigid caste system relied on Negro slaves captured in the south and either kept or sold into Morocco and Algeria. The haughty Tuareg terrorised the peoples who lived on the banks of the Niger and the peaceful populations of the oases into paying 'taxes'. They fleeced the Saharan caravans with opportunistic violence. The beginning of the end of their mysterious invincibility came in the 1880s with, of all things, the threat of a railway line, the Great Sahara Railway from Algeria to Timbuktu, planned to open the interior of northern Africa to French trade by connecting their colonies along the Niger River with the Mediterranean. A military expedition led by Major Paul Flatters was charged with finding a suitable route through the desert. He was slashed to death and his force was reduced to single figures and cannibalism by continued Tuareg subterfuge and sneak attacks. A handful of tattered and shamed men staggered back to tell their story. That they had killed and eaten weaker comrades was covered up. The 'revenge' battle occurred in March 1902 when the cream of the Tuareg fighters was killed near the village of Tit by a force of French Arab irregulars. The railway was never built, overtaken by political indifference, the motor car and then the aeroplane.

Idir explained that the *Alfellaga* rebellion saw, perhaps, several hundred Tuareg warriors take on many thousands of Soviet-supplied and well-equipped Mali troops in 1962. It began with a number of hit-and-run raids. Within two years, with the help of Morocco and Algeria, the rebels had been crushed with such intensity that even non-combatants were embittered. It was camels against armoured cars and jet fighters.

'The *Azawad* flag has been raised,' Idir continued. 'The people are waiting for their next chance. They will be better organised. Your guns bring the day nearer.'

When the deal with the Tuareg was struck, the weapons would be taken by mule again, but this time in long trains, at night across the Atlas mountains and the desert plateaus to the small village of Ben Hado, near the town of Ouarzazate. Loaded onto camels, they would slip two days nearer to the border where Tuaregs waited with their 4WDs for a final trip into southern

Algeria and then to Saharan oases. Little money would change hands; the 4WDs would come laden with African hardwood, ivory, silk, silver and dates.

I swallowed hard, thanked Idir for his confidence and suggested that it had been a long day.

'My uncle has honoured you with his gifts. You are my brother now. You leave for Tangier in two days. We cannot among family offer you money for what you have done for us, but I can ask you if there is any further favour I can do for you to thank you on behalf of my people.'

I thought for a few seconds. 'What I would like, Idir, before I leave for Europe, is a Moroccan passport, with my picture, and a French name and background, a passport that will never be questioned. Something that will allow me to hide from the British. Can you do that?'

Idir smiled in friendship. 'A photographer will be here in the morning. Good night.'

I was asked not to leave the house which I understood, but which disappointed me for I wished to see something of Marrakech, particularly the great square, the *Djemaa el Fna*. I asked Idir if he could make this one exception and escort me late at night. Two days later, my last in Marrakech, we dressed in none-too-clean jellaba and tagelmust which covered my hair and white skin and set off through the dusty streets, packed wall-to-wall with all the exuberance and expectation of the souk. We passed occasional rivulets driven by the fall of melt water from the Atlas into street fountains. Brimming urns were placed around the squares where people came to collect water for their homes. Water carriers with their clinking tin cups were everywhere.

After fifteen minutes, we reach the *Djemaa*, the square of execution, where just fifty years before the heads of people convicted of treason against the Sultan were displayed on spikes. The square lay huge and dark, but sprinkled with lights. My first sight was an experience like no other before or since.[19] It was a world of sound gone mad, tom-toms and drums beating relentlessly in a savage tattoo; weird instruments wailing; chants that started in heart-rending melancholy then fell till all that is human drained away. In the red and yellow flicker of kerosene lamps, the motionless spectators, white turbanned and in djellabas, were absorbed in the performances: black-skinned slave dancers; Shleuh dancers, Berber boys from the mountains in their early teens, skipping between disarming innocence and lasciviousness; the blind man, faced raised to the sky, 'his milky-dull eyeballs lost beyond reach' as he narrated his story; and, on the outskirts, medicine men surrounded by fox skulls, lizard and serpent skins, ravens' beaks, cock's combs, leopard's claws and bottles and bottles of evil-looking liquids. A snake charmer with his cobra placed around his neck in a mimic of ecstatic love-making opened his mouth to let the poisoned fangs shoot into it. Without thinking, I reached out for the snake and did the same to a gasp from the onlookers. Even Idir, perhaps remembering my control of the mule, was wide-eyed.

I was delivered just after dawn with a single suitcase, still reeling from my experience, into Marrakech's chaotic and ramshackle railway station, desperately awaiting its makeover. Idir embraced me and saw me into a first-class carriage. We said farewell.

'You will be back and you will always be welcome,' he said.

I fell asleep, dozed fitfully during a jumpy stop and start journey, and had to be woken at the Tangier terminus with its equally depressed edifice. I was met by a gentleman called Nizar, as arranged, and taken to a modern house near the port, an office next door, its windows filled with political posters. I had been transferred from one separatist group to another. Nizar explained that *Istiqlal* was a vigorous independence movement that rioted everywhere, but 'not the Tangerines who were known for their civility and tolerance so Tangier was spared the fuss', at least while I was there. The party had helped gain freedom from French colonial rule and was now critical of Morocco's latest ruling monarch, King Hassan II.

'But none of this need worry you,' Nizar said. 'We are doing a favour for our friends in the south. I understand that you wish to cross the water to anywhere but Gibraltar and you would rather not have to show a passport or go through customs. You will leave tomorrow evening so you have a twenty-four hour wait. All is paid for. Here is your room and you will not go out. Meals will be brought to you. Ah, that reminds me, I have a document that has been prepared for you.'

He handed me a passport and turned before I could ask any questions and locked the door.

The tajines were good if unvarying, the toilet little cleaned, the view across the promontory was ever-changing, and I found some dog-eared Dashiell Hammett's on the window-sill so the time passed. At nine o'clock, I was hurried by a sullen young man who said nothing but made abrupt gestures to the right of the main harbour, a fishing cove where a tired motor launch waited. It was American, made by Elco, of World War 1 vintage. The throb showed a well-maintained engine, a smuggler's boat, taking cigarettes, spirits, hashish and silks to the European mainland. I found a place among the boxes and settled down. It was calm, but dark, and we ran without lights. We slowed several times as large ships and patrol boats went through the Straits on their business. On the other side, we slid against a small jetty where an old Ford lorry and two men waited. I helped with the transfer of boxes, squeezed into the front seat, and we drove into Algeciras where I was dropped before midnight near a square off the *Calle Seville*. The tapas bar, *Meson Las Duelas*, was still open. I had a beer, a meal of many parts, a bottle of wine, a large brandy, and was offered a tiny room in a building next door.

I took my time getting to Faro. I travelled by bus and stopped two days each in Jerez and Seville looking at the art and architecture and should have stayed longer in both. My new Moroccan passport saw me across the border into Portugal. I got off at Faro airport late afternoon on Christmas Eve. It was busy with tourist flights. I was in luck as one of the Biafran contacts was on site. Traffic had all but dried up, the remaining Constellations now based in Lisbon.

'We had a Connie go down somewhere end of November,' I was told. 'Never been found. There were too many Americans poking around here. The crews felt that it wasn't safe.'

Back wages in US dollars were paid from a safe in the Phoenix Company office. I offered a couple of passports, which were inspected without a flicker and signed for my money.

'You want me to take you off the list?'

'I guess so. I can always sign on again. All right if I look at the planes?'

It was a nostalgia trip. The two ex-RAF Meteor jets hadn't moved. I noticed one of them had a South Cerney tag in the cockpit. Alongside was the third Lufthansa DC-3 kept ready for spares that would now never be needed.

Time to go. I drifted along the coast to the tiny ramshackle village of Figueira, equidistant between Sagres and Lagos, the latter name causing me a missed heartbeat. I found local lodgings alongside teenage English watercolourist, Clive Cook, who was enjoying his first taste of the Algarve light. I often walked with him and watched his mix of frustration and success, enjoyed his developing technique. I ate at the local restaurant which featured large mussels that could only be collected by men who abseiled down the steep local sea cliffs. The beautiful wooded valley leading to the beach was studded by large caves in the limestone crags and decorated by several dolmen.

On 15 January, the Biafran war ended. It was sudden and unexpected as morale collapsed and the soldiers drifted away. Colonel Ojukwu flew to Abidjan to see the Ivorian President in a last ditch attempt to garner direct support from the French, but his trip turned into exile. Forsyth took the third-from-last plane from Uli. And Chuck? Whatever happened to Chuck?

I could imagine the Igbos crammed into their enclave, hunkering down and waiting for the massacres. They never came, but there were vengeful acts. Hausa soldiers ran exuberantly down the Uli runway firing into the air. Fifteen aircraft had been lost there and thirty-five aircrew, twenty of them Biafran, had died and were buried in the small church cemetery close by at Ihiala, where the two tall spires were a positioning point for landing aircraft. The graves were bulldozed by the Nigerian Army the day after the war ended. The local field commander explained in the press that he wanted the crews to be 'eternally forgotten'.

'We don't want their families poking around here looking for their remains.'

I decided to winter in the Algarve and to go back to England when it was warmer. My earlier meetings with Cook encouraged me to seek out local artists. There were no municipal or private art galleries in Faro so painters and sculptors were encouraged to display in the windows of the tourist office and shop. I made many friends during shared evenings. I also delved into the museums and the cultural associations like the Círculo Cultural do Algarve, the Clube Farense and Ginásio Clube.

It was a welcome change of pace. I needed time to think. It had been a long nine months.

5. FREEDOM TO KILL KINDLY

There will be a time, there will be a time
To prepare a face to meet the faces that you meet;
There will be a time to murder and to create …[20]

When I got back to England at the beginning of July, I made for my home in West Bromwich. I arrived at the door having no key and was thinking which window to break when I noticed the child's swing in the back garden. A young woman inspected me from the kitchen and I realised that in the year I had been away my solicitor had followed instructions, cashed in the trust, sold the house and waited for my contact. I went round to see him. On balance, I would say that he was disappointed to see me.

'Well,' he said. 'I could say that you've grown. I don't know where you have been, you never said, so I couldn't contact you. But I think the callow youth has all but disappeared.'

I never liked him. I decided to be polite, but blunt.

'Thank you for looking after things,' I said. 'How much have I got, when can I have a cheque, and are there any problems?'

He sensed the air, acknowledging he was soon to lose a client.

'I'll answer in the same fashion – about £8,000. I'll be able to tell you accurately in, say, three days after I settle outstanding bills and add up my expenses. The house is all sold and settled. When you come back I can give you the account and the cheque. I am pleased to say there are no problems. I have a few personal letters which I can give you now. Shall we say three in the afternoon this Friday?'

I agreed, left with a handshake, and made my way to a nearby town pub, the *Sandwell*, in the High Street which the year before served good lunches and real beer. The best spot was in the enclosed central snug; that is if you were allowed in. I had a pint and a packet of scratchings followed by pie and chips and another pint. The old landlord had died and the pub madam, who had ruled the place with an iron look, had sold up and moved to Spain.

A young man came over, wearing a suit and tie. 'I thought it was you,' he declared. 'Are you still window cleaning?'

One of my crew from what seemed a long time ago, he was working in a bank and had to be careful drinking at lunchtime.

'Just one pint, you know!'

He was getting married in three months and gave me the girl's name; she had been at the grammar school, but I couldn't place her. He looked as if he had never left school, perpetually hopeful that something better would turn up. I explained I had moved on, been abroad and was meeting a friend. I did not encourage him to join me.

Some of the worst memories of my time in Biafra were fading. People didn't know I had been there so they didn't ask and I didn't have to tell. I was increasingly unwilling to discuss horrors that were too bad to recall and buried them in the forlorn hope they would go away. How much can I remember now of my experiences some fifty years ago? How much has been added or amended by books and articles read much later? What mattered? Things done are done.

My ex-window cleaner-come-banker wandered off and I started on my letters.

The College of Air Training dwelt for a long time on the public money I had wasted for two years while concealing from them my increasing instability. Airline pilots were legally obliged to declare mental illness. My licences might be withdrawn at my next air medical board review. Both BEA and BOAC had a letter from the College recommending that it would be unsafe to employ me in any capacity as air crew. If any airline asked for a reference, this letter would be sent instead.

The letter from the Inland Revenue brought concerns. They had not yet received a tax return from me despite my temporary employment at British United Airways, during which time tax had been deducted at source. They looked forward to my fulfilling my legal duty in the near future. They also wished to be sure that I understood that there were constraints on taking money out of the United Kingdom and strict regulations on detailing the source of money brought in. Money earned overseas had to be declared in full with supporting documents for tax to be assessed.

Here was the worry. Did they suspect that I had been working overseas?

I decided not to take the matter personally and to treat it as a standard warning in those troubled financial times. Anyway, the money from Biafra was either in my pocket or in a French bank account and wouldn't be coming near the United Kingdom.

I bought another pint to wash all of this down. Another lesson was learned. You cannot step casually outside of the rules of bureaucratic organisations. They do not like it and will not stand for it. If they can they will try to hurt you for your impudence. As I later found out, this official intemperance is unchanged to this day. Irritating insects, people who think themselves independent, will be squashed. To make it worse, it was becoming easier through these new computerised files to keep tabs wherever you went.

There was one last letter, scrawled in an unsteady hand to my recent local address. I guessed it had been forwarded by the new owners because it was dated only two weeks before. This one was a shock. It was from Chris Heal back at his home in Bolton after reaching Kashmir, spending almost two years in India, falling ill, then hitchhiking back again. He was in a bad way and would dearly like to see me. If I was around could I travel to him? There was a number and I went to the pub phone after negotiating for three shillings and fourpence. Chris answered within seconds, sounding dreadful, but with relief in his greeting.

'When can you get here, mate?'

'This evening, Chris.'

I downed my pint and made for the railway station. It was a two-hour run with a change at Wigan. I bought a couple of newspapers to pass the time and saw a copy of *Ulysses* in the platform bookshop. I thought I might as well try to finish it.

Tucked away on page six of *The Times* was a story that began with the transcript of an *AP Press* Telex from Marrakech, dated two weeks before, on 11 July.

Moroccan authorities have found a quantity of arms and the remarkably preserved bodies of eight Europeans in the wreck of an aircraft believed to be one of Biafra's grey ghosts … the gunrunners that kept the secessionist state alive during its war with Nigeria. The wreck of the plane, which villagers said crashed last November, was revealed in the melting snows some seventy kilometres south of here in the Oukaimeden mountain range at an altitude of 3,000 metres. The bodies were buried locally. It was speculated that the six passengers in addition to the pilot and co-pilot were mercenaries. But Moroccan authorities would not say if they had determined their identity and declined to provide additional details (END)

A journalist in London added further interesting information. The plane had struck a slope on Tibherine in the Atlas Mountains. Morocco's Air Traffic Control last November had received a brief 'Mayday' from an unidentified aircraft which reported triple engine failure, but the message was garbled by radio interference and was unclear about position or time. Sabotage was not discussed. It was thought that this was a missing Constellation and that it was carrying an unknown amount of weapons to Biafra. The plane was discovered on 18 July by mountaineers.

The journalist noted that Amnesty International had reopened an investigation into the disappearance of the aircraft on behalf of a concerned relative of one of the passengers. The discovery of the wreckage ended widespread speculation that the aircraft had been hijacked and that its crew and passengers were being held at some unknown location. It was assumed that the Moroccan government was refusing to answer any enquiries because they did not wish to admit that they had allowed overfly rights to Biafran planes. Morocco at the time was building a respected position as a non-aligned country which could act with honesty and clean hands as an international mediator.

My musings took me all the way to Bolton. The fact that there had been a mandatory crew of three plus six passengers seemed unknown to anyone, as expected. The false name I entered on the list had died in the snow with an unknown body. The Berbers, Anaruz and Idir and their extended family, had escaped whatever military investigation had occurred. The Moroccan authorities knew there had been weapons from inspecting the empty wreck and seeing the evidence of sustained salvage activity around the crash site. They could only guess what armaments had been there and where they had gone. Disclosure of the loss would not help their international standing. French, American or British involvement may have been suspected, but nothing had come to the surface. It seemed like good news all round.

Chris's house was a four-bedroomed affair with a large front and back garden in Bromley Cross, not far from Last Drop village. There was no car in view. I paid off the taxi and rang the bell, but then realised the door was unlocked. I heard Chris calling from a dining room that led off the kitchen. I found him in a make-shift bed surrounded by half-eaten food and bottles of heavy painkillers, many with French labels.

'About time you came,' he croaked. 'Don't think I could have held on much longer without dialling 999.'

'My God, Chris, what is it? Why aren't you in hospital?'

'Cancer, my boy, the galloping sort. Secondaries, tertiaries. You name it. I don't have long. Diagnosed in Greece on my way back when I tried to sell some blood for eating money. I'd been feeling awful for months. With these bloody Sterling area restrictions, I didn't have much cash. I dragged myself to Paris, collapsed, and woke up in a public hospital where I got the really bad news. After a month, I said I wanted to die in England and that someone was coming for me. Actually, they were pleased to be shot of me, loaded me with drugs for the trip, gave me a bag of painkillers, and poured me into a taxi for the ferry train. I used the last of my foreign money to get to London.'

Telling this story took all but the rest of his life out of him. He went paler than his dirty sheets, coughed blood for several minutes, then seemed to shrink, wrinkled, into his pillow.

'What can I do for you? Shouldn't you be in hospital?'

'No hospital. I don't want to die screaming in some dire ward with a bunch of nurses who don't give a damn. The blessed NHS don't know I'm here or what I've got.'

He paused for a few minutes. 'What I want is to talk to you. Have a glass of beer like the old days. And then I've got a favour to ask you.'

I moved to the fridge, but was interrupted as I reached the door.

'You'll find nothing there. There's a pub just around the corner, *The Last Drop*. Take a big jug and get some Holt's, none of that Watney's keg rubbish.'

I did as I was bid. As I watched the jug being filled I had a premonition: I didn't like the way this was going.

A few strong draughts of beer revived Chris for short periods, but sudden gasps of pain with white-knuckled fists and the rapid changes of pallor, a blotchy yellowing, looked terminal. This was no way to die. He asked me for four tablets and washed them down with more beer.

'How many are you allowed?'

'One four times a day towards the end.'

Some of the old twinkle returned as he told me about his trip. He paused regularly and took the occasional taster.

'I didn't stop much on the way over in May. I left Paris in a hurry after the riots and kept going. That was exciting and bad. You don't realise what thugs the CRS are until you see them laying into the students with their batons.[21] I dug up cobble-stones and stockpiled them for ammunition. Towards the end, I broke a store window to get at blankets for the wounded. Left the next morning. Kept hitching. Every town in France was in open revolt. Got lucky. Just a few bad days. Met an Italian lady up near the mountain pass at Montgenèvre, spent a happy week. She ran me down to Turin. Huge tomatoes in Yugoslavia. Got stuck at Split. Buildings still falling down from the earthquake at Skopje. Lied to the British consulate to get a press pass in Turkey so that I could get half price on a train going east. That's it there.'

He pointed with a shaking finger at a piece of plastic with his photograph and stamped *Basin*.

'Saw Noah's mountain. No ark. Stopped at a place called Erzurum. Had a sauna in a hothouse built over the town's rubbish tip. They said it had been burning for over a thousand years. Had an awful night in prison in a dump called Zahedan in southern Iran. Got buggered and it hurt.'

He paused and took deep breaths, his face creased with pain.

'Spent many months in a village in the foothills of the Himalayas called Shamipur building a mountain road for 4X4s to get in and out. Slept in a mud hut. The kid next door had cholera. Walked to Dharmsala and got an audience with the Dalai Lama. He was ripping into one of his gardeners. Blessed a prayer scarf for me. It's in that rucksack. Lots of prayer wheels and noodles. Kashmir's the place to die: Victorian houseboats, complete luxury, acres of water lilies, fresh walnuts you can snap with two fingers. Wandered around India by train. Got sick.

'Up the Khyber Pass on the way back ...'

```
MARRAKECH, MOROCCO, JULY 11 (AP)   MOROCCAN   AUTHORITIES
HAVE FOUND A QUANTITY OF ARMS AND THE REMARKABLY PRESERVED
BODIES OF EIGHT EUROPEANS IN THE WRECK OF AN AIRCRAFT BELIEVED
TO BE ONE ▆▆ OF BIAFRAS▆▆ GREY GHOSTS...THE GUNRUNNERS THAT
 KEPT SECESSIONIST STATE ALIVE DURING ITS WAR WITH NIGERIA.
THE WRECK OF THE PLANE, WHICH VILLAGERS SAID CRASHED LAST
NOVEMBER, WAS REVEALED WITH MELTING SNOWS SOME 70 KILOMETERS
SOUTH OF HERE IN THE OUKAIMEDEN MOUNTAIN RANGE AT AN ALTITDE
OF 3000 METERS.
THE BODIES WERE BURIED LOCALLY.  IT WAS SPECULATED THAT
THE SIX PASSENGERS IN ADDITION TO THE PILOT AND COPILOT
WERE MERCENARIES.  BUT MORROCCAN AUTHORITIES WOULD NOT SAY
 IF THEY HAD DETERMINED THEIR IDENTITY AND DECLINED TO
 PROVIDE ADDITIONAL DETAILS.  (END)
                                JULY 11
```

The first announcement of the finding of the crash site of the Biafran gun-running
Constellation made by Associated Press Telex in 1970

Many years later, about 2015, one of the engines of the Biafran Constellation on
the slopes of Mount Tibhirine near Mount Toubkal, Marrakech

St Mary the Virgin, Old Alresford, Hampshire. The grave where Heal borrowed the identity of a dead child is on the high ground behind the church

Ray Tindle on his retirement as head of his newspaper group in 2017

Security personnel assess the damage after the bomb attack at the Norfolk Hotel in Nairobi, Kenya, on New Year's Eve, 1980. Heal's escape drainpipe is thought to be in the centre background. His wife and daughter's bodies were found in the restaurant to the left

'Facebook chief Mark Zuckerberg refuses to talk to UK MPs about fake news.' *The Times*, 14 November 2018

The Snake Goddess, Heraklion Archaeological Museum, Crete. *Olaf Tausch*

The moonstone at Polonnaruwa, Sri Lanka, where Heal met Harshani and the monk Bahalika

St Jerome Writing, Caravaggio, in the oratory of St John's Co-Cathedral, Valetta, Malta

Mongol nomads moving their felt gers, 1243; 'when they travel, whether to war or other places, they always take their homes with them.' *William of Rubruk*

Gypsy Memorial, Museum Square, Amsterdam

Women of Ravensbrück at the Museumplein in Amsterdam commemorates the 90,000 women and children and 20,000 men who were killed in the Nazi concentration camp

Vincent Van Gogh's *Landscape at Twilight* in the collection at Amsterdam, 'almost always reaching out to the horizon'

Martyn Selmayr and Jean-Claude Juncker

ABOVE: The scene of the assassinations of Jean-Claude Juncker and Martyn Selmayr in 2018 outside the champagne bar, *L'aube sur Aÿ* in the *Galeries Saint-Hubert*, near to the *Grand Place* in Brussels

RIGHT: Russian semi-automatic Makarov 9 mm pistol

He suddenly grabbed my arm with a strength that hurt, knocking over his beer glass. 'You know why I asked you here, don't you. You do understand.'

'Yes, I do know, Chris. It's a lot to ask.'

'I wonder how Philippe is getting on. Do you think he cares? He's long dead. Out of all this shit.'

Another great heave of agony. 'I've not got a will, but I want you to have what you want. There's no one else. No one else. No one ...' and he passed out.

I went upstairs to find somewhere to sleep. The bedrooms were dust-laden, untouched since Chris left for Kashmir. I lay down for ten minutes then, hearing nothing, went back downstairs to check on him. He was still unconscious, twitching and moaning. I watched him for a few more seconds and took my handkerchief and put it over his eyes in case he opened them. Then I pinched his nose with thumb and forefinger and covered his mouth with my palm. He struggled only once, whimpered a bit, went quiet and in two minutes he was dead.

With another beer, I sat down beside him and told him how much I was going to miss knowing he was around. I felt tearful. Then I went to bed and tossed through an awful night, my brother, my mother, my father, Philippe, and all those black faces with popping staring eyes, pleading with me.

Well into the morning, the sun poured through the window. It was going to be a pleasant day. I thought I would start with Chris's papers. I found his passport, his bank account with a few thousand pounds, the deeds of his house which he owned outright on the death of his parents, some tax and national insurance papers, and his address book which was almost empty: a few tradesmen, medical numbers from a year ago and me and nobody else. I'm sure I hadn't thought this through, even in the back of my mind, but, as I flicked the passport, looking at all his visas from his trip, it fell open at the main page. Even though he was a distant cousin, he did look a lot like me. And nobody in this country knew he was dead or even that he was ill.

I walked back to Bromley Cross and caught a bus into Bolton. At an ironmongers, I bought a couple of screwdrivers, a hammer, cutters, tape, some wire coat hangers and then walked around till I found a large multi-story car park with minimal security. I edged through the cars trying a few doors on older vehicles after checking from the parking tickets that they had been stored overnight. I had no luck. They were all locked, but one black Anglia van had the passenger widow slightly ajar. I opened a coat hanger and made a hook out of one end, lowered it in and worked the door catch up. I hammered a flat screwdriver into the ignition and turned it, but the engine didn't catch so I used the Philips screwdriver to take off the steering cover disclosing the wiring. In the little cluster were two red wires from the battery which I stripped and wound together. Then I cut the single brown wire connected to the starter motor and sparked it against the twisted power wires. The Anglia jumped into life. The bare ends just needed taping to stop them rubbing against each other and shorting while driving.

I took the van to a luggage store and bought a large travel trunk and went back to Bromley Cross. I used the hammer and screwdriver to knock several big air holes into the top and bottom of the trunk, unclothed Chris's body and loaded it inside, and waited till nightfall before putting it into the van. I wanted to lose the body far away from Bolton. I decided on the Bridgwater Ship Canal and after driving around found a quiet bridge in Back Lane near Dunham. I added some road stone, said 'Goodbye' to Chris, and, after a bit of heaving, dropped him from the central parapet. The trunk floated worryingly for a few seconds, but then went straight down. I stopped at the *Rope & Anchor* for a meal and drove to my new home.

The next morning, I emptied all his drawers and stripped the house of its few personal possessions, loaded everything into black plastic bags and took them to the municipal tip. I spent that afternoon with an eager estate agent who wore white socks with his black suit. We toured the house, agreed some cleaning and a few remedial jobs, and I was taken to the seedy office to be introduced to his partner solicitor who agreed to handle the conveyancing. I signed the papers for sale in advance and I gave him the deeds and Chris's bank account details. I explained that I would be travelling abroad on and off for the next few months and would phone in to check on progress. I was after a quick sale and would let him know where I would be staying when he had some good news.

It was Friday. I dropped the house keys off and drove to West Bromwich for my brief afternoon meeting with my solicitor. In central London, I dumped the van in a side street with the windows down. I decided to catch a few shows, joined the list of people who had seen the *Mousetrap* and caught an early performance of *The Great Waltz*, which I thought poor although the music was good.

My real task was to see if Frederick Forsyth was in town for I wanted some career advice that didn't involve flying. It was easy to track him down after enquiries in a few Fleet Street bars. 'Freddie', as I now called him, was open to lunch as long as I paid the bill. He freely admitted to being short of money. We got on well from the start. He had decided to write a novel to try to raise funds and was busily and unsuccessfully hawking it around London publishers, a period when the sole copy of the manuscript would languish on a junior editor's desk and he had to be patient as he waited for the rejection. Within a few minutes, Freddie launched into his continuing disgust with the British government over its duplicity on Biafra.

'What happened could not have happened without the wholesale and covert contribution of the Wilson government,' he said. 'Nor was it necessary to protect some vital British interest, and what interest merits a million dead children? Britain could have used its huge influence with Lagos to militate for a ceasefire, a peace conference and a political solution. It chose not to despite repeated opportunities, pursuing that racist Hunt's conviction that Biafra must be crushed no matter what the cost, but without ever explaining why.

'This is why I believe that this coterie of vain mandarins and cowardly politicians' – a clearly much-repeated description – 'stained the honour of my country forever and I will never forgive them.'

For the Nigerian government, rationale, motive, strategy, military supplies and blockade were all taboo; in Whitehall circles the whole subject was the best conversation-stopper since Burgess and Maclean.

I agreed with him, but gently moved him onto my chances of a job in journalism. He was pragmatic. The best way to get started was to apply to a newspaper in the provinces and spend a couple of years picking up the basics of the trade. Because of my age and background, it would be best to steer clear of a paper that was strongly unionised as I didn't want to enter into an indentureship. He gave me a couple of contacts in East Anglia where he started his trade before moving to the BBC.

What did intrigue him was that I was no longer 'Philippe', but 'Chris'; no longer French, but English. I told him that this new identity was to break with my past in Biafra. He had been a foreign correspondent, but I had been a little more involved.

'Do you have a passport in your new name?' he asked.

'No,' I lied. 'I didn't know how to go about it.'

'Well, the only way I know is illegal,' he said.

Then he laid out the path for what became known as the *Day of The Jackal* identity scam. It was a fundamental part of his book where an assassin gets a false passport using the birth certificate of a dead child. It was a fiddle well-known to criminals and Mossad. The authorities were slow to plug the gap. It seemed an excellent opportunity to add to my collection.

To start the process, I needed to visit somewhere I had never been before. I chose Alresford in Hampshire at random. The next day I got a train down to Alton from Waterloo and caught a bus out to the colourful little town, full of designer boutiques and small eating places for ladies who lunch. Down Broad Street to Old Alresford is the old church of St Mary the Virgin. Through the lychgate, high and to the right, I found what I was looking for, the grave of a three-year-old boy, born in the same year as me. Using a form collected from the General Register Office (GRO) at Somerset House in London, I applied for a copy of 'my' birth certificate. An obliging solicitor in the High Street was only too pleased to act as my letter-box when I explained I was travelling and looking to buy a house in the area. When successful, he would be delighted to act for me. There was some delay in the GRO's reply because at that time they were moving across the road to St Catherine's House on Kingsway. I completed my passport application with the details from the birth certificate, the boy was born in Brighton, and the obliging lawyer, with a wink, was happy to endorse my photographs so that I could replace my 'stolen' passport.

The process worked as smoothly as Freddie outlined. It seems I had brought him luck for the week after our meeting he sold the book rights for *Day of the Jackal* to Hutchinson in Great Portland Street for an advance of £500 and expenses of £6,000 against a three-book deal. Shortly afterwards, through the introduction of a friend, he sold separately the film rights. He had to decide between £20,000 outright or £17,500 and a small percentage of the net profits. He chose the former to his long-term regret and loss.

I sat one evening in my small hotel room in Bayswater and laid my entire possessions on the bed, clothes and suitcase apart. There were three piles. The first contained my silver pendants, The *Hand of Fatima* and the Berber *aza*, both of which I usually wore around my neck, Chris's blessed Tibetan prayer cloth, and a B-Uhr Observer Watch that I had bought in Biafra in an auction of a dead German flyer's possessions. The watch was too big for everyday wear as it was designed to fit outside a pilot's gloves and I was thinking of getting rid of it. The second heap contained the bank statement and identity papers for Chris and my own banks in the UK and in France. The statements reflected the sale of two houses, and the US dollars I had brought back from Portugal. The whole was a little shy of £15,000.

The final group was my collection of passports: my original name (French), my adopted name (British), one from Philippe (French), one from the Red Cross, one from the Connie wreck (American), one from the Berbers (Moroccan), one from Chris (British), and one courtesy of a dead boy in Alresford when it arrived (British). All were either new or renewed. When I came to renew the second passport from the Connie, the German one, I sent it off to Berlin and it never came back. I was philosophical as it wouldn't have stood much scrutiny as I could only just order dinner in the language. That made eight working passports in total. From a novel I was reading, I adopted an additional 'proof', that of an address associated with the name in each British passport. I did this with accommodation addresses and used that address to place the British passport names on the local electoral roll. I could let them lapse, knowing that I could re-establish them, given they now had a voting history.

I went back to Alresford to collect my passport and, as I quite liked that part of the world, called into Farnham just over the Surrey border to see if they were hiring staff on the local newspaper. I knew from the *Guardian* that, the year before, an ex-Army captain called Ray Tindle had bought the *Farnham Herald* group and was installing computerised production equipment. I stopped at the *Bishop's Table*, a grand old town centre Georgian house, for a beer before trying the *Herald*'s offices in West Street. I was in casual conversation with a fellow drinker when I recognised Ray Tindle from his photograph in a newspaper cutting going into the dining room. My companion agreed to a free lunch and I tipped the waiter a quid to place us at the table next to Tindle.

'I'm going into the *Farnham Herald* to see if I can get a job as a reporter,' I began, alongside Tindle's left ear. 'I hear he's going to modernise the place with the latest machinery and I'd like to get in now on the ground floor and learn from him.'

My partner grunted approvingly in the right places like a professional.

'Do you know that he bought his first paper in Tooting for just £250 when he got demobbed after the war', I added. 'Must have some real get up and go. He's got hundreds of titles now.'

When Tindle got up to leave, he gave me his business card and I was employed that afternoon.

I spent two years with the group. Understanding the machinations of local politics and county-town businessmen left me highly cynical and with even less respect for those who wielded power. After twelve months, I was given my own comment column at the bottom of the leader page. My views often got me into trouble, not for inaccuracies, but for challenging worthies who thought it insulting that in a conservative town their opinions could be questioned. To give Tindle his due, he always backed me, or at least, never disciplined me.

My other main task was a weekly series where I visited some local institution. The plan was that over a year I would have covered most of what makes an English town tick and, I suggested to Tindle, the collection might make an interesting book.

Some of my visits were to places outside the circulation area, but with local involvement. One such was Knowle Hospital, near Fareham, Hampshire County's Lunatic Asylum from 1852. The building was part-constructed by Russian prisoners from the Crimean War. It had its own pub in the grounds, the *County Arms*, and its own railway station, *Knowle Halt*. When I visited, its cemetery held 6,000 inmates. It was one of my more interesting features because of the many difficult social issues that flowed. I had meetings with both Dr Ronald Sandison, who investigated psychotherapeutic approaches to mental illness, and Professor James Gibbons who headed Southampton University's department of psychiatry on the site.

During my quieter hours, I reflected on what I had seen and been told and compared it to my own life. Many of the inmates had endured brutal childhoods, beaten or abused by their father. Other patients suffered from an early and traumatic loss of both parents for which they struggled to compensate later in life. There was a long list of possible psychoses, some serious.

I also thought about adding to my passport collection. Could I improve upon Freddie Forsyth's methodology? At Knowle, I found a way. Among the patients was a young man I was only allowed to view through a thick glass window in the doorway to his padded cell. He was classified 'most dangerous' and, when his door was opened, three attendants had to be present. He was physically fit and would likely live a long time, but would never be released. I took a note of his name, ordered his birth certificate, and then applied for his passport with my picture, endorsed by a pal on the *Herald*. There was no likelihood that the man in the cell would ever apply for a passport.

Forsyth later wrote that he got into a lot of trouble with the British and French governments about the *Jackal*. The Brits never stopped blaming him for saying how easy it was to get a dodgy passport. One day they were going to computerise all dead children starting a hundred years before so they could check if copy birth certificates had been issued after their death. If they ever did find a way to cross-check those birth certificates with passports issued in the same name, a lot of people might be in trouble.

I felt quite smug about my 'lunatic' variation, which I kept to myself. There was no death to cross-check against. But I did start to ponder my first effort through the solicitor in Alresford. I sought a way to cover my tracks. My latest girlfriend was a student whom I had met by chance in a bar a few weeks ago. Out of the din, I had heard this perfect Nigerian accent. Aisha. She was beautiful and willing. The trouble was, she had to go home. Her mother had died and she had family responsibilities and there was little money. I got to thinking. Perhaps I could solve Aisha's money problems and make my Alresford passport less likely to be uncovered. I was extremely protective of my collection; the loss of the German passport still rankled.

I put it to her that evening. Would she like to get married?

'You're joking, Chris,' she laughed. 'What would I do with a white husband? What would the folks back in Lagos say?'

'No joke, but a deal. I'll pay for your flight and give you some cash. We would get married in a London Registry Office. You'd go home soon after, but we would have a honeymoon first, just to say 'goodbye' properly. And that's it. We never tell anyone and we would both be free to marry in the future if we wished. No more contact because there is not going to be any more contact anyway. You can go and marry a rich Nigerian.'

'Why do you want to do this? There's a catch. What is it? Is it illegal?'

'Not for you except that you will have a secret marriage. The catch is that when you marry me I will have a different name than the one you know me by. No one will ever know the actual me. And in the absolutely unlikely event that it came out, you could always say I had died. And you'd have some new clothes.'

That clinched it.

We married a few weeks later in Richmond before rented witnesses, near the end of a long queue of couples waiting for their ten minutes, had a great week in Paris, and she left and I never saw her again.

I saw no reason to delay and changed my name by deed poll to a hyphenated version of our two surnames to reflect our marriage. Once registered, I despatched the deed poll, marriage certificate with the passport for it to be changed. My logic was that if ever the Government did get around to checking my Alresford birth certificate against passports they wouldn't find me because computers weren't yet that clever and Aisha's surname was the first part of my new hyphenated passport name. I also noted the ease of the deed poll process in case I needed it in future.

The 'Jackal' scam came to a head after 2004. The GRO was making a considerable income from the large number of people taking up genealogy. It was driven by the growth in home computers and by the advent of the Ancestry website. There was a lot of money associated with this new mass hobby. The GRO saw a way to save significant cost by digitising birth, marriage and death records and providing a simpler, speedier and more expensive service. The Identity and Passport Service (IPS) was able to piggy-back this work to launch its crack down on its long-standing loophole, codenamed *Operation Wisdom*, first exposed by Forsyth more than thirty-five years before. The IPS claimed that in three years they uncovered 1,200 cases involving the use of dead people's identities and also stopped nearly 700 new fraudulent applications. This success led to 290 arrests, 100 convictions and thirty-eight people deported. The inquiry also uncovered applicants who were connected to Israel's security service.

Executive director Bernard Herdan claimed IPS had now all but ruled out any 'Day Of The Jackal-style frauds'. A database of infant and young person's deaths up to the age of eighteen was automatically updated and anyone applying for a birth certificate of a dead person had to prove they were family.

For several years, stories appeared in the press of embarrassed people caught in the net and publicly exposed. One from Otago in 2010 named New Zealand MP David Garrett who admitted in Parliament that twenty-six years ago, he used Forsyth's method to obtain a false passport. At the time, he thought it a 'harmless prank', never used the passport and later destroyed it.

'To this day I cannot explain the rationale behind my actions except to say that I was simply curious to see whether such a thing could be done. At the time I committed this offence I gave no thought whatsoever to the effect it would have on others,' he said. 'Following my arrest, I wrote letters of apology to the child's relatives expressing my sincere remorse for the pain I caused them.'

Garrett said he would carry this remorse for the rest of his life. I always thought this regret somewhat shallow, brought about by being caught, and didn't credit that a family would be deeply disturbed by the news of misuse of a birth certificate over thirty years after a child's early death. Nor did anyone come to call on me so what did it matter. My 'Nigerian-Alresford' and 'lunatic' identities were secure.

Some years later, I developed another serious hobby: hiding my communications from electronic snoopers, like internet companies and the government. Most people don't know how to encrypt messages, or how to send them by an encrypted email service, to browse the net without being traced, or how to pay for goods and services anonymously. If you are trusting enough to share all of your personal data, believe in the good-heartedness of the organisations who openly spy on you in order to collect your smallest activities, then you have no immediate worries.

For me, the cry 'I have nothing to hide so I'm not worried', is a naive and lazy abdication.

However, if you believe that you have the right to stay off the radar, not be tracked by Facebook and its bedfellows, or be secretly monitored by a myriad of government departments, all of the techniques which hide your identity matter to you as standing stones of freedom. I don't trust any organisation not to seek to increase their power, to act without scrutiny and, when the chips are down, to use my historic information to my detriment.

I was committed to the principles of privacy. I also recognised I might need these skills one day for another reason. I had begun to consider idly whether I could disappear from official records; all these ways of using the internet might become my tools, my passports to independence.

A crypto-party is a free, small workshop which provides answers about the internet. Typically, twenty to thirty people are walked through the basics of online security by volunteer experts. In 2012, spread over several months, I went to several of these parties in London pubs. They were packed workshop sessions of an hour each and hard work, but I got what I wanted.

One of the problems was that it was not only democratic revolutionaries and freedom fighters, and, yes, I had come to see myself as an older armchair freedom fighter, that use these tools. Terrorists, extremists, serious organised criminals and child pornographers, denied mainstream channels, are often early adopters of new technology, because they have an incentive to stay secret and hidden. The extent of the continuing depravity is breath-taking. Instructions and payments for the 9/11 destruction of the Twin Towers were attributed to encrypted channels and covert money transfers. In 1999, the FBI seized the database of a company called *Landslide*, which it suspected of selling child pornography on the internet. The database was found to include the credit card details and IP addresses of over 7,000 Britons, data that was swiftly handed over to the British police who subsequently made almost 4,000 arrests. As a result, thirty-nine people committed suicide while 140 children were 'rescued'.[22]

That is one important side of the argument, but technologies that bring change have always been accompanied by optimistic and pessimistic visions of what they will do to humanity and society. In Plato's *Phaedrus*, Socrates worried that the recent invention of writing would have a deleterious effect on the memories of young Greeks who, he predicted, would become the 'hearers of many things and will have learned nothing'. When books began to roll off Johannes Gutenberg's press, many suspected they would be 'confusing and harmful', overwhelming young people with information. Marconi believed his radio would help humanity win 'the struggle with space and time' but, as his invention became popular, others feared that children's impressionable minds would be polluted by dangerous ideas and families rendered obsolete as they sat around listening to entertainment programmes.

'From its inception, the internet has acted as a canvas on to which we have painted positive and negative pictures of our future.'

In 1992, in San Francisco, Eric Hughes began an email list which predicted, developed or invented almost every technique now employed by computer users to avoid government surveillance. The people who wrote the material called themselves *cypherpunks*. 'Encryption is the art and science of keeping things secret from people you don't want to know them while revealing them to those you do.'

One of the first names on the list was that of Phil Zimmermann who, the year before, engineered the code *PGP*, 'Pretty Good Privacy'. He enabled two people to communicate over long distances without the risk of interception. PGP rewrote the debate.

Public key encryption used two codes, one applied at each end of the transaction; shared keys which can be used to encrypt a message, turning it into a meaningless jumble that could be decrypted only with a private key. Many code writers had strong views and believed every individual had the right to possess strong cryptography.

'Some of us are explicitly anti-democratic and hope to use encryption to undermine the so-called democratic governments of the world.'

Governments did not like it. Many of them demanded the right to perpetual access to internet communications. This battle became known as the *Crypto-Wars*. The British government even briefly considered following France in legislation to control encryption, but decided it was always going to be impossible to remove it from the public domain.

John Perry Barlow issued, in 1996, a Declaration of the Independence of Cyberspace:

Governments derive their just powers from the consent of the governed. You have neither solicited nor received ours. We did not invite you … Your legal concepts of property, expression, identity, movement and context do not apply to us. They are all based on matter, and there is no matter here.

I learned PGP and use it for my financial messages.

Another cypherpunk developed early versions of a secure email service. At one of my crypto-parties, I learned about a much-advanced encrypted system called *Mailpile*. Unnecessary? In 2013, the American National Security Agency, working with Britain's GCHQ and others, was tapping seabed internet cables, installing back door access to private company servers and working to crack encryption standards without legal authority, let alone public debate. Chinese mobile phone providers installed Government-mandated access to personal handsets. In 2015, one cypherpunk estimated that the USA currently spied on every internet user in the world at a cost of about thirteen cents a head a day. Default encryption would not stop people being spied upon, but pushed that individual expense closer to $10,000.

I now use an advanced version of *Mailpile* for sending all my emails.

One estimate is that ninety per cent of all sites on the web are hidden from general view. Some have good reasons for privacy like in academia, financial records, the military; others for bad reasons like criminal organisations and pornography. The key to access here, and to browsing free from government scrutiny, is *Tor, The Onion Router*, which carefully sends your enquires though peels of secure servers around the world to hide your address.

Within *Tor* lies *Tor Hidden Services* which are not easy to navigate. In many respects, they are very similar to websites on the surface net, but are rarely linked. *Tor Hidden Services* sites addresses are a meaningless series of numbers and letters which change regularly. There are, however, several index pages, some hidden. The most well-known in 2013 was *Hidden Wiki* that looked identical to *Wikipedia* and listed dozens of the most popular sites in this strange parallel internet. To even download *Tor* is illegal in many countries, for example China. To go to some of *Tor*'s more disgusting websites, particularly dealing with child pornography, is automatically deemed an offence almost everywhere. But that only means anything if the viewer can be found.

I use *Tor* for all of my internet searches, whether they are pure of heart and mind or when I am looking for more problematic content.

My last series of pub workshops were on bitcoin, a peer-to-peer market with no corrupt or controlling third parties. A quantity of bitcoin is stored at a bitcoin address, the key to which is a unique string of numbers and letters that can be kept on a website, desktop, mobile phone, or even a piece of paper. Every time someone sends bitcoin as payment, a record of the transaction is stored in a *blockchain*. Transactions are collected in those blocks with each representing about ten minutes' worth of transactions. The blocks are ordered chronologically and include a digital signature, a 'hash', of the previous block that administers the ordering and guarantees that a new block can join the chain only if it starts from where the preceding one finishes. A copy of the blockchain record, a list of every single transaction ever made, is maintained by everyone who has installed the bitcoin software. The upshot of all this is that, at any point, the system knows exactly how many bitcoins I have in my electronic wallet so they cannot be copied or spent twice. Ownership can be transferred, but never duplicated.

I speculated with bitcoin in a small way and the currency became a useful part of my eventual money transfer system.

My kitbag was growing. My life had entered a new phase. I found I was re-assessing my views on government and technology in a fundamental way. I spotted a 'Crypto-Anarchist's Manifesto', one of the few original political philosophies to emerge in the last fifty years:

A spectre is haunting the modern world, the spectre of crypto-anarchy. Computer technology is on the verge of providing the ability for individuals and groups to communicate and interact with each other in a totally anonymous manner … These developments will alter completely the nature of government regulation, the ability to tax and control economic interactions, the ability to keep information secret, and will even alter the nature of trust and reputation.

6. FREEDOM LOST

And here is the one-eyed merchant, and this card,
Which is blank, is something he carries on his back,
Which I am forbidden to see. I do not find
The Hanged Man. Fear death by water.
I see crowds of people, walking round in a ring.[23]

I slid with no plan to call my own into the cul-de-sacs of late middle-age, often angry, almost always disappointed.

It was a worm that tipped my frustrations into what my wife said was full-blown paranoia.

'Any sensible adult would have sorted it out without a fuss,' I was told.

This was a worm that was so inconspicuous, so unattractive, that I cannot remember its name or what it looked like, except that it was a dirty brown. In my dressing gown, after a long morning writing on the computer, I was interrupted by a phone call. A builder who was failing on an urgent job slipped around facts to prove his innocence and my eternal stupidity. The doorbell rang as I walked to and fro, phone to ear, slowly losing the will to live. A determined man clutching a clipboard loomed large.

'You do realise,' he challenged, 'that you have a rare worm living in your verge. It is in great danger if not cared for. You need to act responsibly.'

I was in a dispute about working hours. The builder insisted that Friday afternoons did not count as part of a working day and that I should know this.

'What … what on earth are you talking about?' I spluttered.

'Your worm,' replied the man, 'your precious worm. You need to safeguard it for future generations.'

'But you promised that you would give this your personal and caring attention,' I demanded into the phone. 'Why am I having to deal with this?'

'So you are happy if I put in some stakes and arrange for a sign?'

'Yes, yes, whatever.'

And I firmly, and I hoped politely, closed the door.

Two days later a circle of flat white wooden stakes appeared on the grass by the front gate. Somewhere in the middle lurked a dismal worm. A large official sign was attached with staples to the nearby telegraph pole. The owner of the property had agreed a preservation order for a rare animal. No grass was to be cut, nor any car parked, within a metre of the marked worm hole on financial penalty. It took only a week for a police car (another story which comes later) to flatten the stakes and all inside. I then forgot to tell the weekly gardener that no mowing was allowed outside the gate and he trimmed the whole verge. I remonstrated and he retaliated, behind my back, by pulling the sign down and sticking it in the black waste bin. The green bin, as one slowly learns, is for rubbish destined for the municipal dump; the black bin contains recyclable material in line with the local council's green policy. I found two seedy gentlemen checking my black bin watched over by Worm Man bearing his clipboard. They had discovered the discarded white sign, badly torn. My culpability was evident.

I should admit that I have form with waste disposal operatives. I went one day to collect the black bin to find it hadn't been emptied and yet I could see the lorry down the road. I called rubbish control and was told there had been an infringement: my wife had placed a broken plastic flowerpot, unsuitable for recycling by dint of a number in a triangle on its base, at the top of the black bin. There followed one of those unwinnable discussions.

'So, am I being punished?'

'Not punished, trained'.

'Wouldn't it have been possible to take the flower pot out and leave it on the grass?'

'Then you would not have known that it was an offending article.'

'You could have left a note.'

'We're not a bureaucracy.'

'So, shall I just leave the bin outside until you come again in two weeks?'

'No, that would be against the bye-laws. You could be admonished or fined.'

'Do you have any positive suggestions, then?'

'This is your waste!'

I suppose I shouldn't have made the personal suggestions I then did, but I felt the purpose of the conversation was to make me angry. I took the bin down the garden and lit a fire with the contents. Within half an hour a police car arrived, the officer saying that there had been a complaint about dangerous smoke. I pointed to the bonfire, faintly visible forty yards away with its smoke drifting across open fields.

'You can tell the waste disposal people hiding behind their hedge that they should brush up on bonfire law.'

'Sir, I wouldn't like to get the impression that you are not taking this matter seriously.'

'Which matter? Let me put it this way. I've had five thefts from my garden shed and garage in the last two years, all reported, and this is the first police visit I have ever had. At least I now know what you take seriously.'

Worm Man had his clipboard held high as a shield in case of attack.

'Not a very neighbourly attitude,' said the smaller of the seedy ones, inspecting the discarded sign. 'First off, you're destroying council property by ripping off the sign thereby showing disdain for your public authority. No proper respect. Then you go and put it in the black bin when it should have gone in the green one. And, you've gone and sliced up the worm and thrown the stakes God knows where.'

'The stakes are in the green bin,' I offered. 'They were run down by a police car. Do you have the right to come onto my property and rummage in my rubbish?'

Worm Man could hold back no longer. 'It's not rubbish,' he yelled, 'and you agreed I could put it up.'

You get to that time in life, driven by bitter experience, when the truth of the old adage about stopping digging when you are already in a deep hole becomes a lifeline.

'You'll get a letter of admonishment,' he declared in capital letters, 'and the council will review your service provision. You won't get away with this.'

'Please leave my property,' I responded, 'and you can take your rubbish with you.'

Worm Man's parting shot showed a good memory and was decisive. 'You shouldn't open the door at midday while you are naked underneath your dressing gown.'

I share the details of these episodes because, I recognise now, they initiated my descent into a need to get away, to quit all the petty-fogging bureaucracy. There were nineteen follow-up letters of increasing severity over three months. It was still not settled when I actually did disappear and left the council and Worm Man without a decisive victory. I took that to be a petty, but tangible, personal success.

I mentioned a previous call from the police during which the worm and its protection had been flattened. This visit also happened with commendable speed. I have, or rather did have, a shotgun for shooting our plague of rabbits. I was rather proud of it: it was a hundred years old and had a Martini-Henry action, the type in use by the British Army against the Zulu *impi* at the Battle of Rorke's Drift. Shotgun licences need renewing every five years and I forgot as the licencing authority's reminder letter never turned up. No one could believe that I didn't keep a five-year diary. The authority managed to call me immediately the licence lapsed and I was ordered to take the gun forthwith to a safe place. For a number of reasons, this was inconvenient and harsh words were spoken, feathers ruffled. The gun had been safely kept for fifteen years, but overnight I became a potentially dangerous person and was scarcely out of bed the next morning when the arm of the law reached into my driveway and the gun was confiscated. I remarked that I had many reported thefts from the property in the last few years, but had never seen a police car.

'We have our priorities, sir. You have committed an offence by holding an unlicenced gun and it is not relevant that it was licenced a few days ago. We have to safeguard the public.' I felt it was time to shut up,

The *Battle of the Worm* as it became known up and down the road and, I suspect, throughout the village was the first incident in what felt, childishly I know, like a concerted attack on my personal freedom. It also caused the break-up of my third marriage.

My second wife and I were both in our mid-twenties when we married. It was love at first sight. I never mentioned my bargain with Aisha that made me a bigamist. We did everything together and soon had two children, just a year apart. My employer, an American multi-national, offered me a job in Johannesburg for two years and we jumped at the chance to explore southern Africa, the extra money, an interesting job, the warmth and to see apartheid at first hand and to form our own opinions, perhaps to help in small ways. On our way out we flew first to Nairobi and travelled by car to Malindi for two weeks' beach holiday over Christmas. The coast in those days was uncluttered, the resorts mostly a little worn, functioning but unsophisticated. The beaches reminded me of São Tomé.

The plan was always to return to Nairobi for New Year's Eve and then to fly to South Africa and our new life. I booked the iconic Norfolk in its leafy suburb. The hotel used to stand on the edge of the city, acting as the starting point for safaris. My wife took the children to the café near the entrance so that we could put them to bed early and enjoy the gala dinner and celebration. My son arrived breathlessly at my door to let me know they were settled for their meal and ran off. He ran everywhere.

It was not long after eight o'clock. I had just poured a gin and tonic and was in my dressing gown ready for a shower when the bomb went off. I found myself in a cloud of swirling dust, everything obscured, and that acrid never-to-be-forgotten mix of electrical charge and high explosives. The ceiling came down and I was trapped between the bed and heavy rafters which landed either side of my head. A fireball went through the room and took out the window to the courtyard. I wrenched my back badly getting out and stumbled to the door. The wide, carpeted stairs had gone, but I could see my son's torn body at the bottom. It all went a bit numb and confused. I searched the room for my wallet, which I found, stuffed some clothes into one of the suitcases, climbed out onto the tiles and lowered myself down a drainpipe. Someone offered to store the case and I never saw it again. I walked in bare feet across the jagged blast damage to the hotel restaurant. The bomb had taken out the main internal glass partition where everyone, all six sitting for the view, had been decapitated. In the middle of the gory mess were my wife and daughter, their heads beside their uneaten plates of food.

I found myself in the back of a commandeered van being driven alone across town to the hospital at breakneck pace, and it almost did as my head was banged against the walls. I sat and watched the injured and dead being brought in, men without limbs, without skin, women without breasts, without clothes. After half an hour of chaos I had had enough and caught a lift, still in my bloodied gown, to the Hilton Hotel where my American Express card got me the last room. I was woken by the chamber-maid at midday and remember little of the next week.

The bomb was planted by a Moroccan with a fake Maltese passport named Qaddura Mohammed Abd Al-Hamid, identified as a member of the

Marxist Popular Front for the Liberation of Palestine (PFLP). Al-Hamid had a long history of plane hijacks and was involved in a machine-gun attack on passengers at Rome airport in 1973. Al-Hamid checked into the Norfolk as Muhammed Akila, quibbled about his noisy room, 203, and accepted number seven. For several days, he seldom went out, refused housekeeping, and was visited several times by an Arab woman who spoke with a pronounced German accent.

Al-Hamid placed his bomb under a radiator directly above the ballroom. The device would have killed many more except that it was sitting by mistake directly over a metal beam so that the blast went sideways. The PFLP explained that the attack followed the successful storming of the airport buildings at Entebbe in Uganda four years before by Israeli commandos. An Air France airliner had been hijacked by the PFLP and over 100 Jewish passengers held hostage. The bomb was in retaliation for the assistance given by the Kenyans to the Israelis who refuelled their aircraft in Nairobi on their way back home. The Norfolk was owned by the Jewish Block family so the choice of target was doubly appropriate.

Al-Hamid left the hotel on the day of the bombing, walked out without paying his bill, and took a Kenya Airways flight to Jeddah in Saudi Arabia. And I had seen him. As I checked in about midday, he walked past me, well-dressed, carrying only a small personal bag and got into a waiting black limousine. As he entered the car, he glanced back at the hotel and, later, I remembered that look and I knew.

The Kenyan Police kept people out of the hotel's wreckage for some time in fear of a second explosion. They used that time to strip the rooms of their valuables. All my cash, my wife's jewellery, suitcases, camera and the rest were gone. The hotel placed what was unstolen in sad heaps in an undamaged room and there the next day I found our four passports, a chess board bought as a memento, chess set gone, and two favourite furry toys, an elephant and a pig, and I have these still. Before I was allowed to take my pathetic belongings away, I was asked to pay for the room. I refused and was threatened with arrest and was only let go after a large police sergeant forced me to sign a disclaimer against all loss. I had an operation to remove ruptured discs in my back and spent my first two months in Johannesburg in and out of hospital. I soon got a reputation at work for heavy drinking.

For the next thirty years or so, I was probably not a nice person. I took business risks and some people got hurt. I was a poor friend, unreliable, selfish. I enjoyed, mostly, a string of casual relationships, but never got close to another marriage.

In my sixties, retired with a healthy bank balance, and aimless, I turned to travelling. I toured Sri Lanka, taking advantage of the end of their bitter civil war and the favourable exchange rate. I built the holiday around two expert-guided tours of the two ancient royal capitals of Anuradhapura and Polonnaruwa, each steeped in Buddhism and architecture.

My guide at Anuradhapura fell sick over lunch on the first day. Harshani, Sinhalese for a 'delight and a joy', was the last minute replacement and reached me from her home in Colombo that evening. She was in her early thirties with a degree in English, a vision of graceful movement, was tolerably knowledgeable about Buddhism, but knew nothing about architecture and not much more about the city ruins.

I was invited to meet her parents. They lived in a mean two-bedroomed house on the outskirts of town, not a good place to park a car. I didn't like them from the start and I was sure the antipathy was reciprocated. He was monosyllabic, sly, slow to respond, always watching from under his heavy lids. There was a brittleness about the mother's caring, as if it was an act for my consumption. I found it remarkable that an English degree had come from this environment. Harshani asked me for money and I paid for everything, and, I suspect, quite a lot more. There was no sign of work, of love, within the family, visible mementoes, or visits from relatives. We married in a local pseudo-Christian ceremony two weeks later, low-key, few flowers and even fewer friends. I was uncomfortable throughout. I suppose I was committing bigamy for the second time, but I could not bring myself to see this performance as a crime. I wondered how Aisha was faring in Nigeria. I missed my children. I just wanted to get Harshani home.

There's no fool like an old fool. Harshani was keen to live in England and, after some brief posturing from British immigration she got permission, but only because one grandparent was supposedly Scottish, not because she was married to an Englishman. We moved into my home in Hampshire. From the first day, she investigated everything I owned. Knick-knacks full of memories moved to her dressing table; others disappeared and enquiries were met with a blank face and dismissive shrug. As well as some changes to the furniture and in the kitchen, her first major demand was a large television system with four speakers and subscriptions to every channel possible. On my own, I had seldom watched, now the set was on every waking hour.

Harshani was quickly pregnant and insisted on going home to Sri Lanka to have the child. It was decided she would travel alone and that I would join them as soon as news came of the birth and bring them back to England. After regular phone calls, Harshani announced the birth of our daughter, Sammi. There was no need to come to Sri Lanka and could I pick her up at the airport at the end of the week.

It was a stilted reunion; I was confused and disappointed. Sammi cried constantly, had a string of never-ending ailments, and clung to her mother for attention. This was, of course, my fault for forcing Harshani to live in England which was freezing and awful with tasteless food. My contact with the child was deliberately limited. To be honest, it was almost as if Sammi was someone else's offspring. Within a month there were daily rows: Harshani could shout louder and hold any grudge far longer than me. Most of the time I didn't understand how I had failed and caused such misery. By the time Sammi was one-year-old and getting about under her own steam, I was a foreigner in my own house.

This background is not meant as an excuse for what happened. I am still deeply ashamed about it. As I came in from my worm skirmish, Harshani attacked my cantankerousness, my trouble-making, my always picking fights with reasonable strangers, about trapping her away from her own mother. She had a piercing tone, capable of reaching deep into my consciousness and festering there. Two days later, without respite, I lost it. I hit her. Not a punch, you understand, but a solid, powerful slap. She wasn't big and I am. She stumbled across the room and hit her head with a crack on a skirting board. I thought I had killed her and I had to push Sammi off as I tried to give her attention. My thoughts filled with awful images of my father standing over me while I lay in a mirror position as my mother tried to stop him doing more damage. I was near speechless. Was I an abuser? Had this terrible secret lain with me for fifty years and only come out when I finally had someone that I could abuse in turn?

Harshani was groggy when she came round, her speech slurred, and I rushed them both to A&E. There is no one so low as a wife beater in the casualty department of a provincial hospital staffed, it seemed, entirely by female nurses and doctors. I was open about what had happened. No recriminations were made directly to me. In fact, no one spoke to me at any length. Harshani was taken straight to X-ray while a scowl-faced social worker on night duty took Sammi into care, behind my back and without discussion. That made me lose my temper and the police were called. I found, thanks to the shotgun licencing department, that I had a record of instability and, therefore, potential violence.

Harshani and Sammi came home a week later and for a while we received daily visits from social workers and district nurses, always female and working in pairs, to check that my wife and daughter had received no further beatings. All talks took place with me firmly excluded from the room. My opinion was never asked.

Harshani announced that she wanted a divorce and that she was taking Sammi back to Sri Lanka. She was scared of me and for her daughter's life. If I paid her money for Sammi's health and education, she would go quietly. One part of me was still in shock at what I had done. I gave in almost immediately, sold some shares, and gave her a third of all the money she knew about. The next day she left in a taxi for, I thought, the airport. There was no contract, no written agreement, no access rights, no contact address, just space.

When the social workers next came to check on Harshani, I told them she had gone back to her parents in Sri Lanka. Their faces shone disbelief. An embarrassing difficulty was that I didn't have the parents' contact number in Colombo. To my pleasure, Harshani had always looked after the relationship and the phone calls.

Then the police arrived. After a brief interview, they walked the garden, prodding loose earth. I spent the next night in a noisy, smelly cell in Winchester. Harshani's phone was switched off. No flight records for the pair could be found; lengthy enquiries were initiated in Colombo. The parents' house was empty.

How much time you can spend with a person and still have no idea who they really are?

I was never arrested, but was warned not to leave the country. I had to surrender my 'Chris Heal' passport. After a month, no trace of Harshani and Sammi had been found. The only slight evidence in my favour was that all their clothes had gone, all pictures disappeared and a significant sum in cash had been drawn from my accounts. But, as the detective inspector said, 'That could mean one thing or the other, couldn't it, sir'.

The investigation was not closed; there were no inquests as there were no bodies. It became a cold case.

I came to believe that most of the world ran on lies and deceptions, people pretending to be one thing when in truth, inside, there were always someone different. I also felt that these lies were acceptable, indeed, necessary. I lied, I had always lied, but I never thought that I lied to myself. Everyone else lied. Deception mounted on deception. People were never who they seemed, never really shared, nor wanted what they claimed. What they presented was a front and who knew what truths or further layers of evasion with sharp-edged corners lurked beneath.

I wondered if I had been the victim of an elaborate confidence trick. Was the scheme set up before my arrival in Sri Lanka? Had my guide in Anuradhapura actually been sick or had he spent the morning assessing a possible 'mark'. Was Harshani all the time waiting around the corner for her lonely, gullible and elderly prey to be delivered? Was Sammi really my child? Was she really Harshani's child? My mind started to swim; the truth, what truth, floated beyond reach, never coming into focus. If you want the truth about others, you have to develop it for yourself and still be prepared to be disappointed.

Were my imaginings covering another reality, one that I would not, dare not, let come close?

The mistakes I made with facts, with memories, when talking to the police came home to haunt me. I have one piece of advice for anyone arrested. 'Say nothing'. Police interviews are about false friendship, deliberate misunderstanding, and entrapment. You make your choice: be a fool, lie to yourself that the world is good, and bare your soul. But if you do you will lose as I did and everyone and everything might be destroyed. You begin to see the world for what it often is, a nasty place where you are unimportant, a statistic to be used. At the time, I did not recognise how far through a process of disengagement I had travelled.

A number of different matters intruded into this personal maelstrom, each in their own way confusing, worrying and demanding. For almost two years, I had been researching and writing a book on the First World War called *Sound of Hunger*.[24] It was a personal project, unsolicited, complex, involving travel to France and Germany and visiting many libraries and record offices. People who don't write books, but possibly know they can, may be surprised at the degree of commitment required. When the computer is switched on, as the writing continues with re-reads, improvements, edits, checks, double-checks, it becomes another world into which you slip; food, sleep, telephones, letters with demands, become irritations. Harshani and Sammi must have suffered from this, but after they had gone I began to welcome my daily falls into my one-hundred-year-old construction. It felt stable and safe.

The police leaked many details of the disappearance of my little family to the national and local press. I thought it was a blatant and vicious attempt to force me to error, perhaps through an emotional reaction. For several days, journalists and photographers camped at my gate doing terminal damage to any worms which may have poked their noses above the turf. I regularly saw cameras pointed at my windows from my garden. The doorbell rang and rang till I disconnected it. The chimes were replaced by loud rappings. It was a happy excuse to play Scriabin, Mahler and Wagner in a robust response. I complained to the police, but their only interest was in a confession. I closed the curtains, lived from fridge and freezer, and withdrew from the outside and got on with my work; my contacts were through the computer and the post-box, which contained only books, invoices and hate mail.

At first, I read the hate mail avidly. The notes contained intimate details unknown to anyone who had not read, or spoken to someone who had read, the police interview reports. Here was a conflicting subject: someone in the police force abetting a hate crime, for I was surely hated. Some letters were classic melodrama: green ink, capital letters, pasted magazine cuttings, lurid half-truths, complete lies and drastic threats. God appeared a lot and often provided a personal guiding hand. It took several weeks to tire of the sadistic rubbish; further letters were placed in a cardboard box, unopened. At the back of my mind was an idea to write a book one day on this frenzy.

It was from one of the early notes that I first realised I was a subject of widespread condemnation on the internet. I had found YouTube by occasional accident, but had never Twittered or been on Facebook or Instagram, their $1 billion acquisition in 2012. In fact, I was so ignorant of social media that I hardly recognised its existence or purpose. I saw usefulness in the internet in the early 1980s when I used it for booking holidays, which I discovered, made me a proud early adopter. On the other hand, my family didn't have a first house phone until I was twelve-years-old. It sat prominently on a lace doily on a table in the hallway. I didn't have my first personal phone until I was in my forties and driven by business. I valued privacy.

However, I was prompted now to investigate social media. My publisher had suggested it would be useful in providing publicity for the forth-coming book.

I wanted to see how it all worked at first hand. I opened Facebook and Twitter accounts, placing the minimal amount of personal information without yet mentioning the book. I was introduced to what I have seen since several times described as 'the Twentieth Century gangrene' that is 'killing us, mind and body'. As someone said, 'I wish we could uninvent it altogether.'

I did a lot of background reading. Early hopes of the internet were that anonymity would allow explorations of identity, without the fear of being held responsible. In stark contrast, a study of the behaviour in the first chat rooms showed participants were more aggressive and angry than in real life. Protected by a screen, people felt that every day social restrictions and responsibilities didn't apply. As online discussions grew longer, so did the probability of a comparison involving the Nazis or Stalin or Pol Pot. In short, the more anyone talked online, the more likely they would become nasty. If they argued long enough, it was a certainty.

John Suler came up with a famous seven-part 'Online Disinhibition Effect': any actions can't be attributed to me, nobody can tell what I look like or judge my tone; my actions do not occur in real time; as I can't see these people, I have to guess who they are and their intent; this is not the real world nor are these real people; and there are no authority figures here so I can act freely.

As word spread of my electronic availability, I was plunged into the court of Facebook and Twitter, charged as a murderer and an abuser and suffered the attack of the 'isms': ableism, classism, homophobia, racism, transphobia and worse. Any action or statement has an 'ism' about it somewhere. To be accused is to be guilty: a 'digital Salem'. All that mattered was that I was accused with enough force. Denizens of the internet with minority opinions have power over anything they choose not to like. I was left in the poorest of positions as, while there was no evidence of what happened to Harshani or Sammi, there was sufficient public information through the press to encourage legitimate speculation as to foul play. If one added police leaks, deliberate lies, malicious fire-stoking, and a general hysteria, I really had nowhere to go.

What was clear was that retaliation was equivalent to throwing fuel on the fire. For someone like me, a businessman and latterly an historian, any response would be amplified, twisted, held as evidence, and used to convict. I was used to handling critics, other than the police, by reasoned argument so I had no idea how to handle a Twitterstorm.

Humans, especially the less mature, are creatures that like to copy and watch each other and Facebook, with its co-travellers in the social media, is the greatest system ever invented to allow us to see and be seen. But the platform includes every trick in the book to keep you hooked. Nothing is left to chance. It is certainly working.

In 2004, when the first 4,000 users signed up to Facebook and began submitting their personal data, Mark Zuckerberg said in a private email, 'They trust me ... dumb fucks.' Zuckerberg claimed that his site was solely a platform and that it did not act as a publisher. His company did not edit content placed by users. However, the innocent platform behind which Zuckerberg hid was totally within his control; he built it and his company constantly changed what people could see and could not see based on its own secret algorithms and direct interventions. The intention was to reward what was most engaging, because engagement is fundamental to the company's growth strategy and it has profited greatly.

Google, Snapchat, Twitter, Instagram, Facebook, and the rest, have long since ceased to be simply technology firms. They are not altruistic free social services. The aim is to know so much about individuals that they become the channel of choice for anyone who wants to influence behaviour through precise advertising or manipulation.[25] Around ninety percent of Facebook and Google's revenue comes from selling adverts. For Google, in 2017, this meant $95 billion of their total revenue of $111 billion. Why wouldn't these businesses want to live in a Wild West environment that keeps costs low while maximising profit and to portray criticism as an attack on free speech?

Where you find a combination of great need and ignorance, you are in the land of predatory adverts.[26] If people are anxious about their sex lives, advertisers, using Facebook's identification technologies, and constantly fine-tuning their approaches, will promise them blue pills or a penis extension. A slow-running computer may be because of an implanted virus which prompt calls with instant fixes. In the US, for-profit universities are being fined for their practices. They seek people living in the poorest zip codes with special attention given to those who have clicked ads for payday loans or are concerned with post-traumatic stress. Damaged ex-servicemen are prime targets because they can receive government finance for education. The online habits of friends and families are dredged to cross-match their hopes, fears and desires.

The founder of the original Facebook, Aaron Greenspan, claimed that the platform had led to 'countless deaths' as Zuckerberg had developed it to be as 'addictive as tobacco'. Greenspan alleged that Zuckerberg 'sacrificed safeguards on cyberbullying, extremists and data security to pursue growth at all costs ... floored the accelerator for fifteen years straight to achieve maximum quantity.'[27]

The cat was out of the bag. Sean Parker, the founding president of Facebook who left the company in 2005, said that the original thought of social network inventors was 'how do we consume as much of your time and conscious attention as possible?' These media all decided they needed to give everyone a 'little dopamine hit – the pleasure chemical' – every once in a while as someone liked or commented on a photo or a post or whatever. The aim was to create a 'social validation loop' that exploited a vulnerability in human psychology. Anticipation of information is deeply involved with this reward system and 'that addictiveness is maximised when the rate of reward is most variable'.[28]

The truth is sinister. Dopamine circuitry seems to predict how much we will enjoy something and, when it falls short, we feel a dopamine plunge. 'And so we keep going, hoping to ramp it back up. The rush we feel of someone posting on our feed is the anticipation of how good it will be. The reality is never quite as good.'

Zuckerberg insisted that his company was trying its best to rid itself of the unsavoury. However, critics argued, that his business model mitigated against doing what it takes. The likes of Zuckerberg were as responsible for what was pasted on their sites as an ordinary citizen would be for permitting racist haikus to be painted on their roof.

Zuckerberg's great scandal of 2018 was the claim by a whistle-blower that a company called Cambridge Analytica, a 'truly despotic outfit', acquired and exploited the data of fifty million Facebook users in an attempt to influence the outcome of the US presidential election in 2016 in favour of the Republican party.[29] These users were manipulated unwittingly through the data they had themselves offered up. This was no 'breach of security'; it was Facebook's business model in plain view.

The risk of Facebook working hand-in-hand with governments to monitor and influence citizens is real. Nation states are already seizing the opportunity. Cambridge Analytica's parent company, the SCL Group, is a military contractor and claims to have 'conducted behavioural change programs' in over sixty countries including for clients in NATO, the Pentagon, and in the UK defence ministry and MI6.

Thousands of activists have eschewed the traditional stomping grounds in favour of Facebook, Twitter and YouTube. They have become vital platforms for political groups around the world. The battle for ideas, influence and impact has moved online. One-time leader of the UK Independence Party, Nigel Farage, was clear that his message about the perils of the EU became mainstream and helped secure Brexit due to video-sharing on YouTube. Twitter gave rise to propelling Donald Trump into the White House. Facebook was instrumental in turning Beppo Grillo's Five Star Movement into Italy's biggest political party in just three years. 'These three examples of anti-establishment triumph prove the supremacy of digital platforms today.' Add to that Google's pre-eminence as the preferred gateway to information and news with 3.5 billion searches made every twenty-four hours while, in the same timeframe, 1.5 billion people log into Facebook, and five million tweets are sent; one begins to feel the power.

Slithering through this freedom is the 'troll', the anonymous generic given to a very broad church ranging from bullies to amateur philosophers, from the mildly offensive to the illegal, to knights of the internet who see themselves acting in the public interest to expose hypocrisy and stupidity. At the core are those who cannot be argued with, who do not care which subject is chosen. They are the gutless, the inept and the plain sick whose lives are spent scanning the horizon for any offence with the intent to crush debate or variety, or through the enjoyment of pure malice.

Trolling is not going away anytime soon. It has been a central feature of online life since the mid-1970s. An increasing desire for digital affirmation, very like the continuing desperation among many to appear on television, is leading more people to share their most intimate and personal lives online, often with complete strangers: what we like, what we think, where we are going. The more we invest of ourselves online, the more there is for trolls to feed on and the more likely we are to be offended.

As a result of my study, I decided to fight back against my hate mailers, but finding trolls is difficult. Many use proxy servers to mask their addresses and they have dozens of accounts with different names for each platform they use. If they are banned or blocked by a particular site, they re-join under another name.

I set up, easily, fake Facebook and Twitter accounts, explored the settings and was taken aback by the potential volume of information collected by Zuckerberg. An account's index shows twenty-four categories with at least thirty-six further sub-categories. One user wrote that she found 324 MB of data collected by Facebook after twelve years of membership that took forty minutes to download. Facebook knew every personal contact and the identities and contact details of all parents, siblings and cousins. It was the 'huge' list of contacts and friends which shocked the most. Years before, she had downloaded the Facebook ap to her phone and allowed it to synchronise with her phone contacts. 'Basically it sucked up all the contacts in my phone and stuck them on a contact list', numbers lost years ago, boyfriends, people met in crises, relationships ended unfairly or in anger, all permanently recorded by Zuckerberg and shared with whom?

Data is actually not numbers, but friends, relationships, memories, ups and downs, life's dilemmas, successes and catastrophes. And then there was every Facebook 'like', cookies collected through web browsing, Uber taxis, Google maps following every movement, pizzas ordered.

Speaking of pizzas, this parody was floating around the internet at that time:

CALLER: Is this Gordon's Pizza?

GOOGLE: No sir, it's Google Pizza.

CALLER: I must have dialled a wrong number. Sorry.

GOOGLE: No, sir, Google bought Gordon's Pizza last month.

CALLER: OK. I would like to order a pizza.

GOOGLE: Do you want your usual, sir?

CALLER: My usual? You know me?

GOOGLE: According to our caller ID data sheet, the last twelve times you called you ordered an extra-large pizza with three cheeses, sausage, pepperoni, mushrooms and meatballs on a thick crust.

CALLER: OK! That's what I want.

GOOGLE: May I suggest that this time you order a pizza with ricotta, arugula, sun-dried tomatoes and olives on a whole wheat gluten-free thin crust?

CALLER: What? I don't want vegetables. I want meat.

GOOGLE: Your cholesterol is not good, sir.

CALLER: How the hell do you know?

GOOGLE: Well, we cross-referenced your home phone number with your medical records. We have the result of your blood tests for the last seven years.

CALLER: Good Lord! Anyway, I don't want your rotten vegetable pizza! I already take medication for my cholesterol.

GOOGLE: Excuse me, sir, but you have not taken your medication regularly. According to our database, you only purchased a box of thirty cholesterol tablets once online four months ago.

CALLER: I bought more from a drugstore.

GOOGLE: That doesn't show on your credit card statement.

CALLER: I paid in cash.

GOOGLE: But you did not withdraw enough cash according to your bank statement.

CALLER: I have other sources of cash.

GOOGLE: That doesn't show on your last tax return unless you bought them using an undeclared income source, which is against the law.

CALLER: WHAT THE HELL!

GOOGLE: I'm sorry, sir, we use such information only with the sole intention of helping you.

CALLER: Enough already! I'm sick to death of Google, Facebook, Twitter, WhatsApp and all the others. I'm going to an island without internet, cable TV, where there is no cell phone service and no one to watch me or spy on me.

GOOGLE: I understand sir, but you need to renew your passport first. It expired six weeks ago. Do you still want a pizza?

You can never escape your past. Social media providers always know where you were through your phone and also where you are now. You can only try to limit them learning much that is new. Facebook always tries to keep any information that passes by. It will also hamper efforts to get information on others, even when they are suspected terrorists. While they knew who was attacking me, in fact, had considerable information on them, Facebook would not tell me who they were. I had to find another way. Facebook may respond promptly for information about 'imposter' accounts after a report of a fake profile. However, first, you do have to prove who you are and I wanted to be sure that I was separated personally from this research.

I went back to first principles. I downloaded all of the aggressive postings and tweets onto a spreadsheet, noting the source, date and content and I added the new items that came each day. Then, with some enthusiasm, I opened my box of hate mail and entered that also, but included franking information and physical characteristics, like the use of green ink. Across all three sources, I developed another spreadsheet that noted each 'fact' connected with my crime and which communications included it.

I love a chase, the pursuit of connections that are not immediately apparent, the skill that results from many years of lengthy, sometimes tedious, but finally rewarding historical research. Time spent poring over old documents, disparate sources and other people's opinions in books and scholarly articles, was not wasted.

What I saw was that there were far fewer humans challenging me than I thought. I was looking at over 500 items, but with a reasonable degree of certainty there were a maximum of thirty-two perpetrators and, excitingly, a minimum of twelve. While there was some ingenuity in the content, there was also a laxness, probably through an over-confidence, a surety that their identity would not be uncovered. Of the twelve, it seemed likely that eight were camp followers, trolls in it just for the fun and hurt. Or perhaps not?

Catfish, or fake accounts, persuade people to join a witch-hunt by setting up dummy profiles and interacting with themselves, not just talking to themselves, but also following themselves. They make 'friends' of themselves on Facebook and 'like' and 're-tweet' their own tweets on Twitter. This incestuousness can also give the game away as careful investigation of their 'Following' and 'Follower' lists shows the degree of interaction and high level of support that is indicative of a 'fake'. I confirmed this by using the *Tweepi* website to go to the very start of these catfish Twitter accounts. When people follow themselves they mostly do it very early on and so the initial followers repay attention and can reveal interesting information that was thought long buried.

I was left with four primary targets and I re-concentrated my efforts on them alone, their letters and their Twitter and Facebook posts.

The mail showed a variety of media. For instance, one was my green ink specialist, but that person also used magazine cut outs and stencilled capital letters. Envelopes for these four also showed a pattern. While their posting points were spread, it looked probable this was deliberate. I placed all of them on a wall chart with four differently coloured pins. There could be no mistake: three were local, one from Winchester, one probably from my own village, and one from north Hampshire. The fourth was centred in Reading, while none of the letters actually came from the town. As new insults arrived day by day, there was no serious deviation.

I went back to the letters cut from magazines by three of my trolls. Two of them used glossy paper that seemed similar; one was more basic, but heavy-duty paper, possibly a cheaply produced, limited circulation publication. A visit to the newsagent provided a clutch of likely candidates.

In fact, the answer was simple to spot, the glossy papers came from two cooking magazines aimed squarely at women at home; the paper product was my own village magazine. The cooking magazines did not necessarily imply that the writer was a woman, but if it was not then they likely lived with a woman who did not mind her monthly magazine being cut up. An order for recent back numbers of the three publications showed that the cut outs were used within the month of publication, not treasured possessions, but possibly bought for the purpose by people who knew each other.

I then stood back from these accounts and assessed them. Genuine online account holders place their own needs, prosperity and self-image at the forefront of what they do. These accounts had glaring omissions of expression of personal interest. They had one purpose only: to denigrate Chris Heal, the murderer. There was no attempt to hide their intent; they were a crusade.

Why would they care? Troll fakers have a weird motivation and so exhibit weird behaviours. It doesn't seem weird to them, but to perceptive onlookers it appears as a branding. As these people think their behaviour is normal, they are not aware how many clues they leave.

Unless intent on confusion, one of my four was less well-educated, probably achieving no more than a few lower GCSE examination pass marks; one I felt sure had a degree, probably in a specialist vocational subject. Two frequently used formal trite expressions which suggested a bureaucratic background that was not in senior management. These two almost always posted their messages after six o'clock in the evening, which suggested a return home from work. My bet was that for one of these, English was a second language. All showed a paucity of imaginative word use; their vocabulary was limited. And all four were slapdash with word choice, spelling mistakes (and some defining errors were always repeated), and grammatical construction. One was left-handed. The likelihood was that two did not write regularly, say as part of a job. That suggested they were non-clerical, non-management, possibly in manual work or out of work altogether. Perhaps this general laziness extended to their computer or phone controls?

After some hours of speculation, I posited that these were not four casual trolls. If not co-ordinated, or known to each other, they knew of my case personally or directly through another who did. My money was on a male police officer or associate from north Hampshire and a graduate female social worker from Winchester, one of whom knew the person in Reading, who was possibly out of work. The person in my village knew me or Harshani and Sammi. I felt the connection had to be with Harshani who had made no local friends that I knew of: so a female who worked in a local shop she visited or, perhaps, and more likely, someone who worked in or around the local medical centre. Could one of them be Sri Lankan?

Before pounding the streets, I travelled out-of-county to Esher and bought for cash a low-level laptop and used it to develop further false email, Twitter and Facebook accounts. I joined the criticism of Chris Heal and added additional juicy insights, suggesting insider knowledge. I let my outpourings increase in vitriol, especially when I saw a drop-off in contacts from my four main suspects.

After four weeks of steady self-establishment, I hit gold. One of my suspects asked me on Facebook to be a 'friend'. I had been building to 'pinging' them and asking for a chat with the intention of gathering their IP address, the numerical identifier of their device, be it a computer or mobile phone. You can only gather an IP address while the personal interaction of a chat is in progress. At other times, Facebook is the channel, or stands in the way of, a contact with another user. Here, you use a 'netstat' command covertly whilst chatting, standard fare on Windows, and then type the IP address into a purpose-built website to give a location, which may be the device's actual location or may be that of its internet provider.

I accepted the hand of friendship and began a careful correspondence. What I now had was an IP address based in Basingstoke in north Hampshire. It was, I hoped, the policeman who was intrigued by how I knew what I knew. Facebook friends for their false account were limited, but one was in Reading and clearly family. I placed a formal subject access request to the police for all of the papers about me connected with my arrest and investigation. I explained I was preparing my defence against a possible charge. When these papers arrived, within the month, I listed every policeman connected with the case, which produced seventeen names. I then cross-checked these names with the Basingstoke voters' register. There were only two matches and I could remember one of them clearly, a constable, foul-mouthed, unbelieving, and who evidenced an immediate dislike of me. I recorded both addresses. I had a bundle of social work papers, medical reports, formal warnings and instructions for meetings, and, similarly, found four women who lived in Winchester.

Calling on my waste disposal expertise, I checked the days for rubbish collection in Basingstoke and Winchester. To the credit of both towns, green bins were for recyclable material. In the early morning on the day of emptying, I drove to my selected addresses. At each address, I checked the names on letters and packages in the bins, found my targets, and emptied the contents into large black plastic bags. I only needed to empty one in Winchester as the bin contained near the top a cooking magazine with letters cut out.

Back home, I sorted through my bags and confirmed my two trolls. Detective Constable Ray Strange of Hampshire CID, whose bin also included confidential papers relating to my case which he had copied and taken home. Strange had a disabled younger brother in Reading whom he supported, paying £300 a month towards his rent. They met every weekend, followed the local football team in season, went fishing otherwise, and did their drinking at *The Village* at Station Hill and drank Carling Black Label. Strange ran a pub tab and paid through his credit card. Social worker Janet Brimsmore had several photo printouts in her bin and I recognised her straightaway as the woman who had taken Sammi into care. She was Sri Lankan by birth, had a BSc social work degree from Portsmouth University, and was forever posting pictures of her latest culinary creations.

The next night I drove back to her home, parked outside and, as I hoped, found that she didn't log off her computer and had no password connected with it. Within five minutes I was in and browsing her personal Facebook page. I saw an individual I knew: Worm Man. They were friends and had a combined interest in me through their conviction that I had murdered a precious worm and both Harshani and Sammi. Their co-ordinated trolling was laid bare in email correspondence.

I discarded my laptop in a municipal tip having put a six-inch nail through the hard drive. I then bought another, loaded it with pictures of my targets culled from their bins, and added two false Facebook and Twitter accounts. Strange's computer was password-protected, but his brother's in Reading was not. As an anonymous 'Concerned Citizen' I posted on the brother's and Brimsmore's covert and open accounts, and sent emails to their entire contact lists, especially their work comrades, and to the press. I made explicit accusations of each other's complicity in computer trolling, based on confidential work papers and knowledge, of an unfairly pinpointed Chris Heal who had been driven into seclusion and deep depression. I added damning written evidence, facts and pictures. I then destroyed this second laptop and burned all of my evidence.

The results could not have been more dramatic or immediate. The disclosures made national news and were raised in parliament. Photographers parked in front of the four homes. After two weeks, Brimsmore took a drug overdose and died in agony. I was investigated, of course, but the coroner offered me an official apology. The cold case was parked. Following an internal police investigation, Strange was fired. His brother was taken into a sordid care home as his brother, unemployable, could no longer support him. I left Worm Man to sweat, sending him a few weeks later a birthday card with a worm on the cover, wishing him health, and signed anonymously in a combination of green ink and cut out letters. I hope that the rest of his life was miserable and lonely.

And yet I realised that in the middle of everything, I had some sympathy, respect even, for the trolls who scour the internet seeking to disarm the pompous. I had become anti-authoritarian. I saw myself as a minarchist who believed in the smallest possible government. I just wanted someone to protect my privacy, private property and safety and if government wasn't prepared to do this for me, I was increasingly happy to look after myself as judge and executioner. Broadly, I wanted government to leave me alone. Trolling was a way of causing trouble for an over-zealous and arrogant system.

I was happy to be the itch, the grain of sand in the machine so long, of course, as my identity was not compromised.

7. FREEDOM REGAINED

The nymphs are departed.
And their friends, the loitering heirs of city directors;
Departed, have left no addresses.
By the waters of Leman I sat down and wept ...
Sweet Thames, run softly till I end my song ...[30]

Tipping points: the unheard ripples caused by butterflies' wings beside the Amazon that cumulatively build to a hurricane in the Caribbean. My ripples were two minor confrontations involving my car. Resolution would cost little but time and temper. The long-term effects, however, helped change my life. No doubt, you will have similar irritations to share.

A self-elected team of ageing urban vigilantes decided to police the thirty mph limit in my village – the SpeedWatch scheme. These enthusiasts claimed that local speeding was a 'major problem and concern'. No one could remember the last road death in the village side roads until someone recalled a drunk who had fallen off his bicycle into the path of a passing car, perhaps thirty years ago.

'Foreign' vans which sped through the rat-runs were the target, but it was local cars like mine, well used to the route and conditions, which were mostly caught. The 'watch team', three or four men clad in yellow jackets, stood on the pavement. With no official powers, they could not stop anyone, but had a large device that flashed the speed of oncoming vehicles whose licence number they recorded and passed to an administrator at police headquarters in Winchester. A warning letter was sent to the vehicle owner. If anyone stopped to remonstrate, the team hid behind a hedge and this became a local game.

Criticism of the initiative was met by condemnation: the scheme was only opposed by the selfish and the dangerous who cared little for the lives of blameless tots walking to school. You cannot debate speed limits, whatever the political and historic nature of their introduction. If this group needed to find a purpose, some suggested, how about curtailing the drugs sold openly each morning to the children waiting for the bus to the secondary school? What about the small group of perverts who enjoyed mutilating horses in the fields? Then there were teams of burglars who toured the area by day looking for targets to hit by night? Petty break-ins, opportunistic theft, and burglary were now so endemic that it went unreported other than to get a crime number for an insurance company.

I had two arguments against the watch team. The first was that the police are paid to stop crime against person and property and they have lost the plot. Resources are placed against low-hanging fruit, managing the numbers, and dealing with political and social correctness. This failure means increasing amounts of police work carried out by non-policemen including the burgeoning number of special constables. Authority rests with the police and it should stay there. This delegatory practice has spread to councils who farm out Public Spaces Protection Orders to incentivised private companies and to GPs who rely on ill-trained pharmacy assistants, triage nurses and practice receptionists.

But, really, this was about a misunderstood private howl for the freedom of my youth. Too many people seek or accept restrictions that take away from the pleasantness of life. Show me a road and I'll paint a yellow line, stick up a restriction sign, parade in an unnecessary yellow jacket, and threaten fines for non-compliance, but ignore the potholes and crumbling curbs. Proportion has gone out of the window.

I allowed myself a smile when news reached me of a fire that had burned to the ground a locked garage next to a private house in the village. Someone had stacked old tyres along one wall, doused them with petrol and set them alight. By chance, the garage was the storehouse for the equipment of the SpeedWatch team, including their yellow safety jackets. The police have yet to visit.

The second car problem came from a research meeting with a Royal Navy submarine expert to discuss technical detail for *Sound of Hunger*. We decided on the Roadchef service station at Clacket Lane on the M25 and we got on well during a discussion which lasted over three and a half hours. Later, we each received demands for a £100 payment for overstaying a two-hour 'free-parking' period. I refused outright.

Some internet advice suggested that the demands would stop and this is what happened almost five months later. In the interim, there was a flow of letters which ignored everything I wrote and used carrot and stick: further reduced payment options to avoid court action, increasing the demand to include solicitor's fees, threatening my future creditworthiness and employability, enforcement proceedings, use of a Supreme Court judgement as justification,[31] and passing the demand to collection agents.

The RAC said that parking should be a small, inconsequential part of our lives. The Supreme Court judgement would stir up totally disproportionate anxiety and anger, opening the door for parking companies to make sky-high charges.

Even more disturbing, in my view, was that the government was happy to sell my personal information, given in confidence to the vehicle licencing authority (DVLC), to parking companies, accredited, but not regulated, so that they could make these parking demands of unsuspecting travellers. The companies take pictures of number plates on all cars entering and leaving a lot they manage and, if they decide they have suffered a loss through a long stay, pay the DVLC £2.50 for the name and address of each car's registered owner, including live-alone single females and the elderly. This business is worth almost £7 million a year to the DVLC so they and government are not about to stand up for individuals any time soon.

A quick trawl around the websites found dozens of complaints ... ripping off drivers ... scum ... scammers ... shame on the companies who use them ... wankers ... cretins ... don't respond ... wrong car ... wrong place. And what of the firms that employ them regardless: English Heritage, Morrisons, Waitrose, Moto, BP ... and the NHS.

It was the NHS that was seized on by the *Daily Mirror* in 2018 while describing Ian Langdon and Ellis Green as the 'fatcats' managing about forty car parks for twenty hospital trusts. More than £147 million was demanded for hospital parking that year and this was blasted by charities, unions and MPs from all sides, as a 'tax on the sick'. Health Secretary Jeremy Hunt called increased parking charges a 'stealth tax on the vulnerable'. The *Mirror* reported that Langdon and Green each earned £6 million in the previous year and also had a property investment firm worth more than £14 million. Langdon, sixty-four, was worth £32 million, with a townhouse in St John's Wood, while Green, sixty-two, and associated with at least nineteen companies, had a £5 million home in nearby Hampstead and drove a Porsche with the word 'RAT' in its number plate.

I might have made a mistake in decrying 'two-hour' parking companies when I made some pointed comments in a letter. About that time, I received threatening phone calls, surely not associated, some heavy breathing, some challenges to 'watch it'. Another caller claimed that 'it's not over yet, you know', number withheld. Then there was an unusual car parked outside three early evenings in a row. Two large gentlemen sat in the front. I made some coffee and took it out on a tray but, as I got near, the car was slammed into gear and driven off with a tyre screech. I managed a picture of the number plate. Sadly, I couldn't pay the DVLC £2.50 and get the vehicle's registered address. The police weren't interested when I left a message which is the way of things these days; no one called back.

Were they suspicious SpeedWatch members? Perhaps the gentlemen had something to do with my missing family? I bolted the doors a bit earlier each evening for a few days, had a few weapons to hand – assegais, heavy torch and the like. It all went quiet.

Why spend time on the detail of these two motoring rants? Because they prompted the first real steps in the journey I describe in the rest of this book.

I decided to stop driving. Was this a victory for the village SpeedWatch team? For Langdon and Green? I thought it was something more important. To earn the right to crawl along the M25 behind a horsebox, you have to pay for and pass both a theory and practical test, purchase insurance, get an MOT, and buy vehicle and fuel tax. The Government not only tells you what speed to drive at, but regulates it punitively with cameras and makes you drive on roads that are as well maintained as the surface of the moon.

Columnist Tim Stanley asked, 'Who will act in the individual's interest? For decades we have seen the expanding power of the police, teachers, civil servants, social workers and tax collectors, all protected by the deference thought due to public servants, and who always claim they are acting in the individual's interest?'[32]

Well, they seldom do any more. Public servants act in their own interest and in the interests of some unhealthy and unsavoury bedfellows. I sold my car, informed the DVLC that I no longer wanted my driving licence, destroyed it, and smoothly cashed in my car insurance and tax. I made an arrangement with two local taxi companies, settled for home-delivered groceries, and walked to the pub. It was also another small nail in the coffin of my local town's economy.

Then I relaxed and went on holiday for two weeks to Crete and Malta. I encountered anti-German feeling everywhere as the Cretans rued the businesses, hotels, bass and bream sea farms colonised after the EC-imposed crash of the Greek economy. The fish for dinner at the shore restaurants was still good if expensive. At Rethymno harbour, the waiters lied noisily about the poverty of the cooking of their competitors. Victory with a new customer was celebrated with shouts and rude gestures. Valetta had far too many steep hills for everyday living and so was crossed off my 'where I might live one day' list. One day, four cruise ships, each with over two thousand passengers, docked and the town centre became a jostling horror. The many smaller archaeological sites around the islands were a joy and the museum at Heraklion is one of the great wonders of the world. Personally, I would give the teeming tourist trap of Knossos a miss.

The two Caravaggio paintings in the Oratory of St John's Cathedral were my personal pilgrimage. *The Beheading of St John* is dominant and glares down from above the altar, declaring to new members of the Order of St John that they, too, must be prepared to die horribly for their faith. The executioner has botched the job of severing the head for Salome's dish and pulls out his knife to finish the job. Caravaggio depicted his own name, the only one of his works that he signed, in the blood flowing from the neck of the martyred saint. The signature, beginning with 'F' for Fra, brother, was added later to celebrate his own acceptance into the Order and the forgiving of his many sins. My favourite, however, is the facing picture of *St Jerome Writing*, a copy of which used to hang in my lounge. 'The face is the mirror of the mind, and eyes without speaking confess the secrets of the heart.' It is a striking and sombre work with the wracked Jerome, a repentant pederast, bent, I hope, to his long task of translating the bible into Latin, the *Vulgate*. His own head mirrors the skull lying on his desk, foretelling his imminent death.

On the flight back to London from Valetta, an advertisement in the in-flight magazine, made me reflect on my travel collection. I was giving a run-out for this trip to my Moroccan passport. I had added nothing new for many years. The article encouraged the take-up of a Maltese passport. 'In a unsettled, ever-changing world, acquiring a second residence or citizenship is a wise decision and an investment in the future.'

Back in England, I made some semi-formal enquiries and received a phone call from the firm in Quebec. I soon realised that a Maltese passport was beyond my purse: altogether over one and a half million euro. The scheme swapped citizenship for investment: a non-returnable contribution of 650,000 euro to the National Development and Social Fund for distribution at the ministry's discretion, due diligence fees of 7,500 euro, real estate ownership on the island for at least five years which cannot be sub-let during that period, a five-year investment of 150,000 euro in a prescribed financial instrument, global health cover including 50,000 euro for medical expenses, and fees of 70,000 euro. Criminals were not allowed to apply, an amusing restriction, and residence for one year prior to naturalisation was obligatory. It also brought back unpleasant thoughts of Qaddura Mohammed Abd Al-Hamid.

I expressed disappointment at the time it would all take. Estonia was a problematic alternative because of the language. Perhaps, the West Indies would suit better and it did. Antigua, St Kitts and Nevis, and Granada all offer passport opportunities. The best option required buying property worth at least $400,000 which could be sold after five years and a non-refundable contribution to government of $100,000 plus due diligence and fees. I saw the property as a returnable investment. It was a place to park some spare cash for later use.

I flew to St Kitts via Antigua and was able with some ease to make a private case when I introduced my American passport, a descendant of the one salvaged from the Constellation wreck in Morocco almost fifty years before. This opened a back door into the island and saved a considerable amount of money.

I found a property and returned with the cash in a small suitcase to frustrate the money trail. My new passport was expedited. The one drawback was that parts of the deal had to be done in my Chris Heal name so that I could provide enough evidence to pass minimal suitability checks. I planned to stop using that passport in the near future so I disinterred the device of the deed poll that I had used after my first marriage. As St Kitts was in the Commonwealth, I arranged with a welcoming lawyer to change my name in St Kitts and received a new locally issued passport. When I returned to London, I changed my name by deed poll again, followed by my passport, and went back to St Kitts and did it again. My bet was that the international paper trail would never connect the beginning and end of these name changes.

My collection of passports now stood at nine, important when it came to arranging my money and gaining credit cards so that I could access money when and where I wanted.

I reviewed my wealth. There was my $400,000 property on St Kitts, now safely under the care of a local estate agent and self-funding. I had a few thousand euro in a French bank account. My combined UK bank accounts contained just shy of £500,000. I had a further £200,000 in a variety of small investments, ISAs, premium bonds, soft loans and shares. I cashed up the lot.

The house was unmortgaged, paid off during my business days, and I placed it on the market to see what I might get. I was assured it would fetch at least £750,000; I made it clear that while I invited interest it could be at least six months before I was ready to leave.

That left my pension trust fund containing shares at that time worth a little under a million pounds. This I could cash in, but it would be hit by the top tax rate of forty per cent which I considered unreasonable.

I had by now all but decided that I wished to disappear, to lose all the petty bureaucracy, and SpeedWatch, parking companies, shotgun licences and worms, and Facebook and the rapid erosion of freedom. The decision was not an epiphany, but a slide. If nobody knew who I had been then I had only to choose who I was at any one moment. Tomorrow I could always be someone else. I would have no property to live in, no responsibilities and no long-term relationships. I could choose where I stayed, for as long as I wanted, depending on what I wanted to enjoy. I would declare an identity as I needed. Then I could move, paying as I went and leaving nothing behind except footsteps in the sand.

Before, I was never overly worried about consequences, about conscience. Rats of guilt gnaw at people's happiness, nibble away at their self-worth. The cause could be some catastrophic event, an awful mistake, or some sudden and later regretted decision based on greed or neglect. Happily, I always found myself free of this weight except for the mind-pictures that lingered from Biafra and Nairobi. My decisions had all been made, I felt, in my reasonable best interest. Nobody had suffered unfairly. However, I knew some might see what I had done as beyond what was acceptable and there were so many 'bad things' in my past. Was there a pattern that could be noticed by others if they cared to look, a shape that I could not see, but that could be followed? If I was found, could I be forced back to the world I had quit?

Were these thoughts the first stirrings of conscience? Of fear? Of lack of resolve? Might the unease be my first worm cast of some repression that I was only now beginning to face? Could I leave it all behind? Could I strike out free, unencumbered, with no identity that could be tied to what I had left behind?

I ran a small experiment; I suppose to prove to myself what I already knew. I spent a week trying to live rough. It was early summer and in and around Winchester was not a time or place of great hardship.

The first lesson was that it was tougher than I thought. Daytime is all right, begging is easy if boring. It's at night that the trouble starts. I collected some cardboard boxes from the back of the Iceland store and set up my sleeping bag in a large shop doorway. After I had spent an hour staring at a window mannequin dressed for the beach, an aggressive and determined young drunk arrived and accused me of stealing his space. At my age, I wasn't looking for a fight, but I got one anyway. He was too confident from the alcohol, swinging wildly, and didn't have my training. One slow sidestep and I hit him in the midriff and then jammed a forearm in his face. He vomited and I caught him in the jaw with my knee as he went down which hurt us both. I didn't wait to collect my pieces of cardboard and legged it. A few streets away, I got lucky and a lonely dosser called Adam suggested I joined him in his patch as he had spare boxes.

'It'll be safer mate. Almost throwing out time', he said.

Around midnight the pubs and clubs began to empty. A group of jeering young men unzipped their flies and emptied their lager and vodka onto us and then threw in a few kicks for good measure. Then it was the girls' turn as they dropped their knickers and urinated while taunting us with their bare sex.

'We'll be all right now,' said my wet friend. 'People will stay away because of the smell. Unless someone decides they want to beat us up.'

The next evening, Adam and I joined a group of four others. He knew them all and they argued intermittently through the night: small debts unpaid, cigarettes promised, two of them sharing a tired-looking needle.

'Be better tomorrow,' I was told. 'Hope Church will be round with some grub. Then it's the Sally Anns with soup and sandwiches. And then there's someone else on Friday.'

I gave it one more night, but I was already almost at the point of giving up, finding a taxi and going home. Begging is cold work in the rain. I had a pitch nobody else seemed to want. Perhaps I needed an unwashed dog with a piece of string for a lead? After a couple of hours, an old woman with short white hair bustled up, her red rucksack bobbing on her back. She hadn't put her hand in her pocket so I knew she wasn't going to give me anything.

'You know about Trinity then,' she asked? Oh Lord, some sort of religious nut about to hold forth about God and the Holy Spirit and so on. I could do without that. I tried to ignore her.

'It's a drop-in centre for homeless people over near the old Police Station down by Durngate. Go and see them. At least they will give you something to eat, and some help if you really want it.'

After another cashless hour, my backside was numb so I took her advice and, clutching my sleeping bag, found 'Trinity' in a leafy street just off the city centre. After mumbling a few words, I was welcomed at the reception and a 'key worker' called. Mary was a delightful middle-aged lady with a caring face, ready smile, and a hard edge. She carried a pre-printed questionnaire and offered me a plastic cup of tomato soup.

'Shall we start with your name?'

I looked worried for a second, concentrated on the soup, and then offered, 'Basil'. I think it came from the tomatoes.

'Well, that will do for now, Basil. Have you got any identity papers, anything with a picture, your name on it?' I shook my head. 'Have you got a last name?' I shook my head. 'How about a birth date.'

'Can't remember.'

'How long have you been on the streets? Remember, I meet a lot of people that are in your position. To be honest, you don't look like you've been homeless for long.' I managed a small guilty smile. 'Can you tell me anything about why you're on the streets?'

'Things got too much,' I offered. 'Needed to get away.'

'Have you got a home somewhere? Any family? Anyone who will be worried about you?'

'Not anymore.'

'OK. Look, I can maybe get you a bed for a night or two, but during that time you must come back and see me every day so that we can talk some more. If you won't tell me who you are then it will be difficult to help you much. I don't care how long it takes to get you settled. We'll always be here for you. But, you have to help us help you. Lots of doors will be closed, like the Council, until you do.' I nodded.

'Do you want to talk any more, now?

'Perhaps tomorrow'.

'Do you want to see a doctor?' I shook my head slowly.

'Or for me to let anyone know that you are safe?' To my surprise, I started to cry, just small tears, but they found a steady course down my cheeks.

'Nobody,' I said.

I was given some sausage and chips and a piece of paper with the address of the Winchester night shelter in Jewry Street and I limped off, knee and elbow throbbing. The place was run by a consortium of local churches.

'You're in luck,' said a lady called Michele. 'Come on in. You'll have to share a twin, but you'll have nice sheets. You'll be safe here for a night or two.'

After the last two days, it was heaven: a television room, quiet room and an internet lounge. I headed for the hot shower, cleaned my teeth, enjoyed sitting on a toilet, washed my urine-stained rags and was offered spare clothes which had seen better days, but were clean. I devoured the evening meal, ignored my room partner's snoring and occasional sobs and dropped into a deep sleep.

The next day, I slipped away, experiment over. I found Adam near the Butter Cross in the High Street and gave him my news.

'You are much better off in Winchester', he decided. 'I was in Southampton last week and there are a lot of people who come through the port from all over Europe and beyond. Poor buggers. They don't survive for long. If you can't look after yourself then the Border Police take you away and you get shipped home, wherever that might be. Another of Theresa Remainer May's cock-ups.'

I gave him a packet of cigarettes and a fiver and said goodbye. When I got home, I sent large cheques to Trinity and Winchester Churches Nightshelter.

It was clear that I wanted to live in some comfort, not too conspicuous, not first class hotels, not luxurious restaurants, well, maybe now and then. There would be no flying except in an emergency and, therefore, greater freedom by train, taxi and ferry to carry what I wanted in my luggage, which would be limited.

Jack Reacher had always interested me with his folding toothbrush and his single shirt; to go into a shop and come out wearing new clothes, leaving his own gear in the waste bin.[33] As he drifted the length of the United States, a crime-solving nomad, I never thought of him as lonely, only with envy that he was free of all ties and responsibility. He was as pure an avatar of freedom as can be found in modern fiction: no wife, no kids, no mortgage, no domestic entanglements, and no rules except the ones he made himself. He didn't look for trouble, but it followed him anyway. His flaw was that he carried a bank card in his own name and, from time to time, made withdrawals and, therefore, could be found. Reacher, though, is fiction, a series of popular stories. This book, my book, is as true as I can admit.

Philip Larkin describes how he felt when he heard of an acquaintance who 'chucked up everything and just cleared off'.[34] There was an expectation that the nomadic act would be approved: 'this audacious, purifying, elemental move' when Larkin was left 'flushed and stirred' as someone 'walked out on the whole crowd'. Settled people fear moving people, but they can also envy and half-admire them. In envying and admiring, they invent the sort of travelling people they prefer and hold up a cracked mirror to examine themselves.

To do all I planned, I needed money that was not associated with me and where I was, but with my passports. I reasoned that the money must be spread across many places. The property in St Kitts was a good start. I had to be able to drop any of my resources at short notice, to walk away and never go back. It followed my money pile had to be as large as I could make it, yet split into small pots, and that meant evading the punitive forty per cent UK pensions tax.

What I did next was simple and legal. I wanted a new pension from which I could extract its entire value. I registered a limited company; I thought 'Nomad Enterprises' sounded good. I used 'Nomad' to set up a Self-Administered Pension Fund (SSAS), an occupational pension scheme run by employers. There used to be a requirement that the Fund appointed a pension trustee, a pension professional or actuary. This had been relaxed and the Fund administrator did not need to be a third party. It was possible for any individual to take on the role on the grounds that only technical matters need be outsourced to advisers. This was my opportunity. I appointed myself as the scheme administrator for *Nomad* and set up a trustee's bank account that required only my signature. As the scheme administrator, I controlled my own bank account and my own pension arrangements. I arranged for my existing pension fund to be closed and the money transferred to my SSAS account. Once the funds had cleared, I would be able to write cheques and transfer funds without any initial scrutiny from the pension's regulator. I would be required to provide an annual scheme pension report, but I knew that these were seldom audited and by then I would be gone. I discovered that the Revenue was aware of the loophole I was exploiting, but had not yet closed it. I acted at once so as to get the money to the account that I controlled.

My illegality would occur when I cashed in the whole of the account and distributed it out of harm's way. The tax consequences of this evasion would be considerable to a law-abiding citizen, but not to me. I could never return to the UK as Chris Heal, but then I never intended to. Chris Heal would become a non-person. I would always be someone else. With the lack of an audit and my disappearance, the Inland Revenue would become interested and would decide that what I had accomplished was a tax fraud.

The questions were, 'How hard would they look for Chris Heal?' and 'Who and where was he'?

I could now see my anticipated cash pile of £2,185,000, not counting my property in St Kitts or the French account:

Net house sale	850,000
SSAS transfer	930,000
Cash at bank	195,000
Cashed in investments, etc	210,000

The amount surprised me at first, but I reasoned there must be many people in the south of England with houses worth nearly a million pounds and pensions pots pushing a similar amount. The difference for me was that I had no mortgage and I was acquiring the full amount of the pension. My bank agreed to facilitate large cash withdrawals on suitable notice. On several occasions I walked out with £250,000 in used £50 notes.

I did not want to carry a large amount of cash, but I needed to be able to access money whenever I wanted by a variety of different routes to suit the occasion. I had to split the money so that the loss of any one or two parts through discovery by unfriendly parties would not lead to others. I needed an appropriate passport for each stash. I now had nine passports, but one, Chris Heal, was going to be destroyed.

Here was my headline distribution:

Cash in hand	5,000
Swiss bank account	500,000
Cayman bank account	500,000
Hawala transfers	390,000 (in three accounts)
Credit card placements	700,000 (in seven accounts)
Bitcoin	100,000

The Swiss and Cayman Island bank accounts were straightforward to establish with cash deposits. I say Swiss and Cayman Islands, because these may or may not have been the actual destinations. The money is still there, untouched, and these are my bolt holes. They cannot be touched by using a name, but only with a number which I have memorised or in person by two physical recognition tests. There, I will let these two accounts rest.

Hawala, 'trust' or 'change', may be strange to a European who is captive to large and avaricious international banks. Indeed, if you are not part of a Muslim community or a security agency then you may well not have heard of this way of money transfer. It operates parallel to, but outside of, the traditional Western system. It originated in India in the eighth century and was a major component of trade between Muslims and Arabs on the Silk Road to China (where it is known as *fei qian* or 'flying money'). Today, it is used throughout the world with complete legitimacy and, in some countries, is advertised and supported as an efficient and frictionless alternative to 'morbid and corrupt domestic financial institutions'.[35]

In the USA, India (where it is known as *Hundi*, based on 'chit', a word which is still used in English to signify an IOU), Pakistan and parts of western Europe, *hawala* is seen as facilitating money laundering, drug trafficking, tax evasion, and the anonymous movement of wealth and can be illegal. The American government suspected al-Qaeda of using *hawala* to fund the 9/11 terrorist attacks on the Word Trade Towers in New York. It is also thought that the system facilitated the payment of ransoms to Somali pirates. However, in Afghanistan, it is used by NGOs for the delivery of emergency relief. It was also the financial system used in 2012 after the chaos when Tuareg and jihadist forces captured Timbuktu and much of northern Mali and left the country without an official money transfer system for many months. These Tuareg attacked using in part French M1 carbines and heavy weapons destined for Biafra in 1969 and salvaged from a plane wreck by their brother Berbers.

For me, *hawala* was a means of transferring money across borders, avoiding taxes, the need to bribe officials, or to pay high bank fees without the need for physical or electronically transferring the cash. Moneychangers, *hawaladar*, would receive my cash in the UK, no questions asked, and correspond with an *hawaladar* in another country who would dispense the money. Minimal fees and commissions, about one percent, were deducted and the exchange was effected at a much better rate than a megabank would offer. The transfer would be conducted in PGP code, and this would also be used to identify the eventual recipient. The *hawala* system requires unbounded trust and so *hawaladars* are often members of the same family, village, clan, or ethnic group, but large *hawaladars* use a chain of middlemen in cities across the world. For large amounts, *hawala* transfers are fragmented into 'starbursts' and wired to hundreds of international recipients. Formal records are sparse. Settlement of accounts between *hawaladars*, which may come months or years later, can be in any form – cash, goods, services, properties or discounted trade.

I went to London in search of three *hawala* brokers between whom I planned to split £390,000 in cash. They were easy to find in the ethnic areas of London. I made my selection based on their geographic strength, one in

North Africa with an agent in Morocco; one for the Indian sub-continent where Bangladesh was the obvious choice; and one for south-east Asia, which had to be Vietnam. My amounts were large compared to their usual fare, but they were unfazed even when my unusual requirements were discussed. No questions were asked as to my identity or sources. The bank contact with two back-ups would be reconfirmed each year, also by email.

Eventually, I wanted money transferred of an amount, on a date and to a place all as yet unknown. The transfers would be triggered by me with a Mailpile-encrypted email using a PGP code and this was agreed on the spot. The response to my call would detail the local *hawaladar* who could give me or a nominated recipient local currency against an agreed code in whatever town I found myself in need.

Even with all the implicit work and secrecy, the charges agreed in advance were still less than twenty-five per cent of those requested by Western Union when I had made sham enquiries there for a single transaction. The whole set-up took less than a day. I left an adequate personal thank you in each case as a gesture of good faith. As I said, *hawala* depends on absolute trust.

My *hawala* accounts were a half-way house, back-up money, but also available whenever I was able to make contact with London. Apart from my small, though exposed, hand-carried personal cash, my main source of income would be my credit cards. Ubiquitous holes-in-the-walls would give me an instant supply of money in the right currency. I could also use them for hotels, restaurants, clothes, admission tickets and travel if I had to, although I planned to use cash whenever I could to break any paper chain. The trick was that I wanted several cards, each with a name that matched one of my passports so that, if necessary, I had proof of identity. These cards would be from a mix of card providers, never the same company. I also did not want to settle each month's statements myself as to do that I would need a bank account or another credit card to transfer the money. I needed someone else who would do that for me, a different person for each of my identities.

I nicknamed these people my 'helpers'. If I could pull it off, no helper would be known to another, and none of them would know me by any other name than the one on the passport associated with 'their card'. The cards themselves would be used haphazardly. The disconnect would be absolute.

Any official inspecting one of the card statements would see only a variety of overseas purchases and would have no reason or way of associating the statement with another statement with a different name on another card.

My immediate need was to find this set of individuals who would be prepared to take out a card in their own name and then to apply for a secondary card in one of my names for which they would be financially responsible. For this service, I would give them £100,000 in cash of which £10,000 was an up-front personal payment. This left a pot of £90,000 which they could place where they wished, my only condition being that as each month's statement arrived, they would be responsible for making any payment due in full without quibble. When the pot fell below £10,000, which may not be for many years, they were to email me at a non-personalised, agreed address. They would signify whether they were happy to accept a second batch of money, in which case, if I agreed, they would be called to collect a second cash payment of £100,000 and the cycle could repeat.

The safeguard for each helper was that if, at any time, official contact was made to query the use of the credit card, they were to admit the complete truth. The truth, that is, except for my covert email address and, perhaps, the amount of money they had received, given that the £100,000 could be entered in their finances in a number of ways. The helper would send to me a discreet email with a code word indicating that the card was suspect. Whatever money remained, either undeclared or unconfiscated, was theirs to keep. The arrangement was at an end and neither of us would contact the other again, unless, of course, there was a question in my mind of duplicity on their part. I would then consider what action best suited my interests.

All that remained was to find my helpers. I decided to see if I could enlist an author I had met by chance at a Southampton University academic conference earlier that year. He was an established writer of historical investigations, fortunes made and lost. Contact was a risk, but we had got on well over dinner and I thought it a chance worth taking. We met in London. He was morose as Brexit loomed large in his thoughts and government perfidy was on his mind. I had sent him a draft of *Sound of Hunger* and he was complimentary with a few suggestions for improvement. I said I hadn't started looking yet for a publisher. He picked up his phone and I found I had an appointment for four o'clock that afternoon a short taxi ride away.

While he was in decisive mood, I asked for his advice in finding my seven helpers. I didn't share the whole story as I did not want to implicate him and, with sadness, realised for the first time that 'disappearing' meant 'disappearing'. This could well be our only lunch.

The puzzle appealed to the master plot-maker. After a few chuckles, he gave me three names: a well-known politician, long out of government and now bitter at being out of favour with little hope of return; a solicitor with a small public reputation for managing the defence of ham-fisted habitual criminals who, in a blow to his income, were all serving long sentences; and a struggling authoress in north London, the sole support of her dying mother.

'The point,' he said, 'is that your helpers should need money now and be encouraged by the chance of some more coming. What you are asking from them is not in itself illegal as they are just providing a financial service and don't know the background or the intent. There's no cost to them and they have the chance of a gain if there is a problem. But, and it's a *big* but, it is in their interest for their own involvement to be kept quiet. At the slightest whiff, they'll try to dampen things down if only for their own good.'

He offered to speak to the politician and I gave him two names of people I thought good prospects, but did not want to approach personally. In return, he gave me the phone numbers of another two names that occurred to him.

'Don't mention my name,' he said. 'That'll keep it all secret and separate. Once it's done, I'll forget about it.' He took a large sip of red and looked at me with intent through hooded lids. 'I hope to read the book one day.'

How far ahead of the game was he?

The introduction opened all the doors with the publisher. The book was never going to sell in huge numbers, but I had put two years of care into it, so I wanted good production values and some promotional vigour to find appropriate reviews. I stayed in town having made appointments with my two prospect 'helpers'. The solicitor was the easy one. The authoress needed to think it over, but when I called two days later and we had gone over it all again, she was firmly in favour. My author friend netted the MP and the two other names I had supplied, I posted all of them a copy of their appropriate passport number, along with the name, age and address they should use if asked. They all then applied for new credit cards for themselves and asked for a secondary card. The cover I suggested, but I don't know if it was used, was that I was someone who would be helping out on the domestic side and that included doing all of the shopping, hence the need for a card.

I contacted the last two prospects myself. One was a recently widowed woman who was trying to set herself up as a potter, her husband never having taken out any life insurance. She lived some distance away from me and I had only met her when I bought a goose eggcup. She had been on a down day and poured out her heart over a cup of tea. The other was a young man I had met at one of the crypto-parties and who had declared his dislike of the western financial system. Both were easy sales.

As my last financial string, I dabbled in bitcoin. Volatile for sure. It seemed certain that I would lose money, but the reason why bitcoin is so beloved by libertarians is because it takes control of money away from the state. These were people like me who hated that bankers and governments held the keys and always manipulated the rates to their own ends. When the markets were all but destroyed in 2008 and 2009 by the chronic greed of bankers, governments arranged the bail-out so that those responsible were not imprisoned, but instead remained Midas rich, the vast bills paid by taxpayers. I have come to believe that if bitcoin were to become a major alternative, with equal status to the dollar or the euro, central banks would lose their power forever. These central banks are the only institutions that can print money and for actual spending money provide the only option. Because of this, the banks have the power to set interest rates and to finance deficits or to run surpluses whenever they like to the detriment of personal finances. As someone said, 'If bitcoin deprives central banks of the ability to finance catastrophic wars by printing money, it will be the best bargain humanity ever got.'

I watched the bitcoin market rise and began to buy in January 2017 from a personal broker at just over $200 and ended with fifty-nine coins. By November 2018, bitcoin had fallen by over eighty per cent from its peak, losing one-third of its value in the previous week as the impossible bubble burst. I was still about flat on my investment. Then it started to rise again. We'll see how it goes.

With pleasing timing, I received three offers on my house; the lowest by a few thousand was not dependent on a mortgage approval. I accepted on the condition that the sale included all the furniture and white goods and then I waited for the final month before I had to move out.

I started to wade through the long list of petty chores I had identified with my disappearance. House bills – gas, electricity, council tax, home phone – were all easy enough and, as the rebates involved were small I wasn't going to be anxious about any that did not arrive in time. I reduced my bank accounts to near zero and cancelled my own credit cards, bar one. I then sat down with all of my personal papers and the computer and stopped all memberships, standing orders, in fact anything left that had any life. I lit a large bonfire of all my papers and threw the computer on it and cancelled my internet provider. I used an internet café two towns away to set up the series of email addresses that I might need and committed others from contacts like the *hawala* brokers to memory.

I worried a lot about the next step, but decided that I would need some back up if for any reason my memory failed. I used a PGP code to record on three unconnected Tor Hidden Services websites the separated parts of all the information I might need to activate my finances. I also committed the information in code onto a single sheet of paper and took it in a sealed envelope to a solicitor in Guildford and, for a small sum, he agreed to keep it for twenty years and only to release it through a convoluted arrangement we hammered out. The name on the envelope was not one that was used by me anywhere else.

Where might one expect to find the greatest difficulty in this whole process of disengagement? A bet at odds of fifty-to-one would be safe, I suggest. It was the television licencing authority. They were unable to accept that life could be lived without a television and so declined a refund. They asked me to declare three times that I no longer had a television or other receptor and accompanied each request with threats. I noticed that the fine could be up to £1,000, but £2,000 in Guernsey.

Proving a negative is always an interesting conundrum. There was only two months' money left on my licence, but I continued my demand to be set free with a rude letter. It was with some amusement that I then received a nasty letter from TV Licencing with 'Official notice: investigation opened' visible on the envelope; the BBC and its capitalist running-dog agency thereby publicly declaring my guilt. A day later, my refund cheque arrived with dire warnings if I broke the law.

I decided to switch the set on every night when I went to bed until the day I quit the property. Two days before I left, I noticed an under-cover van with its discreet roof aerial stopped a short distance away. I offered the men coffee and suggested that late evening might be a better time to catch me and would also give them some welcome overtime.

'Smug bastard,' was the response. 'You realise that we can get you from quarter of a mile away.'

'Does that mean that you don't want the coffee?'

Much later, it caused me sleepless nights, tossing and turning into the small hours, because, as I had deliberately broken the law, a TV Licencing summons was probably somewhere waiting for me.

Thinking about the television took me back to Harshani and how I thought for a mad few weeks that I loved her. I cringed at my naivety. What of her mask, that convincing face? Could I ever relax into a relationship like that again? Dare I? I remembered how she had slowly worked her way through the things that I owned, she saw herself owning, choosing and assessing as many items slid into her control. At first, I was pleased that she cared, but soon felt an irritation at her acquisitiveness. Now I was going to walk away from all my possessions.

The morning when we first visited Anuradhapura, we stood in front of the site's famous *sandakada pahana*, a moonstone, based on its shape and design. It lies at the bottom of a wide, brief stone staircase, the old entrance to a Buddhist temple. The carvings of these semi-circular slabs evolved through other great Sinhalese cities and I saw examples at Polonnaruwa and Kandy.

Harshani was struggling to answer my questions. She was, at first, authoritative and then spoke with little pauses as she sought explanations that would satisfy me. She was so beautiful that I forgave her, didn't realise or even notice the deceit. A young Sinhalese man in jeans and T-shirt came and stood beside me and asked if he could help. He was a monk called Bahalika, not long passed his initiation, who was released from his temple for two days a week to act as an interpreter for the site and in the process gather money for his order.

The centre of the *sandakada pahana* at Anuradhapura is a half lotus, nirvana, enclosed by four concentric bands, each with their own repetitive design: the outside depicts flames around an altar; then four animals – elephants, lions, horses and bulls – standing for the four stages of life:

birth, decay, disease and death; an intricate floral design, worldly desires; and on the inner band, a procession of swans, good and evil. There are many variations. The *sandakada pahana* symbolised the Buddhist cycle of *Samsāra*, a fundamental concept in all Indian religions. Its meaning is subtle, but 'aimless wandering' is the one that stuck with me, being a nomad without direction. All beings go through these cycles of mundane successive existences, birth, death and rebirth. The Buddha reached nirvana and therefore escaped and was not reborn.

After twenty years of failing to write his first book investigating nomads and their lives and finally claiming that he burned it, Bruce Chatwin declared the term useless. 'The word *nomad* must go'.

Chatwin was struck by the analysis used by zoologist Desmond Morris in *The Naked Ape*. There was a fundamental psychological difference between wandering away and then back to a fixed base and wandering from place to place without a fixed base. When man became a hunter, Morris thought he 'had to have somewhere to come back to after the hunt was over'. It was an essential development from an ape-like existence. He suggested a vaguer term like 'human wanderlust'.

Anthropologist Jeremy Swift met Chatwin in Tehran and disagreed with his 'romantic' definition. Real nomads would 'move to places that they knew about, would understand the space involved, would not go in search of sensations'. Real nomads were not like Arctic terns that were pulled along a magnetic highway, a beautiful white bird that flew from the North to the South Pole only to return.

I discussed these thoughts with Bahalika and admitted that I knew little of Buddhism, but claimed that it had always fascinated me. It seemed the hardest of religions to follow. Even knowing where to start was problematic.

'For most western people, but not all, you are right,' he said. 'For you, it would be hard. You could not do it without a teacher. To discover if you are ready, listen hard to a teacher for you would not know enough to carry on a conversation. You might start with something which might seem easy, but which would be hard in reality.'

'Like what?'

'You cannot travel on the path before you have become the Path itself. You must give up your collections of goods, one by one. Collections are not needed. They are a devotion to property. They are a good example of what is wrong with your way of life, I mean by that, the western approach to civilisation.'

'I'm not sure I have any collections,' I said, without thought.

'Today,' he said, 'more than ever, men have to live without things because they fill a man with fear. The more they collect, the more they have to fear. Things have a way of burrowing into the soul and taking control.'

He paused, offered a look that was shy and built on sorrow. 'It was pleasant to meet you. I will leave you now to your guide,' and he was gone.

'Nice man,' said Harshani, 'but you need to be careful with monks. Never trust them. Too many of their lamas drive around in big cars.'

On the flight home with Harshani, I started a list of all my collections: books by subject, books by author, cds, paintings, archaeological memories and thefts, holiday mementoes, love tokens. I thought I would start cutting down on the books.

'I wouldn't throw anything away,' offered Harshani, 'until I've had a chance to look at things, see if there is anything I like, and', recovering flawlessly, 'so that I can learn more about you, of course.'

My last task proved personally the most difficult. I say 'personally' knowing its Latin root, *persona*, meaning a theatrical mask. The persona in everyday usage is the character played by an actor. I was shedding my mask. Would I accomplish it only to replace it with another mask, even less truthful? Was there a person of any real character beneath or was I just a straw in the wind, a grain of sand in the desert, near identical to all the others once the deception of the mask was lost?

Now I had to leave all of my collections and take a first lonely step into a life of wandering and try to live without the comfort of collections or masks.

Too fanciful?

We shall see.

8. FREEDOM OF SPEECH

Here is no water but only rock
Rock and no water and the sandy road
The road winding above among the mountains
Which are mountains of rock without water
If there were water there we should stop and drink.[36]

My two-year endeavour, *Sound of Hunger*, a biography built around the First World War, was published in June and received some kind comments. The book sold slowly, typical for its type, written more for curiosity than any hope of recovering expenses. The UK parliament went into summer recess. EU negotiators waited for more British concessions on Brexit. The BBC was scratching around for news so I was asked in for a short-notice author's interview. I was not enthusiastic. I've always found that when a project is complete, I move on so quickly that within a few months the detailed memory fades and enthusiasm drains away. Some years ago, I made one-off original oak furniture for my home – kitchen dressers, beds, chests of drawers, a roll-top desk and the like. Later, I looked at the individual pieces and struggled to remember how I had made them.

A large gin and tonic, which kept me company while I waited for the call to the studio, may have been part of the explanation for saying what I did on air. I didn't plan my contribution. I expected to wing it. Adrian, the presenter, all bouffant hair, printed flower shirt and fake friendship, had skimmed the book; he couldn't be blamed for this as it was over 700 pages. After three dry questions about submarines and naval training, showing that he had missed the point of the story, he suddenly switched to Brexit.

'Tell me, Chris, you have written this book about a period one hundred years ago from the German perspective. Do you see any lessons, any continuity, between then and now, between the reign of Kaiser Wilhelm and the people who now run Germany and the people who run the European Union?'

It was a trap, of course, but I was happy to dive straight in.

'There are significant similarities,' I explained. 'The people who run Germany are largely the people who run the EU. They are by far the biggest funder and so they pull the strings. Nothing of importance happens without German consent.'

'But the EU is a democratic institution,' Adrian offered.

'It's interesting that you think that. The structure the Kaiser and his lackies used to run Germany in the years up to and including the First World War is remarkably similar to that of the EU today. The Kaiser and his inner team equate to the oligarchy who now run Brussels, both unelected and largely untouchable. No political party that you can vote for can, or could, unseat them. They are, and he was, above democratic reach. Both understood this and luxuriate in it. Like all power of this nature, it corrupts, it develops feelings of superiority in the ordained and produces disdain for people who think for themselves.'

'So you think, Chris, that there is a natural conflict between the EU and the people?'

'The real power lies in searching for the truth, in a willingness to look beyond this story, any story. And as long as people keep searching, they are dangerous to the EU elite. That's what they're afraid of – people and democracy. In response, the elite denigrates truth-seekers; the 'populists' are seen as less-knowing, less important and are treated as an inconvenient irritation.

'Bismarck's constitution made the Kaiser the most powerful ruler in the world, not quite the case for Tusk and Juncker, but comparable. The Kaiser and his Chancellor, the federal executive, stood giant-like over both the *Bundesrat*, the moribund executive body of the empire, and the *Reichstag*, which, like the sop of the EU parliament, could not initiate new legislation. By privilege of *Kommandogewalt*, the royal command, the Kaiser could appoint and dismiss his chancellor, all federal officials, and all officers in the military, a state within a state. He held complete control of foreign policy, could declare war and make peace, and was the supreme commander of all imperial armies. He was answerable to no-one.'

'But, further down the hierarchy in Brussels, there's something different today?'

'The EU elite appoint their head of departments, with Jean-Claude Juncker even ignoring his own laws to anoint the institution's civil service leader, Martin Selmayr. Now, the Germans want their own European army shorn of the Americans. As Lord Ismay, the first secretary general, said, "NATO's mission was to keep the Russians out, the Americans in, and the Germans down".'

Most interviewer personalities see their own questions are more important than any guest's rambling answers. Adrian was champing and I felt I should let him back in.

'But how come, then, that the Kaiser was able to join a war and persuade millions of his subjects to fight and to die?'

'It's important to correct part of your question. The Kaiser didn't join the war; he and his generals, industrialists and politicians started it. Deliberately and with arrogance, despite what some modern-day revisionists argue. Many Germans agreed with him as they were miffed that all other, lesser, powers on the western European seaboard had colonial empires. Germany, largely, did not and this was intolerable to the German self-view. They demanded their place in the sun.

'Their war aims were inconsistent, but their proposals included emasculating Britain, swallowing up Belgium and the Netherlands, and impoverishing France for decades as part of an economic vassal state, annexing most of the French channel ports, as well as seizing extensive colonies around the world.

'The levers of power were almost all in the Kaiser's hands, directly or indirectly. A "good" German obeyed orders, a respect for authority that took them to war again within twenty years of defeat. They started planning and building for the Second World War before the ink was dry on the armistice.

'Does any of this seem familiar to you?'

'Yes, Chris, but about the EU ...'

'Wilhelm was suffered, not enjoyed, by most Germans, as is the EU by a climbing number of Europeans. Nonetheless, there remained a loyalty to the royal ethos and to those in power. Wilhelm's chancellors were weak, not the men to direct an all-powerful general staff, an arrogant navy, a confused foreign office, and an increasingly divided Reichstag. There was and are delusions of either prosecution or grandeur, charm on the one hand, rudeness, vulgarity and even cruelty on the other, utter conceit, and all of these have worrying echoes in the upper floors of Brussels' ivory towers.

During the war, according to Max Weber, it seemed as if they were ruled by a bunch of delusional maniacs. What's different now with the current group of zealots?'

'Strong stuff. Are you saying then, Chris, that this EU could end in revolution. I mean that's what happened in Germany after the first war. Surely it's not comparable?'

'Absolutely it is comparable. There is and was profound disaffection and anger. From the perspective of 1919, millions of German soldiers were dead and maimed, hundreds of thousands of non-combatant German children and their mothers were brought to near starvation by the British-inspired and managed economic blockade, not an episode, by the way, that any British government is happy to talk about. There was increasing internal dissention, growing insistence on electoral and financial reforms, and increasingly powerful trade union demands for industrial and agricultural legislation. Liberal Reichstag members wanted to bring imperial Germany into the modern political world. A ruling aristocracy wanted imperial Germany to remain in the Junker tradition of government by the few for the few, and the industrialists were largely supportive of repeating the war. For the war, substitute today the mass youth unemployment of the northern Mediterranean'.

'But, are you really suggesting that a lot of the current ills lie at Germany's door rather than the EU?'

'If you want the dramatic headline, I think that the EU has become the continuation by other means by Germany of two world wars where it sought world domination. It is, in fact, what they should have done in the early 1900s. Not start an EU, but let their economic muscle do the talking, not seek victory on the battlefields of 1870, 1914 and 1939, but take the fight to the heart of the competitions' marketplace.

'If you like, you can take it right back to the Roman historian Ammianus Marcellinus, "The Huns burn with an insatiable lust for gold".'

'So, what's your diagnosis, Chris?'

'A Euro with exchange and interest rates designed to further the Deutschmark. Mediterranean states pauperised by monetary union, the 'German cage' as it was so colourfully described by the man who would have been Italy's economic minister if the EU had permitted it. Now the EU elite wants fiscal union so that German bankers control the entire edifice. This would be a uniform tax and expenditure policy to embrace all of the member states, no matter how disparate their economic conditions.

'Go to Greece and see the assimilation of what remains of Greek industry by German money – tourism, infrastructure, fish farms. Germany owns Greece and is on the road to owning Italy.

'Europe's migration crisis was sparked by Merkel without request or discussion with her partners. In 2015, when the immigration crisis began, more than 1.8 million people were detected crossing Europe's borders. She sought to bring cheap labour into her country to soften the lives of her ageing population. That selfishness alone has quickened the populist advance across the continent. The Hungarian government is busy vilifying immigrants and minorities while the Italian prime minister talks about drawing up lists of Romani gypsies. For the first time since the Second World War, Nazis sit in Germany's Reichstag. And even in the great liberal and illusional victory won by Emmanuel Macron, one third of the electorate voted for the French National Front. Macron admits that if the French were allowed a vote they would leave the EU.

'The crisis is not abating. By 2020, the German government will have spent an estimated £74 billion dealing with the domestic costs of the crisis that Merkel caused. And in the midst of this Merkel sideswipes her neighbours, particularly Hungary, by setting up bilateral deals with Russia against EU law to get cheap energy through new pipelines – up to 75 per cent of her natural gas needs. Germany is heavily dependent on Russia which is now doubling its energy supply capacity by building the geopolitically critical Nord Steam II pipeline to Germany. As someone said, "It is one of the most politically divisive projects in European history." Poland and Lithuania have gone the other way and weaned themselves off Russian energy.'

'Surely, surely …,' stuttered Adrian. I wasn't going to stop now.

'Donald Trump went so far as to accuse Germany of being "totally controlled by Russia", captive because of these joint energy deals. He questioned why America was spending billions of dollars countering the Kremlin through NATO while European countries handed similar amounts to Russia in business deals and were unwilling to meet even a two per cent target for military spending.

'This European money, mainly German, has been used by Russia to prop up its brutal colonising government: to annex the Crimea, instigate a proxy war in the Ukraine, conduct a failed putsch in Montenegro, and lead Georgia to war in 2008. The Kremlin also attempted to manipulate the 2016 American presidential elections and all of this against a backdrop of subversive information campaigns waged via Kremlin-controlled media, mass killings in Syria, continual undermining of NATO, and cyber and naked poison attacks on Western targets.

'Putin's United Russia party is allied to two fringe groups that are now in power in Austria and Italy. It is forging closer ties with Greece, Hungary and Turkey. Russian money is highly significant in Cyprus and Russian loans have been used by the French National Front. Russia has supported anti-EU politicians in the EU parliament on both the left and right fringes. The Russians have closed the international waters of the vital Kerch Strait joining the Black and Azov Seas to all Ukrainian vessels. The French and German governments advised cautious negotiation and rejected a military solution.

'It is an unholy alliance. The German government has a lot to answer for. I suggest two lessons immediately learned, as pertinent in 2018 as their mirrors were in 1918: first Merkel will always act to save her own skin and, second, Germany will always dictate terms to neighbour countries whatever the legality when it wants to advance its interests.'

'Well, Chris, thank you for the polemic. We have to end now, but I have a feeling that your comments and this debate is not about to end any time soon.'

'Thank you, Adrian. I hope that you learnt a lot about my book.'

I was glad to be pulled up. I was out of puff and beginning to think about repercussions. If anyone questions the accuracy of my recall of these on-air conversations, they can all be found tucked away in the recesses of the BBC's online archive if they have not been quietly excised as an embarrassing memory? And, yes, of course, I've cut some of the interviewer's interruptions and tightened up the language a little to make me appear more lucid. What did you expect?

I had hardly left the studio when I was confronted by an enthusiastic young lady who said, 'Fantastic, wonderful, absolutely wonderful.'

'What?' I tried.

'Your views, so refreshing, so different.'

'I didn't think they were so different to what a lot of other people have said.'

'But it's the way you say it. People will sit up and take notice.'

'I thought that most of it was seriously off message for the BBC? And, to cap it all, I'm male, white and over sixty.'

'Don't be daft. Come and have a drink. What I, we, would like you to do is come on a news discussion programme in an hour or so. Talk some more about Brexit. Get your point of view across.'

I am going to share, perhaps remind you, of what happened next. The debate continues to be vital, but in retelling it I want you to recognise what drove me to the edge, confirmed to me that, despite my own two days in the sun, I wanted to leave all this pettiness and falsity behind.

No politician is ever to be trusted. They are all to a degree dishonest and many close to power are calculated, compulsive super-liars. They will do whatever they can to keep their jobs and to protect themselves from harmful criticism. Some very powerful, immoral people told me directly and indirectly that week that they wanted to see the back of me. They made it clear that they would be very pleased if I went away and was never seen again. *Ever.*

I relished the drinks. I didn't believe a word of what the young lady said. It was the silly season. The BBC was short of news and here they could manufacture a frail controversy, their particular expertise, if they played it right. It was another trap and I walked right in again.

However, for once, the BBC got it badly wrong. I had been hastily drafted into the later programme because of the sickness of a prominent Remainer MP, who wanted to reverse the British referendum because voters were not capable of deciding on so complex an issue. Another 'second referendum' Remainer pulled out at short notice. What the BBC was left with, as *The Guardian* put it the next day, was a 'Conference of the Fruitcakes' although none of us that I could see were paid up UKIP members.

For an hour, the British listening public were treated to a quartet of speakers queueing up to agree with each other. It was funny in the room as we realised we had the freedom of the airwaves. Politeness and reasonability reigned except with the panel's treatment of the interviewer; this aggressive and shallow piece of work was resolutely ignored. I swear the production team tucked in their glass box were tearing their hair.

This was bad radio, no personality-led disagreements, no angry words, no tantrum-led interruptions, just old-fashioned debate. And, worse, the wrong consensus was reached. A 'no deal' was advocated and welcomed.

I was politely introduced, as much for the benefit of the other panellists, all hardy veterans, as for any audience that may have been out there, and was asked to reprise my arguments from earlier in the day.

I said that there were historical parallels between the period of the First World War and today and that the Germans had taken over the European Union machine. In an end to any pretence of parliamentary democracy under the *Spitzenkandidaten* system, the next EU president would be German and chosen by the elite. It could even be Angela Merkel, increasingly exposed as a flawed chancellor, who might be persuaded to attempt to breathe life into the shaky super-state. If her health does not hold up, 'Mutti' might push for her compromise, Ursula von der Leyen, long-time champion of a United States of Europe with its own army, currently attacked for a departmental spending scandal and ridiculed for her decrepit Bundeswehr with its underperforming submarines and helicopters. The Germans and the Dutch would run the European army which would rely on a British backbone. The next leader of the European Central Bank must then be French with the awful possibility that it would be Christine Lagarde, the failed political head of the IMF, 'Project Fear' leader, neither economist nor banker, but competition lawyer. Add in a likely appointment of Josep Borrell as foreign policy chief, recently fined for insider trading, supporter of the Catalonian clampdown and agitator over Gibraltar, and the coup would be complete.

However, anger was in the air and the coming confrontation between the EU and Italy was more important for the future of Brussels and their project than Brexit could ever be. That was assuming that the British government continued to make a mess of their Brexit planning and negotiation and signally failed to take the opportunity for global growth sought by the referendum majority. Britain would be punished and humiliated for risking the 'project'. This would include forced reparations that would mirror the Versailles 'agreement'.

Economist and *Telegraph* writer Liam Halligan, a fighter for plain-speaking and the truth, leapt upon the role of Italy and described when last year he reported from Rome.

Outside the Palazzo dei Conservatori where EU member states assembled in an upbeat rally to celebrate the EU's sixtieth birthday, several thousand supporters, many excited youngsters, carried centrally issued yellow and blue placards.

At the same time, across the city was another demonstration, many thousands more. This group protested bitterly against the EU amid tight security, including a large deployment of Italy's tough anti-riot police. Hemmed in by armoured vehicles, these 'populists', generally middle-aged and more careworn, marched under various Right- and Left-wing banners shouting their disaffection. They decried Brussels-based bureaucrats and corporate vested interests. They complained that the single currency had benefitted prosperous nations like Germany and the Netherlands while impoverishing the likes of Italy and Greece. They derided the EU as a 'rich man's club' with the banks always getting saved by the European Central Bank while 'there never was any money for the people'. There was no hint of celebration, just smoke bombs and barely controlled rage.

The panel quickly accepted that Brussels wanted 'more Europe' and 'even closer union', but the project had decreasing popular support. The EU had become the focus of massive popular dissent. The centrepiece of the project, the single currency, had for many millions been an unmitigated disaster. The EU had again usurped democracy and vetoed the appointment of veteran eurosceptic Paolo Savona as the country's finance minister. Italy's pro-Euro elites had over-reached disastrously. President Sergio Mattarella asserted the extraordinary precedent that no political movement could ever take power if it challenged the orthodoxy of monetary union. Financial markets took fright with short-term Italian bond prices suffering their biggest one-day fall in a quarter of a century fuelling a broader sell-off of Italian assets. The push to smother Savona and exclude him altogether and in doing so try to smother the eurosceptic rebellion, as Yanis Varoufakis and Syriza in Greece had been subdued, came from Berlin, Brussels and the EU power structure. Varoufakis also predicted how the EU would dictate the Brexit negotiations with the price of divorce agreed first, followed by a withdrawal agreement, wherein all the traps were laid, and lastly the trade agreement, where punishment would be administered.

'This is the darkest moment in the history of Italian democracy', warned

Luigi Di Maio, leader of the Italian Five Star party, as he called for mass protests. 'Italy is not a colony, we are not the slaves of the Germans and the French', raged an impotent Matteo Salvini, head of the anti-immigration League party. The Italians, temporarily whipped back into line, waited for their next election. It would be the 'People versus the Palazzo', a plebiscite against Merkel, Macron and the financial markets.

Would democracy prevail?

The EU needed to decide whether to make major concessions to Rome and its collision course manifesto or risk destabilising the entire project. If Italy's financial goals were crushed, the prospect of their exit from the Euro might be resurrected. Initial enthusiasm has been eroded by anger and bitterness over the years of sluggish economic growth and the burden of almost a million migrants and refugees. As usual, Juncker approached the conflict with his blinkers firmly set. 'I expect Italy to stand in the way of the populists otherwise populism threatens to destroy our Europe.'

Here was the iron intransigence that became so familiar to British negotiators. One result of social media and regular polling was that people were now used to expressing opinions. Populists questioned the idea that someone elected for five years could, during that time, decide what was best for you. This arrogance was out-of-date. Parliamentarians should be compelled to listen to their voters.

It was about this time, I heard later, that the EU press office in Brussels, fingers on the British broadcasting pulse, realised what was going on in a radio programme of their sponsored and funded ally, the BBC. Senior politicians called the BBC's top management and action was urged to constrain this anti-EU free-for-all and restore 'decency' and 'respect', favourite EU requirements when they face criticism they do not like. The producers decided to introduce an instant 'phone-in' element to the programme to provide the necessary balance demanded by their political leaders. Young BBC staffers, sympathetic to the 'project', were deputed to act as public callers. Sadly, for the BBC, the first caller introduced, despite the panel's protests that this change of programme direction smacked of censorship, was immediately recognised and challenged on air. She mumbled off into silence.

Some panel members then challenged the producers through the glass either to allow the programme to continue as announced or to pull the plug and face public ridicule. Frankly, I thought it all looked pretty silly already. When the right-wing and pro-Brexit press got the story, as they surely would the minute the programme ended, the furore would take many weeks to die. Some radio careers might receive long-term, even terminal, damage.

American-born Janet Daley, *Sunday Telegraph* columnist, and a life-time observer of the British scene from the inside, weighed in.

'You might have thought,' she offered, 'that the EU could at least have considered reforming itself. Given that so many of the problems which it finds infuriating – Brexit, the Italian election debacle, the rebellions in the eastern bloc over migration, the rise of antagonistic populist parties – all come down to the same complaint, that the EU Commission is seizing too much power, there seems to be clear remedy. Why on earth, then, are they not even prepared to countenance the obvious option? Couldn't the EU just give way a teensy weeny bit on its relentless centralising project?

'No apparently not! If there is a difficulty with the inexorable progress of ever-closer union, the cure must be ever-closer union.'

Janet pointed out that the consequence of this 'insane idea would be to render national elections almost pointless'. On what basis do you generally decide which party will get your vote, she asked? Surely, it is largely on the grounds of their tax and spending policies. And if those policies are taken out of the hands of national governments, what is it exactly that you are choosing?

'That's not just a democratic deficit,' she decided. 'It's the outright abolition of democratic accountability in the area that most voters believe to be central to the electoral mandate.'

Janet felt that the question had to be repeated, 'Why is the EU so purblind to the disastrous political consequences of its remorseless drive to unification, and so oblivious to the rage it produces?

'To listen to the remarks of those philosopher kings in Brussels, you would think that this was pure arrogance: that the EU attitude was a product of bureaucratic power mania and personal vanity. The Barniers and

the Junckers scarcely bother to conceal their disdain for those office-holding upstarts sitting in their absurd state capitals, surrounded by the anachronistic machinery of national mythology, who presume to challenge the authority of the great supranational body which is the only possible future.

'Perhaps surprisingly, I do not think it is the peculiarly vainglorious nature of one particular bunch of commissioners which is wilfully driving this strategy, however much their public posturing might make it seem that way. The deliberate undermining of the national states – and the power of their elected governments – is not a silly mistake, or historical accident: it was the whole point of the project.

'The EU was designed, quite consciously, to put a permanent end to the dangers of nationalism and the cult of the powerful individual state government. That these governments were democratic was thought to have little redeeming value, since left to their own parochial inclinations, electorates had shown an alarming tendency to vote for the wrong people. Germany infamously did so in the 1930s, and Italy has just done so, by EU standards, this year. No, the people were definitely not to be trusted. The European fear of the mob would finally be codified into a system that would prevent forever the kind of benighted rule which could too easily be legitimately installed by an inflamed populace.'

This was too much, unchallenged, especially for the BBC. There was a technical problem, we were cut off, and listeners were provided with the final movement of Beethoven's Ninth Symphony until it was time for the next programme, *The News*, which did not mention our discussion at all. We were ushered out of the building, worse than naughty children, no gins, no taxis, and we drifted happy, chattering away into the night.

The ordinary man, in this case me, knows very well most of the time what he ought to do, but he may not be able to defend himself against criticism. You could well take the view that, as I mostly started it, I should take the consequences, but I was completely unprepared for the co-ordinated torrent of abuse I received. It seemed that everything that was said on the programme was laid at my door. To my pleasure, the BBC also got it in the neck. The EU's bloated neck followed when it was discovered they had manipulated the closing down of a programme of the national broadcaster of a nation shortly to leave the EU altogether, or so the story went.

What had been wrong with what was said, anyway? What role did free speech play? Questions were asked everywhere. Parliament introduced an emergency debate which overran despite all attempts by Speaker John Bercow to bring order in a pro-EU context. Heads were demanded. Virtue signallers, with no workable policy at the best of times, were rampant.

My house was again besieged although, to my great surprise, there was no mention of the disappearance of my wife and daughter. My 750-page factual social history was dissected overnight, no mean feat, and pronounced a 'brilliantly original view of the German psyche' and a 'steaming pile of petty, borrowed and inaccurate rubbish not fit for the shelf'.

Sales soared.

I also agreed, next day, to do one more programme, this time on London City Radio. I suppose I had a taste, but I should have called it a day. I was joined by the editor of *The Sunday Telegraph*, Allister Heath. To my surprise, my only condition, designed to forestall the event, that the half-hour should be a conversation between the two of us with no arbiter, was agreed. After a short introduction, we were given the studio.

Allister, naturally, had the lead and asked me to expand on my BBC interview of the day before.

I suggested that, in all the current debate and anger, there was a great irony. Historic arrogant and insensitive rulers with disdain for the great mass of the population had led to murderous, destructive uprisings and left terrible memories in the collective European conscience. Perhaps the entire history of human misery could be traced in some way to smart and pushy people whose lack of humility allowed them to believe that they should force their ideas on everybody else. The EU had done more than any other institution to undermine genuine liberal democracy. Its nomenklatura had deprived the European public of any say in the biggest questions of the day, from immigration to economic policy. The introduction of an inflexible and supremely confident ruling class had turned the masses. Our leaders' contempt for real democracy was matched only by their preposterous self-regard.

William Buckley, the American conservative sage and despot, was spot on when he said that he would rather be ruled by the first 2,000 people in the Boston telephone directory than by the 2,000 people of the faculty of Harvard University. The EU elite had fallen foul of the same rebelliousness they had tried to circumvent. The EU version of benign oligarchy, built on the premise of social solidarity and shared prosperity, was not being accepted as a trade-off for national governments answerable to their own populations.

The result was the EU's worst nightmare: the populist mob was back. No sooner was it crushed in France and Greece, than it popped up in Eire, then in Italy, Denmark, the UK, in Catalonia with its elected leaders imprisoned without trial, in Sweden and in Hungary. The democratic vacuum created by the EU's ideological drive for political union and its undemocratic law-making procedure was driving the rise of the far right, not only true in Germany, but throughout great swathes of the EU. Proponents of European integration could not grasp that elected individuals, such as those in Italy who wished to run their own economy and political system, regarded being in the Euro as inhabiting a 'German prison'.

I majored on the shift to extremism, right and left. I predicted that people would take the law into their own hands. Targeted violence was not just possible, but probable. I borrowed a quote from Shanker Singham of the Institute of Economic Affairs, 'The more you discredit and despise the concerns of the people, the more they will hate you, no matter how benevolent and conscientious you think you are.' Self-respect and self-determination were more important to the populations of advanced countries than the patronising architects of the EU understood.

I even tried words from Goethe and suggested that the EU and Germany's government should take them to heart. 'The revolution from below is always due to the sins of omission of those above.'

Heath described the EU as an example of those democracies which were becoming more authoritarian with power concentrated in the executive. Even the great democracies like the UK were becoming steadily less libertarian and democratic, with political central banks that egregiously manipulated the economy, unelected judges, and a swelling surveillance state. At the same time, the rising Asian autocracies were becoming more liberal as they engaged with capitalism.

The self-proclaimed 'lowly academic', Clay Fuller from the American

Enterprise Institute, called this phenomenon 'authoritarian liberalism'. There was a convergence of all government types: from supposed democracies, like the EU and its constituent countries, and from despotic regimes, like China to a central meeting point, loosely occupied by countries like Jordan and Singapore.

Unless true democracies stood up, this reconfiguration could mean that effective global governance would be possible for the first time in history. It would offer a nightmarish choice, possibly more peaceful, but with little meaningful democracy and no national identity. As these two models met in the middle, political systems were becoming less distinct. Bruno Maçães, a former Portuguese minister, talks of the rise of a Eurasia, dominated by the EU, China and Russia, three entities that share a distrust of liberal democracy.

Allister and I said farewell and shook hands.

The immediate outpourings of an unholy collection of unlovely individuals, pressure groups, politicians of every stripe, government departments that had long since forgotten their duty of service and independence and, of course, every arm of the European Union was like a tsunami of indignation against our poisonous views being allowed air time. In this world of instant news, moralisers, trolls and other bottom feeders rose to the surface. People who never knew I existed, lacking evidence or reflection, short of accurate detail, passed harsh judgement and sought to harm me. Personal history, quotes and motivation were invented. Condemnation delivered. Punishment sought.

Righteousness was everywhere and I had no chance or opportunity of reply. That's not strictly true. I was invited to attend some public media assassinations, mostly at impossible notice so that my cowardice could be exposed. I was told that Facebook and Twitter frothed with their highest-ever non-celebrity usage, all of which of course I failed to see and only heard about second-hand. Parliament, newspapers, magazines, trade union meetings, in the UK, in the USA, in Europe and, particularly in Germany, picked over every aspect of what had been said. I read that death threats, some from right-wing German political groups, were normal occurrences. I was offered doctorates in several overseas universities. Had there been any statues or portraits of me in the UK, they would have undoubtedly been torn down by enraged students.

In the midst of it all, I had one great stroke of luck, irritating when first discovered, but perhaps life-saving later. I had met with the publishers of *Sound of Hunger* only once, and then only with one director and she had just left the business. Most of my detailed correspondence had been by email and only occasionally by telephone. When it came to publication, I was asked for a short personal history and I was free with the truth. I did send in a reasonable photograph, but in the publisher's rush during ever-slipping release dates, they picked up the wrong picture and it was this that was used in the book and in all of the press articles. I don't know who he was and I apologise and thank him for the mistake. None of my fellow radio commentators, that I know of, ever sought fit to comment.

Two nights later, I walked home early from the pub and noticed the light on in my study; a light I knew I had left switched off. I let myself in quietly and picked up a black wood *iwisa* – a Zulu souvenir – and walked into the room. A man in his thirties, dark hair, short, clean-shaven, was pushing my laptop into a black plastic bag, which was already, it seemed, quite full. He wasn't fazed to see me, finished his packing and told me to get out of his way.

'You've made a mess of my study,' I accused him. 'And I know you from around the town.'

'So, fucking what, you old git?'

I moved towards the house phone.

'You touch that and I'll break your arms. You call the police and I'll come back later with some mates and do you proper.'

'I think I will call the police. This is the eighth time I've had a break-in in the last months. I am fed up with it and that means I'm fed up with you, moron, and the fact that you live off the backs of people who don't steal for a living. And, my dim friend, the people I know will chase you to the end of the world and then eat your children.'

'Stupid idiot,' he lectured. 'I'm not frightened of you. I've got important friends. You weren't chosen by accident, you know. Anyway, the police won't come. And if they do call by, they won't bother. They never bother around here and they'll be kept in their place. I've been to court and they just let you off, anyway. So you can't do nuffin', fuck face.'

'Someone, sometime, has to stop a low-life like you. If the police won't do their job, then I guess, sooner or later, someone like me has to step up.'

'You touch me, I'll say you started it and it'll be you what the police arrest.

You'll end up in the nick. I'll get off because they'll feel sorry for me.'

'Sadly for you I think you're right.' And I hit him on the head with the *knopkierie*. There was a satisfying crunch. I picked him up and carried him into the garden then got some plastic ties and bound his hands behind his back. In a pocket, I found his car keys. The vehicle was parked a few yards down the lane. I took it into my driveway, bundled him in, collected some things, and drove to the outskirts of a wooded area about a mile away. I cut his clothes off and tied him tightly to an oak tree, naked in plain sight of the road. He started to groan as I placed a large card around his neck on which I wrote, 'THIEF'. In the boot of his car I found five swag bags which I arranged at his feet, hopefully for eventual collection by the owners.

I placed a noose around his neck, waved the free end of the rope in his face. At this point he broke down and began sobbing. I dropped the rope at his feet and put my *iwisa* and his clothes inside the car and set it alight. Leaning close to his ear, I told him that if I ever heard from him again he would die slowly and in great pain. Mumbled obscenities followed me as I walked home to clear up the mess.

Screaming sirens woke me from a deep sleep the next morning. Around lunchtime, the police called on door-to-door enquiries.

'Had I had a break-in?'

'Yes, seven, all reported, but you are the first police I have seen that have asked me about them.'

'Sir, where were you last night?'

'At the pub, couple of pints, walked home, had a sandwich, went to bed, got woken by sirens, been working on my computer in my study ever since. I live alone. Why do you want to know?'

'This is a murder enquiry, sir. A man has been found hanged from a tree in a wood down the road.'

The conversation rambled on, notes were taken and the officers left. I wondered if there would be any reason for them to come back. Probably, I thought, when they checked my record.

Someone later wrote that my two radio programmes signalled the real beginning of the fight back of the usually acquiescent majority against the destruction of freedom of speech in the UK.

Never before has it been so easy to communicate, to express one's views, to write, publish, talk or broadcast. Yet instead of ushering in a golden age for free speech and rational inquiry, these very technologies that were meant to liberate us were being used to stifle expression and stamp out dissent, particularly mine. You can't say or think that; you must say or think this. In social media, in universities, in the BBC, and increasingly in most institutions across the land, a hideous battle was raging and liberty was losing. The range of views that can be expressed without fear of reprisal had narrowed dramatically. There was no longer any sense of proportionality, just all-or-nothing, snap assessment. Whoever holds a different opinion on anything is dismissed as bonkers, laughed at out loud, declared stupid and chased out of the global village. Like in the witch-hunts of yore, the burden of proof is reversed: you must prove that you are not guilty of offending others' feelings. The strategy for the tens of thousands of activists working in digital packs is to bully, shame and destroy anybody who doesn't agree with them, who dares to express a different opinion or who fails to signal their virtue appropriately. Attacks against a person rather than their arguments was once seen as bad form, today they are rationalised using fake news and bogus theories. Reality no longer matters. If someone believes that someone said or meant something, then it must be true. A vague feeling is enough.

There used to have rules, standards, but these seldom now apply. This ability to publish freely had appealed to those with a lack of maturity. The people now writing on internet social platforms seldom have the training, the self-restraint, or often the intellect, to use their freedom wisely and for the public good. Irony is well and truly dead. Humour is not understood, often not deliberately, but the listener lacks the intelligence or the ear. Mainstream Britain was quietly withdrawing, because they didn't know how to use social media to fight; it is not their natural home. Dissension is stoked by the media and led by the BBC and the tabloids; minority views are given unnecessary and wrong-headed prominence.

Real freedom of expression implies some measure of openness, of curiosity, the ability to listen, at least occasionally, to others and to learn to live with the difference. It is an approach, an attitude, not merely a set of laws. It is also not anarchy.

At the end of the week, I was sitting at home in a chair by the window soaking the morning sun, mulling over my options and my burglar. I had stopped answering the phone. After the first few dozen calls, the threats about my broadcasts lacked originality or interest. Opinion in the village was divided about the hanging. I wondered who had had the guts to do it. Everything taken together, I was all but decided.

A long Mercedes drew up and four large men got out, looking like a hit squad. I was a little frightened. One of them demanded in a French-accented voice that I open my front door as they had 'something personal to give me'. I declined and said I was armed. They laughed.

'Well you can't say that you haven't received this. Read it or you will know the consequences.'

They dropped an embossed letter through the box, taking several pictures as they did so, presumably to prove delivery. It was addressed to me and came from the European Court of Justice, the political institution constructed to enforce EU law over the rights of countries and individuals. I was to present myself in four days' time to a specially appointed judicial committee in Brussels to answer charges of subversion and of activities designed to undermine the European Union. I was not to disclose the contents of the letter to anyone, nor to discuss it in anyway. I would meet my approved legal adviser just before the investigation began. Accommodation would be provided. It was signed by [*two names redacted by the publisher on legal advice*].

The message was clear. Criticism of monetary union and the Germans was *verboten*. I had joined the ranks of the unstable and had not only thought, but also said, the unacceptable. Perhaps as a legal test case, I was to be punished.

It was time to go.

Everything that smacked of Chris Heal and his life was burned, including the EU's letter. I packed a small suitcase, binned my mobile phone, activated my money helpers, collected my passports and money and went north into the night.

9. FREEDOM TO TRAVEL

And indeed there will be time
To wonder, 'Do I dare?' and, 'Do I dare?'
Time to turn back and descend the stair,
With a bald spot in the middle of my hair ...[37]

The noisy bar skirted one side of the yacht marina in Hull. It was a sunny and cheerful evening. I took a seat outside the refurbished steak and burger *Green Bricks* pub, the old *Humber Port*. Small boat owners were pottering, some leisurely maintenance, but more holiday listlessness. I looked for a tired seaworthy boat in need of marine paint. There were just a few among the new money and polished steel. If I had no luck here, I planned to visit another old town pub, the *Dairycoates Inn* on a street corner in the midst of industrial units by the Alfred and William Wright docks. This was the landing point for the much-reduced Hull fishing fleet.

I saw a promising candidate, a timber-built North Sea trawler yacht. A stocky man in his fifties, short white beard and hair, an untipped cigarette stuck to his bottom lip, stood on the deck. He sawed at a length of cheap pine. Two wood-horses sat on a grey blanket to stop his deck varnish being scratched. I walked slowly towards the mooring pontoons while I waited for someone to press the buttons on the keypad security. It's easy for older people to tailgate, but the trick here was simply to ask for the name of a boat. A yachtie in captain's blue cap and brilliant sneakers waved vaguely in the direction I was to go and let me follow him through.

'Labour of love,' I asked the perspiring man as he wrestled with his tenon.
'You gotta believe it.'
'What gets me is how these boats with a history swallow the money.'
'Ditto.'
'Would you like me to give you a hand? Hold one of the trestles still?'
He sawed. We chatted. Then I made him a proposition.
'Do you do any chartering?'

'Never have. I would if I could, but who'd want to go out on an untidy bucket like this?'

'I might, but it would be a one-off trip.'

He looked askance. 'Don't do drugs. Don't do crime,' he warned.

'Nothing really illegal,' I said. 'Scout's honour. Might be 250 miles one-way. I'm the passenger. No cargo apart from my suitcase with my clothes. I'll need a dinghy to lift me ashore because it's a long, gentle beach – Zandvoort near Amsterdam. Prefer no record of my leaving the country.'

I had decided on a clandestine start. I could have taken the ferry, but I didn't want a precious passport compromised if anyone started checking. I had toyed with arranging a lift somewhere less well monitored than Hull. A little research showed that there were sixty-two normally unmanned ports on the east coast with almost half unvisited by Border Force Officers. During 2015, just over 400 clandestine immigrants had been caught and this was touted as a triumph of detection. People leaving these shores were not so important. Small boats and trawlers travelled all the time for continental destinations. The best place to hide a pin is in a needle case.

As I went off grid without warning, I hoped that no one would be looking for me with any great intent. If they were, then visual recognition was the first threat. Automated devices were everywhere in the UK. Cameras were installed with impunity by state security, the police, private security companies, commercial businesses, and individuals, just about anyone who had a mind. They lurked or hung proud in most town streets or half-hidden at sensitive points like ports and air terminals. Even Hull marina had eleven cameras that I could see.

These systems were now so smart that people's faces could be matched in real time against watch-lists. Captured images could also be biometrically scanned and stored. It was a primitive version of these systems that was used to identify my car number plate at the M25 service station. The most-advanced are being trialled by the police in Cardiff without request, or any lawful basis or guidelines, and were used at the O2 for the BRIT awards.

Public or parliamentary debate has been sidestepped. To my mind, these cameras are dystopian and authoritarian tools that turn us into walking ID cards. So far, despite the spy movies, it is still dangerously inaccurate in the UK with high misidentification rates. On the basis of an incorrect match, the police have the power to stop you in the street and it is up to you to prove that you are not the person that the computer claims. In five minutes at last year's Notting Hill Carnival, two innocent women walking down the street were identified as men on the watch-list. Images of those wrongly picked out are still kept on file. On Remembrance Sunday in 2017, the Metropolitan Police used facial recognition to find 'fixated' individuals, people not suspected of any crime, but who typically suffer from mental health issues and have fallen through the care net. Function creep is already plain to see and the technology is barely out of the box.

China is the leader in recognition software with a network of over 170 million CCTV cameras. Specially trained street police are issued with dark glasses linked to their system and which act in the same way as a camera. A man wanted for 'economic crimes' was identified by cameras when buying a ticket just before a pop concert in Nanchang city. By the time he reached his seat, the police were waiting for him. In Hangzhou, the state school's pupils are tracked so that teachers can be told if they are late for lessons while, in the café, menu choices leave a digital dietary footprint to see which child is eating too much fatty food and, in the classroom, facial expressions are assessed for 'engagement' and so identify underperformers.

Facebook is also using the technology to scan the billions of private photographs that it stores, ostensibly so that people can be alerted to photographs in which they appear and may not know about. In reality, it is designed to get more users to spend longer on the website, the longer the visit the more that can be deduced to produce targeted advertising.

There was a moment's pause on the marina. 'How much?'

'Well, if it's 250 miles, 500 round trip, we'd average about fifteen knots. Take me up to a day to get there. Probably need to stop for diesel on the other side. Need to take my son along for crew. Some lies to tell. There's food. Any alcohol you want.' He paused, took a deep breath, 'Seven hundred.'

'I'll make it the round thousand to include a bottle of whisky, some steaks and the ride ashore. I want to get in around seven in the morning before too many tourists are up.'

He stood up straight for the first time. 'When do you want to go?'

'Early evening tomorrow? I've got a few things to do first. Here's a couple of hundred to get things moving.'

He did some quick calculations on his piece of half-sawn wood. 'Be here at three to be on the safe side. We'll leave as soon as you're stowed.'

The moon was strong over a flat calm. The trip was uneventful although crossing the shipping lanes needed close attention. We were warned off by radio and klaxon a dozen times. The son in his thirties was quiet, obedient and hard-working. I browsed *haiku* written by the Japanese master Matsuo Bashō, one of the world's most famous nomads, in his travel sketches. I was idly looking for a propitious seventeenth-century thought to set me on my way. What surprised me was that even though Bashō wrote almost daily on his months-long meanderings well off the known path, his subjects were more the shrines he visited, the people he met, the plants and countryside he saw, and seldom his thoughts on his rootlessness. I found only one:

> *From this day forth*
> *I shall be called a wanderer,*
> *Leaving on a journey*
> *Thus among the early showers.*
> *You will again sleep night after night*
> *Nestled among the flowers of sasanqua.*[38]

We were lucky with the tide and switched off our radio as we got close inshore just after seven in the morning. This was a small gesture of invisibility: the UK relies on old-fashioned mobile-phone technology to monitor fishing boats instead of the leading Automatic Identification System that is British-manufactured and sold globally.

The sun was already breaking through. It was going to be lotion time for the beach lobsters. The skipper did the rowing. I took off my shoes and trousers and placed them with the suitcase in a large plastic bag and tied it tight with plenty of air still in so that it would float. I had about twenty yards left to wade. We shook hands.

'Best of luck with whatever it is you're doing. I guess this trip didn't happen?'

'Probably best,' I said. 'But, then, you don't know who I am or what I look like.'

I gave him the rest of his money, neatly bundled. He smiled and, after a quick goodbye, I plodded my way towing my bag to the military ranks of empty sun loungers. I had cast away my earthly attachments, one by one, in the preceding months. As I trudged ashore, I set adrift my identity, a precursor perhaps to finding myself.

I chose a seat and was half-dressed when an Alsatian dog appeared. I had been in this situation many years before amidst the deserted concrete of a Breton coastal resort in winter. The dog had backed me into a concrete pillar and then leapt at me time and again with its teeth bared and saliva dripping. I thought rabies and was being worn down when I decided to take action. Here it was again. There was no owner in sight. I met the animal full gaze and pointed and it dropped at my feet. Even as I moved my hand closer, it raised its head and tried to bite. It was dangerous and sick. I put my shoe on its jaw, pushed my forefinger behind its trachea and snapped it. It died within seconds.

Distressed, I went in search of a coffee and croissant. No early risers seemed to notice my appearance on the beach. No one I could see had whipped out a phone to take a picture. Had anyone noticed the dog attack? If they had, what did they really see? Did they care? Did they ask questions or look around for someone in authority? In the distance, I heard a woman calling, a whistle, and then a stifled scream. Within half an hour, the beach was thronged with pleasure seekers and sandy feet that kept a respectful gap around the animal's body.

What purpose does the truth serve when to survive we all need to deceive, tell white lies, and wear a mask. Actions mean nothing without context; words are crude metaphors that grope towards an interpretation of the truth, towards a preferred mask. Our words, our actions, our masks take us away from the truth, not towards it. Truth is an unknowable place where only interpretations live. We are all happier when we are liberated from the truth.

An Amsterdam beach bus left every fifteen minutes and I was in the city centre by nine o'clock. I decided that I would start by being Moroccan and booked into the art deco American Hotel for two weeks.

I did not think of myself as a tourist; I was a traveller. The difference is one of time. The tourist hurries back home at the end of a few weeks or months; the traveller, belonging no more to one place than to the next, moves slowly, perhaps over years, from one part of the earth to another. I enjoyed the vibrant anonymity; a great city is like a great solitude, especially if you like being alone. Amsterdam is as eclectic as London, but more easy-going with its pedestrian streets, almost a million bicycles ridden by megalomaniacs, over half the population under twenty-five, over a thousand restaurants of every nationality, and a trademark relaxed attitude to soft drugs and sex. It is also home to the Rijksmuseum and Reubens and the breath-taking mother collection of Van Gogh's works.

That first evening, I wanted to visit one of the city's undervalued institutions, a juniper bar. My particular favourite among several is the *In de Olofspoort*, which sells home-distilled jenever, best savoured with a beer chaser. Many of the juniper bars have devotee owners and *Olofspoort*'s Raymond Bouquet, or one of his superior bartenders, will give as good a conversation as you can get when trade is light.

I had nomads on my mind, in particular the mare-milking Scythians. These ancient widespread shifting families inform so much of modern European disquiet. They lived above the Black Sea, the Scythian Sea according to Ovid, at times ruling from the Danube to the Don and as far north as Kiev. They moved over their pastureland, richer in those days before the cold winds and rain, over-grazing and over-manuring led to the weakening of the soil. The Scythians travelled with hundreds of wagons, sometimes several thousand, and well-furnished wicker and felt yurts compared by European travellers to 'cities on wheels'. The speed of their ox-drawn convoys synchronised with the grazing speed of the herds, perhaps five kilometres a day. There was little concept of a specific destination, rather a need for contented animals and water and there were plenty of rivers. There was no 'home', no idea of 'state' or 'towns' or static cultural development other than in their burial sites. Was this the way of life I had chosen?

There remains a European conceit that crop-sowing peasants, managed by warrior landholders, represented a seismic improvement from nomadism. Pastoral nomads can and do raise crops. In the fifteenth century, the friar and merchant Giosofat Barbaro wrote that, each March, wheat was planted in patches of fertile ground. When the wheat was ripe, the *Golden Horde* would pass by and reap it from the open steppe on its seasonal journey northwards to the summer grazing. If Scythian nomads were to settle it was not a voluntary change to a more civilised life, but a sign of poverty.

First turn to the sun's rising and walk on
Over the fields no plough had broken: then
You will come to the nomadic Scythians
Who live in wicker houses built above
Their well-wheeled waggons; they are an armed people
Armed with the bow that strikes from far away:
Do not draw near them.[39]

My bartender leant back against his bottled shelves and I, enthusiastic historian, shared the theory and the jenever. Today's European nightmare is a terror of peoples who move, inherited from the great migrations during and after the decline of the Roman Empire and renewed by the Hun, Mongol and Turkish raids into the West.[40] The horror was given an extra dimension by nineteenth-century intellectuals who saw moving people as a physical menace emerging from the trackless East. They incarnated a cosmic disorder in which 'the past rose out of its tomb and swarmed forward on horseback to annihilate the present'. A phase of drought somewhere on the central Asian steppe would dislodge a tribe from its grazing grounds and cause a 'house of cards' butterfly effect with ripples from Europe to China.[41]

Never underestimate your audience, especially in a Dutch bar-room. 'You must come to Amsterdam for Scythians,' offered the bartender. 'After the European revolutions of 1989, they all came here. Had to stop because of the sea and because the British wouldn't let them in. There is a fear of all travelling people, of Merkel's millions, the asylum seekers and economic migrants and terrorists. If Russia collapses, they'll all be hungry and go to Germany and then they'll end up in Amsterdam.'

'Nothing's changed,' I said. 'A thousand years ago their travels were seen as a threat to civilisation, to European culture. A hundred years ago, because of the politics of the day, the Scythians became the butt of the most absurd prejudice. In our lifetime, the Iron Curtain was described as a continuation of the former western boundary of the Scythians' lands.'

'Well, I travelled in the steppes many years ago', said the barman. 'Much of it is truly desolate. It has a flat featureless horizon that sends you drowsy. You can wake suddenly on your horse and gaze around and wonder if you moved at all. I had the same feeling when I travelled by train across Canada.

There is no place where your memory can orientate itself. As a result of the steppes, I don't count sheep when I can't sleep, I count oxen or, on a bad night, blades of wild grass.

'One other thing I remember being told: for a thousand kilometres the land there slopes slowly to the west. The further east one goes the higher, drier and colder the conditions. If you're living on the eastern steppe then the grazing to the west really is greener. Given the choice between living in Hungary or in Outer Mongolia I know which one I'd pick.'

Trade was still slight in the *Olofspoort*. I suggested another round of jenever and beer on me. A bearded man in his fifties, sharp eyes tilted with gin, and his hair unkempt, stepped closer. 'I was listening to you both,' he said, 'and there's one thing about these Scythian nomads that stuck in my mind. It ties in with the terrorists, or the freedom fighters, whichever way your politics lie.

'It's in Herodotus after he visited the Scythians and claimed that they were "wiser than any nation upon the face of the earth" because they made it impossible for any enemy who invaded them to escape destruction. They stayed out of reach unless they decided to fight using their bows on horseback.[42] Because they had no cities or buildings and they carried their felt tents and everything with them, they just moved on, deeper and deeper, and suckered invaders in until their supply lines were too long. Then they hit them. It was about mobility and sudden disappearance and reappearance, of intelligence rather than brutal and unstoppable advance. It is the classic case of the hunted nomad who becomes the hunter.'

'I remember this,' I butted in. 'It was the Persians, yes, the Persians. King Darius sent a huge army, to subjugate them. The Scythians lured the Persians deep into their territory; then they destroyed wells, burned food and trampled their own pastureland. They wore them down and all but destroyed Darius's army.'

The unkempt one agreed. I realised, too late, that he knew much more than me, but had granted me the space. Before buying his round, he added, 'As might be expected, there is no Persian account of this ignominious defeat.' He drank deeply. 'Any cheese?' he queried and received a slow shake of the bartender's head.

'We all had to study Napoleon,' he continued, 'and he was horrified when the Russians set fire to Moscow, their own capital city, in order to force a French retreat. The fire threatened the Kremlin Palace and the great man cried out, 'Quel effroyable spectacle! Ce sont eux-mêmes! Tant de Palais! Quelle résolution extraordinaire! Quels hommes! Ce sont des Scythes!'[43]

At this, the bartender started to attention and served a young American couple looking shyly for the excitement of Amsterdam's red light district. 'It's all the same today,' he told them as he discussed the best streets to visit and warned them of pickpockets. 'Back then,' he said, 'it was Darius's foot soldiers who were outmanoeuvred by the Scythians. Yesterday, your New York Police Department were baffled by the homeless dossers around Tompkins Square. Today, it's the turn of the customs officers and frontier guards of our glorious, democratic European Union that have been outwitted and hunted by a million illegal, inaccessible, fast-moving, immigrants. Scythians all!'

'Aristotle called them the aporoi, the poor, today's nomads,' explained the unkempt one as the Americans, having drunk most of their jenever much too quickly, moved to the door. 'Aristotle contrasted the oligarchy of the EU with real democracy, the kind of government where men who are poor and do not possess much property are in control of the state.'

The bartender waved goodbye to his brief clients and pointed towards the red lights and lubricated skins. 'They could end up the masters,' he mused, 'by sheer weight of numbers.'

I felt that Aristotle writing about the European Union might be a step too far.

The unkempt one picked up his theme. 'Desert people are closer to being good because they are closer to the natural state. They are more removed from all the evil habits that infect the hearts of settlers.'

This was an argument I recognised from Ibn Khaldûn in the Muqaddimah, 'Universal History', in the fourteenth century. Khaldûn was thinking of the Bedouin. His view was reinforced when he witnessed the piles of skulls and devastated cities following the ravages of Tamerlane who had rejected his nomadic roots. Much later, Bruce Chatwin seized on this explanation. Because the rigours of the desert preceded the softness of the cities, the desert was a reservoir of civilisation. Compared to settlers, desert peoples were 'more abstemious, freer, braver, healthier, less bloated, less liable to submit to rotten laws, and altogether easier to cure'. As a general rule, migratory species were less aggressive than sedentary ones.

The bartender leaned forward to make a contribution. 'I read some verses of the Midrash once,' he offered. 'You can find the same attitude in the story of Cain and Abel. Abel was the nomad, his name means 'breath' or 'vapour'; Cain was the man of property as his name suggests. Cain got all the land; Abel all living creatures. And then Cain accused Abel of trespass as he was jealous of his freedom, and killed him. Cain was banished to wander forever in the desert, in the Land of Nod, his brother's home.

I suggested one last cup to celebrate the great connection between our small company and our Scythian ancestors, or invaders, Nod and whatever. 'I have read a little classical Greek,' I stated proudly, as the last round was poured. 'In their eyes, the Scythians were northern barbarians who no one could understand. The Scythians had bizarre and bloodthirsty customs. One of these was their horrifying habit of drinking wine neat which gave rise to the Greek saying "drinking the Scythian way", which meant getting blind drunk. I remember part of a verse from my dear friend Anacreon, and repeat it roughly as a toast to our evening:

> *Fill me, boy, as deep a draught*
> *As e'er was fill'd, as e'er was quaffed;*
> *But let the water amply flow,*
> *To cool the grape's intemperate glow ...*
> *No, banish from our board to-night*
> *The revelries of rude delight;*
> *To Scythians leave these wild excesses,*
> *Ours be the joy that soothes and blesses!*[44]

The unkempt one had the final word as was his academic right and it was a feat of memory at that hour. 'I give you Osip Mandelstam,' he declared, 'and a tribute to taking sad leave and to hard-working oxen everywhere.'

> *I've learned the science of parting*
> *In the laments of the night, her hair let down.*
> *Oxen graze, and the waiting's drawn out.*

The town's last hour of vigil, and I
Revere the ritual of the night when
The cock crowed and exhausted eyes
Raised their load of wandering sorrow,
Gazed into the distance, and a woman's weep
And muse's song combined.
Who knows, at the mention of 'farewell',
What separation awaits us,
What the cock's crow augurs
When flames grow in the acropolis,
And on the dawn of some new life,
While an ox chews lazily in his shed,
Why the cock, herald of new life,
Beats his wings on the town's walls.[45]

Somehow, I found the American Hotel, which let me in even though I was declaiming with some intensity. I slept till midday. It was a good start, but to what: freedom or the start of any holiday?

I had a simple plan for my time in Amsterdam: Van Gogh and Reubens, Reubens and Van Gogh, but there was an immediate problem with access at the Van Gogh Museum. The new building has blossomed to become the city's second most popular attraction. However, their attempt to control queues several-hours long has created an unintended problem. Limiting ticket sales to the internet disadvantages the many who do not have a computer. Overseas visitors can be heard complaining loudly as they realise their cherished day has been ruined because they did not appreciate the booking system. A few unbought tickets can be picked up from machines outside, but again there are long queues, and the allotted time will most probably be late in the afternoon. It was an inconvenience for me, too, especially as I had to find a computer. I worried about the economically and technologically disadvantaged, the poor, the less intellectual, and the old people. I found an internet café with online printers and bought and printed tickets for five of the next ten days using one of my untraceable email addresses and a credit card.

What was forbidden to me was any mobile phone for which an account was needed. It was strictly a case of buy a cheap 'burner' and throw, country by country. I could never risk any contact that might lead to an identity or a place, for instance, through buying tickets for a gallery over the phone using a contact number, name or address which might later be traced. My own cell phone had been dropped in the rubbish in the UK after its SIM card had been destroyed. As no incoming calls were likely unless I gave my temporary number, my current 'Dutch' pay-as-you-go phone was always switched off. If a phone is switched on its location can be traced by a myriad of companies and organisations, not least security services. Many of them use applications, typically over 500 for a well-used iPhone, that log every individual's move, purchase and internet connection and plot them. Photographs are automatically digitally stamped with hidden time and location information. This is called geo-tagging.

Added to facial recognition scans, photographs can offer up your movement history, where you were, at what time and who with. Criminals can check on-line photographs to determine the location of a property where valuable items are visible. Android devices are a little safer. The phone is also used by the big data brokers – Acxiom, Experian, Quantium, Corelogic, ID Analytics – to gather as many as 3,000 pieces of information on any user. At one level, this information is used for targeting adverts, but it is also used to set personal credit scores and includes assessments of race, marital status and religion. If the information flatters, credit cards and mortgages will be cheaper and employment background checks are more easily passed. Many on the inside admit that at least fifty per cent of data held may be inaccurate or discriminatory. The information is so extensive that the British Office of National Statistics is testing with Vodaphone whether to stop the traditional ten-year census by 2023 and instead use phone data collected covertly from individuals which is tracked to where they live and work.

The next morning, I arrived well before the specified entry time. I had a nearby pilgrimage in mind. The Museumplein in Amsterdam is a quiet park in the centre of the city, crisscrossed by the inevitable cycle tracks, and which houses on its edges many of the major museums. In one corner, away from any bustle, is a statue, a monument to the Romani victims of the holocaust, the *Baro Porrajmos*, the great devouring, from 1941 to 1945.

Porrajmos is an ugly word in the Romani language; it can also mean 'rape' as well as 'gaping' as in shock or horror. I made a quick search in the early morning sun, dossers still slept on their blankets, their shoes neatly arranged close by, jackdaws bobbing and pecking, the sky blue and criss-crossed by vapour trails.

The bronze stands on a plinth, three and a half metres high, and shows a man, woman and two children fleeing a blaze. In my respectful opinion, it is a good, but not great, piece of art, but its symbolism pre-empts all discussions of merit. The inscription on the base is taken from a gypsy prayer for the dead:

Putrav lesko drom angle leste te after burma mai but palpale mura brigasa.[46]

The sculptor was Heleen Levano who gave her work to a foundation that provided early advocacy for the Roma people and which, in turn, donated it to the city to be unveiled in 1978 by Dutch Gypsy King, Koko Petalo. It was the first monument in the world for Gypsies.[47] Levano said that the king told her that fire was the Roma symbol for danger. 'So I pictured the fire in the building that the family went through. A lot of people do not seem to know or want to know that so many gypsies were killed. This is my way to draw attention to a forgotten group.'

Each year, a ceremony is held at the monument to remember the night of 31 July in 1944 when 5,000 Roma and Sinti, a Roma sub-group with strong German connections, were gassed in Auschwitz.

The Sinti and Roma are often forgotten in discussions of Holocaust victims as is the Nazi plan for a gypsy-free Europe. Had they been successful, many famous names in the entertainment industry would not have been with us: Michael Caine, Charlie Chaplin, David Essex, Rita Hayworth, Bob Hoskins, Django Reinhardt – even Bill Clinton.

Persecution of the Roma has a long history. In the sixteenth century, the English king Edward VI decreed that Romani should be branded with a 'V' on their breast and then enslaved for two years. If they escaped they were to be branded with an 'S' and made slaves for life. The Spanish passed a similar law. Romani slaves were sold by weight, at the rate of one gold piece per pound. Punishments included flogging; the *falague*, stringing up and shredding the soles of the feet with a whip made of bull sinews; cutting off the lips; burning with lye; being thrown naked into the snow; hanging over smoking gores and wearing a three-cornered spiked iron collar called a *cangue*. By the nineteenth century, scholars in Germany and elsewhere in Europe were writing about Romani as inferior beings and 'the excrement of humanity'; in 1845 in Bucharest, Romani slave sales were openly advertised. Charles Darwin, writing in 1871, singled out Romani as being less culturally advanced than 'territorially settled people'. Chancellor Otto von Bismarck said that Romani were to be dealt with especially severely if apprehended. The Nazis applied the same motives and methods as they did to the extermination of the Jews.

Not far from the Amsterdam statue, in the same park, is another memorial this time to female holocaust victims at Ravensbrück, a place on a small lake near the village of Fürstenberg, close to Berlin. Here, many Roma women endured forced labour, sterilisation and extermination. The monument is a dramatic construction set on a large plinth. A tall stainless steel column, a central tube reminiscent of a chimney, emits endless moaning in the wind, and at night, light that intensifies and extinguishes. The sound and light symbolise the prisoners who were tortured and murdered and is reflected from behind by eleven vertical steel panels.

Chatwin wrote:

Psychiatrists, politicians, tyrants are forever assuring us that the wandering life is an aberrant form of behaviour; a neurosis; a form of unfulfilled sexual longing; a sickness which, in the interests of civilisation, must be supressed. Nazi propagandists claimed that Gypsies and Jews – people with wandering in their genes – could find no place in a stable Reich.[48]

My first visit to the Van Gogh Museum was over twenty years ago and, despite all of the improvements that have taken place with the new building, it was then a more intimate and uplifting experience. In managing the crowds, much of the personal relationship with the pictures has gone. Finding a space to stand in front of what are often small-sized works and to enjoy or study them for more than a minute without being jostled, stood on or interrupted, is nigh impossible. I suspect much of the startling appreciation for newcomers that was a hallmark of yesterday has gone.

The museum is now a considerable industry with a concern for the 'personal experience package' that can outweigh the art. It is one thing to walk around as a curator when the doors are closed and the majesty and curiosity of the exhibits can be enjoyed; it is a much different affair to be wedged into queues for lifts, toilets and the multitude of shops selling sad dross at inflated prices. How many visitors, I wondered, could afford, or want, the personalised prints of Vincent Van Gogh's works on offer for around 25,000 euro?

Of course, there were reacquaintances to be made, old friends to be sought out, but for this visit which way round would best suit: probably at the beginning following the road to the never-fulfilled horizon, or perhaps at the end, progressing backwards into dark innocence? This time I had a vested interest. I was a novice nomad, a man with no tenure or destination, a drifter amid a world of pleasure. I had no time constraint other than that applied by the booking system, the pressing crowds and the museum's clock.

Today's thought was how important the horizons had become. They were enticing, far away and magical compared with what little was portrayed in front of the easel. At Van Gogh's feet there was often emptiness, little of importance, a drabness, while the eye always led through increasing detail, perhaps by an inviting track or road, to a place which was more desirable and perhaps unreachable. Van Gogh seemed dissatisfied with grass-waving steppes and was concerned to reach the fresh pastures of the western slopes.

This vision becomes less evident in his last year at the asylum at Saint-Rémy, which is defined by the sharp and close outlines of the hard-rimmed trees. That last year, despite no great ambitions, was prolific: the contrast of the blacks and reds of his foliage and crows and the sharp yellows of cornfields, a solitary figure working or walking nearby.

In 1890, in a field near Auvers-sur-Oise, a 'broken pitcher' that could never be mended, Van Gogh shot himself in the chest without hitting any major organs. Within two days, he died from infection, his brother Theo at his side. Theo died six months later in a psychiatric hospital in Utrecht, was exhumed in 1914, and reburied next to Vincent in Auvers. Where did

Vincent, just released from a mental institution, get the revolver? It was likely a 7mm Lefaucheux found badly corroded in the field seventy years later. Van Gogh was just thirty-seven and an utter failure in everything that seemed important to his contemporaries: unable to start a family, earn his own living, or maintain friendships. Within a few years, this unloved man was hailed a genius.

Driven out of the Van Gogh each day by late morning stress, I walked across the park to spend the afternoons in the Rijksmuseum, a lovely, airy building redesigned over ten years at a cost of €375 million by Cruz y Ortiz, a Spanish architectural practice. The *Financial Times* described the restored building as 'sophisticated, minimal and understated' as the original by Pierre Cuypers in the nineteenth century was 'grand, eclectic and overblown'. To the delight of the city's cyclists, the building maintains its central ceremonial gateway that allows the public to pedal right through it. Even after a dozen visits, here is a building and a collection to which I could go back many times.

When the nomadic itch returned, I had choices. It was time to leave the canals with their traffic lights and swing bridges, the thousand restaurants. Should I take one of the riverboats and travel the Rhine as far as the Black Sea and the land of the Scythians, stopping wherever I fancied through central Europe? It was tempting, but I suspected that I would not come back this way and so I should pay my last respects to Brussels and to Paris. I crossed the square to Amsterdam's great central station, another Cuypers' creation with its great barrel-vaulted, tiled ceiling, and took the tourist express through the flat and dreary landscape of cows and factories, Utrecht, Breda, Antwerp, to the expensive citadel of the European Union.

Early one evening soon after I arrived, the city exploded with police and ambulance sirens so that I wondered if the world had ended. The noise formed a roof over the centre of Brussels and, reaching down, filled every back-street crevice. I stepped into a café to catch the news. There was only one subject: Jean-Claude Juncker, president and zealot of the European Commission, and his right-hand man, Martyn 'the Monster' Selmayr, the Commission's secretary general, had both been shot dead with single bullets to the head. A professional assassin was sought.

Appropriately, the killings took place among the crowded tables outside a premier champagne bar, *L'aube sur Aÿ* in the *Galeries Saint-Hubert*, near to the *Grand Place*, not five minutes' walk from where I stood. Juncker's bodyguards kept a not-too-close watch, in touch by mobile phone, from behind the window of a nearby coffee shop. The shooter, his face shaded by a baseball cap beloved of teenagers, dressed in jeans and black T-shirt, had appeared, fired his two shots at point-blank range and walked away. No doubt, near-by cameras would struggle to capture the perpetrator's face and digitise it. The well-lit arcade was noisy with live music provided by two musicians playing clarinet and table piano. Some couples had been dancing. On the politicians' table by a blood-spattered bucket of Bollinger lay a small computer-printed poster with the single Greek word, ελευθερία, freedom.

I felt elated. At least the Greek sign would initially divert attention from rabid Brexiteers. Juncker's reputation as a heavy drinker, a gin and champagne aficionado, was well recorded and officially dismissed as 'sciatica' resulting from a car accident. Anyone daring to question this explanation was guilty of 'indecency', according to Viviane Reding, an MEP and former Luxembourg commissioner and political patron of Selmayr. Did I mention that Juncker was a Luxembourger? I remember *The Spectator* magazine thought the 'sciatica' explanation did not really stand up to scrutiny; Juncker's total dependence on Selmayr was no coincidence. An EU spokeswoman put the story down to a British press campaign; these 'insulting allegations' would not be dignified by a comment.

Now, maybe I am paranoid, but I had but recently started on my new life. No one knew I was in Brussels. No one knew who I was or should associate me with the loud-mouth who had so upset the European Union and the BBC just a month before with serial disrespect for the EU and for Juncker personally. But I had been summoned by Selmayr to Brussels to answer the serious charge of abusing free speech and had disappeared. Who knew what details of me were held in the EU's vaults? I thought I should leave the city centre immediately before it was locked down, probably something that would be complete in less than an hour. After 9/11, Homeland Security made every city in the US have a lock-down plan. Downtown Pittsburgh, Philadelphia, Boston and Minneapolis take fifteen minutes. Washington can be closed in under ten. Within thirty-five minutes, there are police at every tollbooth on the interstates and rolling stops on most secondary roads.

Around Brussels, there may not be a good photograph of the killer, but there would be a description. I made my way quickly to the hotel where, by habit, my bag was all but packed. I decided to steer clear of the central train and bus stations. Airports were out of the question. I took a short taxi ride to the suburb of Etterbeek, and from there the local train to Waterloo where I got a room at the Ibis Hotel using a French passport. I lay on the bed, beer bottle in hand, and tried to relax while listening to an hysterical television.

It would be best not to be picked up. After all, I did have a gun. It was a second-hand 9mm Makarov semi-automatic pistol, once the standard issue sidearm of the Russian military, but still widely in use. There was a further difficulty later that evening as *Télé Bruxelles* announced that the 9mm cartridges retrieved from the skulls were Russian and that they came from a Makarov pistol, identified from CCTV cameras in the mall.

10. FREEDOM OF THE CURIOUS

After such knowledge, what forgiveness? Think now
History has many cunning passages, contrived corridors
And issues, deceives with whispering ambitions,
Guides us by vanities. Think now
She gives when our attention is distracted[49]

Identity was the uncomfortable enemy. I no longer felt part of any group, no citizenship, family, bed partners, religion, no lovers of art or fellow discoursers on nomadism. There was no guiding hand, just a flimsy inner conscience; my rule book a void, empty of all but the needs of the moment, transient, pragmatic, utterly selfish. While all the talents of my mind, intelligence, wit, judgement and temperament could be exemplars of the good and desirable, they could as well be forces for evil. Where did I stand? Perhaps, at the end of the day, I was travelling, like T E Lawrence or Bruce Chatwin, as much to leave oneself behind as to find another.

At unexpected times, I remembered shattered bodies. Each time I had washed my hands and moved on. Was there more death to come? From my private list of unnecessary people, would anyone object if I actually killed Qaddura Mohammed Abd Al-Hamid, the man who casually slaughtered my wife and children? Once I placed Al-Hamid at the head of the list, who might follow? Certainly Juncker and Selmayr for they stood against freedom, open speech and democracy. If Juncker and Selmayr, why not Barnier? It would be a small step to include British politicians and gainsayers like Tony Blair, Mark Carney, Philip Hammond, Dominic Grieve, Anna Soubry and the rest. And then, why not add the leadership of Momentum and the far, far left, Jon Lansman, Yasmine Dar and Rachel Garnham. Would their deaths help or hinder the human race? I felt bad will to them all. Only good will can be called good without qualification.

I bought the Makarov pistol at lunchtime in a pub close to Hull's main commercial docks the day after I agreed my passage to Zandvoort. I had

View of La Belle Alliance, in 1815 on the battlefield at Waterloo, today with a Russian pistol buried nearby. *Engraver: James Rouse. Author: William Mudford*

Claude Monet, *Water Lilies,* Musée de l'Orangerie in the Tuileries Gardens, Paris

The Reina Sofia Museum, Madrid, with external elevators

Aluminium and iron sheet mobile, *Carmen*, by Alexander Calder in the inner
garden of the Reina Sofia Museum, Madrid

Picture from Marc Pataut's photographic exhibition, *Grand Stade (Saint-Denis)*, at the Reina Sofia Museum, Madrid, in 2018

Pablo Picasso's *Guernica* in the Reina Sofia Museum, Madrid

Three of the four tempura panels by Botticelli showing scenes from Boccaccio's *Decameron*, in the Prado, Madrid. Heal's unexpected sighting of Morag was through the doorway to the right

The tropical garden in the entrance hall of Madrid's Atocha railway station

Grand Café de la Poste, Marrakech. *Dr Aderfi Hasnouni*

Doorway to Heal's presumed Marrakech apartment. *Dr Aderfi Hasnouni*

Street of the home of Al-Hamid in Traga, Marrakech. *Dr Aderfi Hasnouni*

Famous sign: '52 days to Timbuktu' at Zagora in Morocco

Saharan horned viper

Resurrection plant after a drop of rain

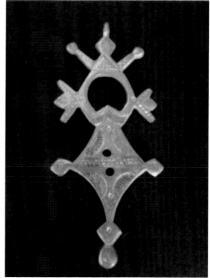

Asso's silver Southern Star.
Dr Aderfi Hasnouni

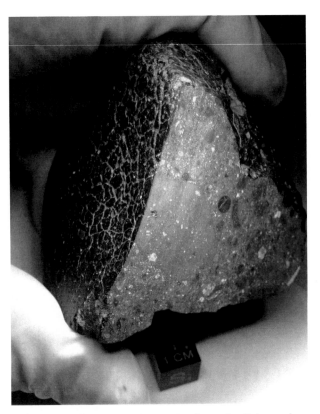

Black Beauty: A water-rich Martian meteorite from the Sahara, determined as 2.1 billion-years-old, offered at auction for over £60,000

Amkssa, 2019. *Dr Aderfi Hasnouni*

been advised that while it was easy to make contact with gun sellers in London, it was also dangerous. The youngsters doing the running were often too high on drugs to conduct a stable transaction without getting distracted by the sight of cash. The best place for a smooth purchase was Hull where the Russian ships docked and their sailors were so lowly paid that they could barely afford the price of a pint. Russia was awash with guns, particularly as the ubiquitous Makarovs were increasingly replaced by the Grach PYa. The evening before, the Russians were easy to spot by their clothes. The only questions I got asked were, 'Which make? How many? What ammunition?'

I reckoned the Makarov, notoriously reliable for a semi-automatic, would be cheap and I also liked that it had been modelled on captured tooling for the German Walther. We agreed to meet again next midday and I said, for safety's sake, that I might want two more if the first purchase went smoothly. I liked the heavy feel of the trigger pull and recognised that I would be trading accuracy for safety. Up close this wouldn't matter; the rate of fire would depend on how quickly I squeezed the trigger. My sailor asked for 300 euro. For £300, he threw in three magazines of eight 9mm cartridges.

Why did I want the gun? Macho stupidity? Hubris? Defence against some unknown threat? Certainly, I was still a little shaken by the phone calls I had received, the late night watchers, the break in and Selmayr's arrogant message carriers at my erstwhile home. Perhaps I did harbour some subterranean thoughts of direct action? Who knows?

What was clear in Waterloo was that the gun had to go in case I was searched. I was in the right place just a few miles from one of the formative battles of European history. The next morning I walked into town and bought a small trowel from a gardening shop and returned to the hotel munching a *pain au chocolat* and looking for coffee. The Ibis was a favourite stop for coaches taking tourists to the widespread site with its superb museum and acceptable restaurant. The Ibis foyer was a milling crowd of complaint and excitement with the guides trying to get their charges organised. It was simple to join one of the more chaotic lines and to freeload a lift. We all got off at the car park by the *Butte du Lion* where I joined a small argument to advise that this was indeed the place where the Prince of Orange was hit by a musket ball and knocked off his horse. British television reliably informs that the musket was fired by Lieutenant Colonel Richard Sharpe who was disgusted by the many lives lost through his senior officer's incompetence. I was challenged by a determined and charming Scottish shepherdess.

'You're not one of mine, are you?'

'It would be easy to answer "yes", but you've got me bang to rights. I'm travelling on my own, saw an opportunity at the Ibis, and couldn't resist. I've found I've got more lawless as I've got older. Put the cuffs on. I'm yours.'

She appraised me in a way that gave me a shiver I hadn't felt for some time.

'I'd like to make amends.' I smiled and meant it. 'If you're going back to the Ibis tonight, I guess you're on duty and food paid for. But if not, I would be happy to buy you a drink, before or after, and possibly dinner to show that my misdemeanour was more about comfort than money. Of course, I'd appreciate a lift back this afternoon?'

I got another appraisal, more sparkle in the eye this time. 'You're on,' she said. 'We go back at four. No dawdling. It's my night off. See you in the foyer at eight. You find the restaurant and it's not in the Ibis. My name's Morag.'

'Geoff,' I said, 'and it will be a pleasure.'

I toured the battlefield first as I didn't want to risk security in the museum with my pistol. I found my way to the inn, *La Belle Alliance*, where Napoleon's Old Guard made their pig-headed last stand. Their commander was General Pierre Cambronne, Napoleon's major of the guard on the island of Elba, and famous throughout France for his rebuttal of the demand by General Colville for his surrender. Depending who you read, particularly that old exaggerator Victor Hugo, Cambronne's response was *'merde'*. 'Cambronne' became a polite but widespread euphemism in France for strong language. He was badly wounded in Colville's retort, but recovered and married his Scottish nurse, Mary Osburn. I decided where Cambronne fell and used my trowel to dig a hole. Archaeologists will have a happy day explaining the Russian pistol if they ever find it. There was an unattended small farm fire burning at a field edge nearby and I threw my baseball cap wrapped around my remaining ammunition into its middle. There followed an excited few minutes.

Cambronne's history was a good story to share with Morag, minus the pistol, as we savoured paté de foie gras at *La Pâte et ose*. We enjoyed each other's company so much that it was an easy, almost foregone, decision to spend the night together. As Morag's coach was leaving for Paris the next morning it solved another of my problems and we shared a further two nights before she ushered her charges to the Channel and home.

The papers were full of the assassinations, of course. Selmayr was much less well known than Juncker, but was hailed as one of the archpriests of an ever-greater Europe. The chattering classes tussled over reputations as details slowly leaked out. The men and the way of their deaths became the dividing line of the European project. One side anointed them saints and argued over the sites for their monuments, which hymns to sing, and dismissed gainsayers as 'indecent' and worse. When you have a non-sectarian religion, know that you are overwhelmingly in the right, there is no end to your hubris. But there were also calming voices. Some saw the dead men as typical of the self-serving unelected politicians of the age. A shocking crime, yes, but what had driven the perpetrator to commit it? Was there anything in what Juncker was, had stood for, that might drive people in desperation to take the ultimate stand.

If democracy is denied, what is left, as the cloak of totalitarianism descends? Why was Juncker, an old man, sick, and soon to retire, chosen to die?

The tussle over their replacements began before the echo of the shots died away. There was no shortage of men and women willing to offer themselves as the perfect candidate to lead the European Federation. In Brussels, where experts worked at getting their way whatever the public thought, the waters closed over, deals were done, and after a month the chosen two emerged without a real vote in sight.

At first, it seemed that nothing had changed, the putative ship of state sailed on, but under the waves there was a hardening of attitude. People who believed in democracy, or in the history and identity of nation states, had had enough.

The rawness of debate increased. As there was no immediate agreement, a shouting matched ensued. Smugness over the failure of the UK's vaunted democratic system was punctured. Some became terrified of speaking out of turn, of causing upset. What often began as a reasonable exchange deteriorated into nastiness with old friends snapping like piranhas. The soft bruised easily, the hard became professionally offended looking to stifle debate, to ban the giving of 'offence' and, inadvertently, to allow extremism to flourish.

People became alone, together. Those on all sides made new tribal bonds of no lasting depth, but which did serve to reinforce views. They stopped hearing those outside the tribe because the worst thing was listening to others, like themselves, who could no longer hear. The ability to discuss, and the skills of listening, of subtlety, disappeared. Families were split by politics. It seemed that everyone had someone they no longer spoke to because of the EU, Brexit, Trump, or nationality. People thought in herds and they went mad in herds and only a few regained their senses, slowly, one by one.

Violence came closer to the surface on the internet, on news broadcasts, in political chambers, and also in the streets. There were copycat assassinations, of course, in Hungary, Sweden and France. In each case, it was the work of amateurs and they were each shot dead by security police within yards of the murders. All were deemed acting alone and all had reported histories of mental illness. No connections were found with the man who dealt with Juncker and Selmayr.

Here was polarisation which lacked respect for individuals, for democracy, for human life and it was only going one way. Violence was again at the heart of Europe. Unless the course was altered, democracy would join feudalism, monarchies and communism as another political experiment that quietly disappeared.

The assassin was never found. He was thought to be an older man, clearly with military training, probably paid by a devious and misguided clique or rogue country. No one went into or emerged from the mall wearing the same ubiquitous clothes. Because the thoroughfare was so busy, there were a dozen suspects, but their faces were not clearly defined. There was always the suspicion that facial dimensions could be altered by a mix of cotton wool, plastic and hair, especially if the eyes were not visible because of glasses. Three men and one woman were identified through recognition software, one of them a career criminal. However, none of them could be proved to be in the city despite some aggressive questioning.

The attack was thought to have been long in its planning with complex organisation and support. It was deemed impossible that an individual could have broken the impeccable security blanket afforded by the European Union to its president and then disappeared. Juncker's visit to this champagne bar happened only occasionally after work as, it was pointed out, he was not a serious drinker. Was the Greek placard a ruse or a statement of that country's anger at their treatment? If you are sure that what was done to Greece by European and German money was all for the greater good, then it is difficult to admit that an assassin and his backers may have had a point. It was easier to ignore difficult truths and to blame outsiders, those jealous of the benefits of living within the Union.

Hotels were scoured and over 400 single men had checked out that day, but then who was to say that the assassin stayed in a hotel, or that he was alone, or that he checked out? The Russian secret service was enjoying a successful spree of assassinations at that time, mostly by poisoning. For the German government, just about to put pen to paper on another unilateral energy deal, the possibility of a Soviet connection was a tad embarrassing. The British were privately suspected because that disrespectful and selfish nation was known to harbour people with unreasonably independent views.

One other theory poked its unwelcome head above the speculation, unwanted by me and, largely ignored, it seemed, by the European intelligence agencies. Its origins were in 1992 when an American, Jim Bell, speculated that if citizens could use the internet to send secret encrypted messages and to trade untraceable currencies, it would be possible to create a functioning market for almost anything. In 1995, Bell set out his ideas in an essay called 'Assassination Politics'. Anonymous digital cash donations could be made to a prize pool which contained a list of public figures. Anyone could enter any name, but it would only become credible when many people chose the same name and the associated prize money became interestingly high. The organisers would award the individual pot to whoever correctly predicted the timing of that nominated public figure's death. This was not illegal, argued Bell, just gambling. But, suggested opponents, if enough people were angry with an individual, each anonymously contributing small amounts, the prize pool would become so large that someone might feel encouraged to make a prediction and then fulfil it. Encrypted messages, secure email, the *Tor* network, and bitcoin made all of this possible.

I knew that the list existed for I had seen it in *Tor's Hidden Services*. What's more, I knew Juncker's name was on it, but not Selmayr's, although perhaps it should have been. Among the many projected dates for the old soak's death was surely one that was close to reality. Had a bitcoin prize payment been made? Without a computer, I had no way of checking, but others surely had.

My fortuitous befriending of Morag, and my fear of being associated with Juncker's death, had proved my precautions on travel. Airports, all major train and bus terminals bristled with security. If a surveillance picture is taken which shows a ticket bought using a credit card then the exact time of that purchase is known. A cross check with the cash machine for that time of purchase will deliver credit card details and a frontal picture. The lesson is to use cash wherever possible. Precious credit cards are to be used for getting cash, not for buying things. Taxis were full of risk as they collected customer details and many carried discreet security cameras.

Uber is renowned for its 'Rides of Glory' internet posting, since denied and deleted, which showed how its data was being used to identify people having one-night stands. As the posting put it, 'One of the neat things that we can do is to discover rider patterns ... a RoGer is anyone who took a ride between 10 pm and 4 am on a Friday or Saturday night and then took a second ride within one tenth of a mile of the previous night's drop-off point four to six hours later. Nearly one per cent of all rides in Boston were RoGers.'

The posting then explained that brief overnight stays 'dropped precipitously' during the days surrounding Valentine's Day on 14 February. The peak was around tax day on 15 April. Rides of Glory had strong seven-day lags. Those districts of major American cities where these 'rides' were most prevalent were plotted and then mapped and it was found that these areas had the highest male female ratios.

I had given up driving partly as a response to petty harassment, but there were other good reasons. To what extent are we all being tracked in ways that are difficult to spot? Cars are still considered private places, but they are the next gold rush for data miners. Car owners have little understanding of the data their cars generate about them, who can access this information and how it is being used, shared, and sold to data brokers. The car might emit a continuous signal to allow it to be traced if stolen;

it could connect to a manufacturer's system to measure usage and wear, including locations, distances and timing. All phone data might be stored through systems like Bluetooth in the car's own memory, the entire phonebook, calls made, numbers dialled, location at the time, and length of call captured from a mobile.

The UK Metropolitan Police's Digital Control Strategy has identified vehicle infotainment systems as a foremost forensic opportunity as it includes details of the driver's and passengers' news and pleasure listening. The data generated can reveal personal communications, including voice, text, email and social networking, as well as web browsing data, personal contacts and schedules and streamed audio and video content. A car owner in Baltimore used the device names stored in a paired list in his stolen car's system to track down on Instagram the teenagers who used it for a joy-ride. Hands-free microphones need not be switched on by the driver for all voice interaction, including personal opinions, to be recorded 'in the background' during a journey. Voice patterns can be used to confirm sex, age and identity, as with fingerprints, or to identify towns of origin and education levels.

All of this information is available to the next user of a car. If the car is a rental, this could be anyone, including people who might seek to do harm. Hire companies are not forthcoming about how to delete data stored during a rent, but insist that it is the sole responsibility of the driver.

How disturbing or embarrassing might a selection of that information be? Best to stay clear of cars or, if you can't, when aboard cover your face and keep your mouth shut.

Can anyone be truly free of registration, of being known? The problem is not limited to the information we knowingly give away, like Uber, or Facebook likes, tracking cookies for web browsing or Google maps. These to a degree we can set out to control. And yet control is in our lifeblood. We build clocks and calendars and we try to predict the weather. What part of our life is really under our control? Is it a sign of naivety to seek to leave all groups? If we choose to exist only in a reality of our own making, like Van Gogh, must that drive us further towards the horizon and to insanity?

Even a nomad is not free when they are with their group. Those outside the clan, the Persians, the other Scythians, do not know where they are, but they can guess. It is July, so the tribe will have gathered the grain crops planted in the spring, left the stubble behind, and headed north. They cannot be pinpointed, but their position can be estimated. Where is north from the crop fields? How many days have they travelled at five kilometres a day? How bad is the weather that might cause hunkering down? Where are the flowing rivers? Is it known where the herds went last year? And the year before? Is there a visible path through the broken and grazed steppe? Cold embers from the night fires? Broken pottery? Snapped yurt poles? Worn-through reins? Ox dung? And all of this was over a thousand years ago and there will be traces even today.

Does anyone have the mental strength to leave all of their groups? Never see parents, siblings or children again? And then be tough enough to abandon a new friend in your lonely world, to push an old lady to the ground to get to the door, to kill? Is that what you have to become?

How likely is it in today's controlled world that there will be a pattern, a bodily record, an electronic fingerpost that points to a trail? Is our personal routine ever truly disrupted? Can even the love of paintings, the frequenting of museums and statues in parks, tell the tracker where we are likely to be tomorrow, especially if where we were yesterday is guessed or known?

I wanted to go to Saint-Denis, the crime-ridden suburb to the north of Paris where getting off the Metro is to feel unsafe. On these streets, the rates of drug-fuelled muggings and murder are almost twice the national average with a less than twenty per cent police success rate. I tried to look down-at-heel, sunk my shoulders and scuffed my shoes. Over half the area's residents were born outside France and most of those in Africa.

The town marketplace may be the most cosmopolitan collection of stalls in all Europe and that was my first reason to visit. You could buy anything. With such a collection of legal and illegal migrants, travel documents were a speciality. I wanted to check the going rate for an EU passport, but I particularly sought a Refugee Travel Document, known in Germany as the Blue Passport or *Blauer Pass*, a substitute for the passport of the state from which you have fled. You can get one if the *Bundesamt für Migration und Flüchtlinge*, the BAMF, recognises your right to asylum or refugee status.

I stood on a street corner near a pirate CD stand, chewed a couple of vegetable samosas, and politely told the line of drug sellers that what I wanted was documents not heroin. Within ten minutes, I was nudged to follow a hip young man with tight yellow trousers and waist-length dreadlocks into the back of a run-down café. The air was thick with cannabis fumes. It was decision time and couldn't have been simpler. I handed over 3,000 euro and went and had my picture taken and was given a mobile phone. Two days later, I got my message and returned and for another 5,000 euro received my Bulgarian European passport and my German refugee document based on my persecution in Zimbabwe. Job done.

I had been in Saint-Denis once before in November 1993 when I did some work for a construction company. *Le Cornillon* in the Plaine Saint-Denis was chosen as the site of a new national football stadium to host France's 1998 World Cup and was named *Stade de France*. This waste ground, wedged in by the Saint-Denis canal, below the A1 and A86 motorways, stood on a former industrial site where the factories had been dismantled in the 1960s and 1970s. Before becoming the high-profile location of a global event, the twenty-five hectare patch of land was the territory of a small number of people who were gradually driven out before the building started and whose huts were demolished when it began. In fact, they were the reason I was there. My job was to advise how to keep a lid on this forced ejection of people from their homes and to keep the focus on the football.

I didn't know what to expect when I tip-toed around the piles of rubbish at the entrance. Inside, I found that the squatters had constructed a maze of buildings using scrap iron. They had an intimate relationship with their surroundings that were clean and well-kept. This was a real community of survivors who had nothing to do with the homeless people who collapsed each night in the Metro. Their life was dignified. They were not like the Eastern nomads of yesterday, although some of their birth areas were no doubt in Scythian territory. Their tribal way of life was not driven by herds of animals needing fresh grazing. But they had moved as a number of groups, family units mostly, to find jobs near to Paris. In valuing their new land, they had lost the prime characteristic of the nomad, but the old fear of the hordes was still evident. Government and society didn't know what to do with them. And, just like the old nomads, they would have to journey again, but this time because they were not valued or respected. Football was more important.

On one visit, I met a campaigning photographer, Marc Pataut, who had just begun what turned into a three-year project to document what was happening. His work mostly consisted of small personal portraits, which, to my mind, captured the essence of these people and their homes. I was so taken by what I saw that I resigned my contract, much to the anger of my employers, and joined Pataut in his condemnation. Football won, of course, and France captured their home World Cup against Brazil.

Buying my fake travel documents provided a good chance to return to the Stade de France. The stadium's offices were open and there was little trace of what had been, except for an advertisement hanging in an embarrassed corner. Pataut's photographic exhibition was destined for a showing at the Reina Sofia Museum in Madrid the following year and, if I could, I wanted to see it.

On the day I picked up my documents, I began a voyage of curiosity through France. I took several months over it. What other nation is the mother of cultural painting, of impressionism, post-impressionism, Dadaism, cubism, Fauvism, expressionism, surrealism, futurism, abstract art, all to die for?

I had a couple of buildings to see and the principal was in the centre of Saint-Denis, the Basilica. This is the unique burial place of almost every French king from Frankish Dagobert in 637 until Louis XVIII in 1824, and a landmark. It is the first major structure of which a substantial part was designed and built in the gothic style. The stained glass roses of the 'Tree of Jesse' and the 'Creation' in the two transepts are masterpieces. I sat in a pew as the building's columns soared and the multi-coloured light flooded in. If there was a place that could encourage prayer, this was it. But, of course, it was also a construct like the *Stade de France* that would keep the peasantry firmly under the thumb.

Autumn in Paris – where to start? I decided to miss the queues at the Louvre, especially around the Mona Lisa. I last visited Sainte-Chapelle some twenty years before to listen to a concert of nineteenth-century French music. The building continued the Gothic theme of Saint-Denis. I managed to stand without too much interruption, gazing up at the extensive stained glass. I still got a thrill as I recreated in my mind the sight of Louise IX, clothed as a penitent, walking slowly the length of the hall to the main altar carrying the 'Crown of Thorns' bought in 1239 from the emperor at Constantinople.

I spent a day at the Musée de l'Orangerie in the Tuileries Gardens, almost devoid of people, and permanent home to Monet's eight large murals of water lilies in two oval rooms. The flowers were reproductions from his garden in Giverny. Displayed in the intended diffused light, Monet presented these works to the nation as a solace after the Great War and this effect continues to this day. Is it possible to have too much Monet? The Marmottan Monet Museum in rue Louis Boilly in what was a private house shows over one hundred of his pictures on its lower floor, just an orgy in beautiful open, uncrowded space.

I caught the bus from central Paris to Giverny itself, eighty kilometres west of the city, which contains the artist's house and garden, and immersed myself in the *Argenteuil Poppy Fields*, *Impression Sunrise*, the *Magpie*, the *Seine at Vetheuil*, the series of *Rouen Cathedral* which gave me a brief connect with my birth mother, *Haystack*, more water lilies and more and more.

I had never been to Arles where Vincent Van Gogh lived for a year from 1888, producing over 300 paintings, and was visited by Paul Gaugin, became increasingly eccentric, cut off his own ear, and was all but run out of town. It should have meant more being in the birth place of *The Night Café*, the *Yellow Room*, *Starry Night over the Rhone*, and *L'Arlésienne*, but when I visited the supposed sites of his rooms, his café, the Old Hospital and the asylum at Saint-Rémy-de-Provence the experience was dispiriting with the crowds, the ever-present tat and the ignorance. You can be very alone in a crowd. I enjoyed the Roman amphitheatre despite its covering of modern seating, but missed the bull fights.

A week's stay at Les Eyzies-de-Tayac-Sireuil reignited my love for cave art. I visited the museum, Font-de-Gaume, Grotte du Grand-Roc, the Lascaux Cave, and the sites of the great discoveries of English Quaker and felt hat-manufacturer Henry Christie and archaeologist Édouard Lartet at Abri de la Madeleine and Le Moustier, where they introduced the system of stratification to date Paleolithic finds.

I drifted to the south of France to winter like some snowy northern bird. I cannot remember a period when I was happier. No worries, no evidence of pursuit, passing friends made and enjoyed, the food and soft sunlight. I visited Paul Cezanne's atelier in the attic home of his father at the Bastide du Jas de Bouffan in Aix-en-Provence. The Renoir Museum standing in centuries-old olive trees at Cagnes-sur-Mer with its superb views all the way to Cap d'Antibes. The Musées Nationaux des Alpes-Maritimes for Marc Chagall, Fernand Léger and Picasso in Nice and Biot. The Musée Jean Cocteau in Menton and a dozen others.

What could be a more splendid way to wait for spring? What could go wrong?

11. FREEDOM OF THE DANCE

But as if a magic lantern threw the nerves in patterns on a screen:
Would it have been worth while
If one, settling a pillow or throwing off a shawl,
And turning toward the window, should say:
'That is not it at all,
That is not what I meant, at all.'[50]

Based in Perpignan, I spent a fulfilled winter along the Mediterranean with many long visits to galleries and museums, the ruins of the Roman and Aragonese empires, a few passing friends, walking the hills, reading, and eating well. There was no sense of pursuit, no strange meetings or coincidences or echoes of the deaths in Brussels where Juncker and Selmayr were being sanctified.

In Paris, in December, armoured cars and some 8,000 police, 90,000 across the country, were moved onto the streets to protect tourist sites and private property from the *gilets jaunes*, the anti-Macron government protests. The riots spread south to Toulouse and Marseilles, but I stayed well clear. Perpignan was untouched, at least in the centre. The older protesters who occupied the roundabout at the toll-gates to the north of the town had none of the anarchists of Paris and Bordeaux. They were friendly with roadside *paella* on offer to share with their tales of *ras-le-bol*, their mix of despair, depression and pessimism.

For years we have lived in a climate of 'You can't say that'. You can't criticise mass immigration – that's xenophobia. You can't oppose the EU – that's Europhobia. You can't raise concerns about radical Islam – that's Islamophobia. You can't agitate against climate-change policy – that's climate-change denialism, on a par with Holocaust denialism, and anyone who dares to bristle against eco-orthodoxy deserves to be cast out of polite society. And yet now, in this populist movement of the gilets jaunes, people are daring to say precisely these unsayable things.

They're standing up to the EU. They're demanding that immigration become a democratic concern rather than something worked out for us by unaccountable bureaucrats in Brussels.[51]

I had no contact from any of my financial sources in the UK so my credit card invoices were being met. The cash machines continued to churn out money on demand and to facilitate this I befriended an Albanian of part-Gypsy stock. Ilia was happy to collect money for me. With each withdrawal, I gave him five euros so that it was his picture, not mine, captured by the hidden camera above the machine.

Even without the all-watching street and travel CCTVs, the business of evading cameras is important. Consider, for instance, refunds made in 2017 by UK banks when they were forced to admit that some customers who had not received pay-outs at cash machines had never been recompensed. The banks backed down when ordered to disclose ten-year-old pictures of users standing at the terminals. Banks never throw anything away.

Anyone who has a built-in camera in their laptop, or attached to their television, or as part of a child's toy, or has microphones in home instruction devices, or in a car, or smart meters, is susceptible to real-time hacking that captures intimate details of personal and family life that can be filed or used for theft or blackmail. The coming world of multi-device interconnectivity will be a time of real hurt for many naive and unsuspecting individuals. And, of course, if an intelligence service wants any of this it can be accessed by force under the cloak of national security.

The regular collection of my cash suited Ilia between his part-time and short-term jobs, especially as he often managed to beg from me a coffee or a meal. Ilia claimed to be an economic migrant, but I suspected he was in hiding for his life from a multi-generation Albanian blood feud, *hakmarrja,* based on the oral *kanun* of Lekë Dukagjini. Ilia's home was in Thethi, a remote mountain village east of Shkodër, unreachable after the heavy snows. It was also notorious for its looming lock-in tower, *Kulla e ngujimit,* where male family members under threat of assassination spent their lives. He spoke Italian as a second language and good French and we established a wary friendship.

It was from Ilia that I heard about the Romani wedding. He had sought me out to let me know that he might be offered a labouring job out of town that would take him away for about two weeks. Did I want to take out a bit more cash than usual to tide me over? It was early April and Gypsies were converging on pilgrimage from all over the south of Europe, *Tsigane* from France, *Zingari* from Italy, Spanish *Gitanos* from Andalusia and Barcelona, *Cigano* from Portugal and, Ilia assured me, from Albania, Macedonia and Romania in small numbers. The occasion was the annual gathering at Les Saintes Maries de le Mer in the Camargue where the Gypsies venerate their saint, the Black Sara. In grand procession, lights in hand, her statue is taken to the shore. The following morning, the faithful, Gypsies and others, take the two Marys, Jacobe and Salome, with their reliquary caskets in a craft to the sea to celebrate the arrival of Catholicism in the Middle Ages. Sara, by tradition, was the servant of the two Marys in Palestine.

The pilgrimage is poignant for the Gypsies because when they arrived in France in the fifteenth century they presented themselves as penitents, condemned to wander the world in atonement for their sins. After acceptance from Pope Martin V, they remained faithful to the famous pilgrimage to Camino de Santiago. Ilia's eyes lit with religious fervour as he told me of the scene: violins, guitars, candles raised to the church nave, loud prayers, shouted invocations, children held high in front of the statues.

I had to disappoint him. Impressive though these events must be, my personal preference was to go to the wedding because I assumed it would be accompanied by a horse fair and flamenco.

'Was this the case?'

'Yes.'

'Where was it?'

'By the side of the Rivière de Tarérach, across the lake from Vinça.'

'Would I be allowed to attend?'

'Unlikely.'

There were several items in my favour, I thought. Ilia called me his *phral*, the Romani word for pal or close friend, all derived from the Sanskrit *bhrata*, brother. I was also a source of income. My black eyes helped and, after I had told him of my Gypsy friendships in England in my early years, he was convinced that I was, at least, part-Gypsy. Also, there was the Roma tradition of hospitality once one was allowed into the inner circle.

There was, Ilia said, a seedy estaminet at the village of Baixas, west of Perpignan on one of the old routes, now just a little-used country lane. The *Zingari* coming from the east by horse and *vardo*, the traditional painted Gypsy wagon, rather than car or train, would use this road to get to the marriage site.

In Italy, the word *Zingaro* is used to describe a slovenly person and may be connected to the Greek for 'untouchable', explained Ilia, and 'nothing much had changed'. We should go to the café, he said, and ask the travellers about permission.

On the second day, it wasn't Italian Zingari who crawled to the estaminet with a tired, paint-peeling *vardo* and strings of horses, but some semi-nomadic *Quinqui* or *quincalleros*, tinkers, who live in the northern half of Spain and along the north Mediterranean coast. They prefer to be called *mercheros* and speak the old form of Castilian, *Germanía*, with elements of *Caló*, a dialect of the Spanish Roma. Their name came from *quincallería*, ironmongers. Because the men were often blamed for petty crime, in modern Spanish their name is associated with delinquents and petty thieves.

One theory, said Ilia, as we idled away our time drinking beer, which I paid for, and playing cards for small change, which he won more often than not, was that the *Quinqui* were Muslims. They became nomads to escape persecution after their expulsion from Spain with the Jews during the Christian reconquest in the fifteenth century.

Conversation was difficult because the arrivals were surly and suspicious. We established they were going to the wedding to do some horse trading. Then, they planned to travel in Spain rather than go on to Saintes Maries. They did not know the marriage couple, but anticipated a general invitation. The ceremony would be a large affair as the bride and groom were from different groups and each had invited favourite and celebrated dancers and singers. The bride, named Preciosa, was coming with her family from Barcelona. The groom was a Zingari and was a day behind the Quinqui with his extended relations, also tinkers.

Ilia and I decided that it would be worth waiting and we spent the time arguing. Gypsies, the Romani people, will argue about anything, but the subjects closest to their hearts are their origins, their horses and flamenco, the last two, along with women and family, providing most of their pleasure.

I was able to tell Ilia from my reading that there were over 10 million of his people, but there could be more than that number just in Europe where they were by far the largest minority group, bigger even than the Czech, Hungarian or Dutch nations. Numbers were vague because many refused to register their ethnic identity for fear of discrimination. Although they constituted a mosaic of languages, religions and lifestyles, they shared a distinct social heritage. Gene studies, backed by investigations in language, dress and customs, showed their diaspora had a single founder population. All originated 1,500 years ago from northern India, either the *Kashmiri Pandit* of Jammu and the North-West Frontier, or the *Meghawal* from Rajasthan. A rapid migration followed through the Middle and Near East and into the Balkans.

Medieval Europeans used 'Egyptian' as a cover term for a number of different foreign populations; one place where the Romani first stayed on the Adriatic coast was known as 'Little Egypt', hence the generic and inaccurate 'gypsy' and the derivation of 'gitano' and other sound-linked words. From there, during 1300–1500, the Romani spread to all the surrounding countries with concentrations in Romania, Bulgaria, Slovakia, Hungary and Serbia and branches reaching as far as Wales, Portugal and Spain, and Estonia and Lithuania. Subsequent tentacles brought substantial populations to the Americas, perhaps one million in the USA. In the eighteenth and nineteenth centuries as the Habsburgs recaptured lands from the Ottomans, including Slovakia and Hungary, and Europe became safer, gypsies were allowed to remain in these countries. Gypsy music funnelled into the theatres of Vienna and Budapest and a romantic image of the Roma emerged: a happy-go-lucky nomadic lifestyle; intoxicating music, with female dancers swirling around a campfire; and mystical powers over Europeans, including the stealing of white children.

The Romani language has always included a set of warrior words that are of Indian origin: 'fight', 'soldier', 'spear', 'plunder' and 'battle-cry'. Some of these words used to refer to someone who is not Romani, such as *gadže* or *das* or *goro* or *gomi*, and meant 'civilian', 'prisoner of war', or 'captive' in original Indian forms. There are more than 250 Greek words in the European Romani dialects, second to the Indian vocabulary. There is also some fundamental grammar of Greek origin; it was probably in the

Byzantine Empire that Romani crystallised into the language of today.

'Travelling is a part of our history,' Ilia offered. 'It may be that our ancestors trekked for thousands of miles from India to Europe and then out into the world, but there's a difference between travelling on a journey with a purpose and travelling because local laws leave no choice and forbid you to stop.'

'There's a third reason to travel,' I countered. 'You can travel for its own sake. Just to travel, to see things, to be free. Pure nomads would never have a fixed home and would sleep where they stopped. They were never going to stay for long. They would know that, sooner or later, a government, or the police, or tax collector, or people who are happiest when telling others what to do, would start to interfere. Then the nomad would no longer be free and would need to move again.'

Ilia was more practical than I. 'But, my nomad friend,' he argued, 'we Romani travel back and forth, follow similar routes during the seasons, stop in familiar places. Is it within a man's soul to be always moving, with no plan to stop for more than a few nights? Is it possible that there is no place on earth, no friendship, where he could be happy? And, if there was not, would he not just get tired of travel and need somewhere to rest?'

We were sitting at a small table under an awning, beers half drunk, with one eye watching the road to the east. We could see the red-roofed village away to our left. It was a drowsy, early-Spring day with lizards motionless on the stone wall opposite, faces to the sun. There was a scent of thyme and the light green and red of budding wild cherries. The fields contained soldierly rows of vines in pebbled ochre ground. Two columns of ants scurried to and from a small road kill. Buzzards mewed, gliding in slow circles pierced by dark kites that flexed their tails to hover and, seeing no prey, moved on. The patron's scrawny chickens pecked in the dirt.

'I can see them, four *vardo*,' said Ilia. Ten minutes later, I made out the shapes near the horizon, inching through the heat haze.

'There's always the problem of making a living,' I continued. 'You know that too well, scratching around Perpignan until you find a *gadžo* like me who'll give you money and beer. You say these *Zingari* are tinkers and that's the Gypsy way of making a living. Because they were travellers their tools had to fit in the wagon. Fixed, heavy equipment was no good to them. So they became skilled artisans, took up metalwork, sharpening knives, horse trading, and,' with a quiet eye on Ilia's face, 'they became flexible with regard to private property.'

He didn't flinch. 'There are far fewer of us who work in metal, now', he suggested.

I said I thought that it was the European Industrial Revolution that had done the damage and removed the Roma's traditional work, something that didn't happen so much in Albania until the fall of the dictator Enver Hoxha. 'Mending things went out of fashion and lots of Gypsies became entertainers: fortune telling, music and dancing, horse shows, dancing bears, and, of course, outlaws.'

Ilia suggested that the best preparation would be to place a dozen cold bottles of beer ready for the arrival. It worked well. There was the smallest hesitation, watchful smiles, and the bottles were all claimed. Ilia identified the groom and I was introduced with a lengthy explanation in a dialect I could not fathom. I hoped most of it was complimentary. There were a few muttered responses. The groom's name was Francesco, perhaps twenty years, dark, wiry hair, brown skin from the perpetual outdoors, coal-black eyes and wearing old clothes that were covered in dust. There was little to separate him from his kin. His father, uncles and brothers, all older, stood around him, ready to protect and to give advice. The women stayed in the wagons with the children, but some beer was passed up.

'It's not personal,' said Ilia, 'but you are not family, not Romani. Francesco has no doubts as to your sincerity and interest, but he does not want to risk offending Preciosa's parents by inviting a tourist. I can explain it like this. We all call ourselves Romani; we all maintain aspects of the same culture and know some of the same words. Despite this, any sense of being once a single people has long been lost. The families of Francesco and Preciosa are not close, but they see themselves as being together. They are together not because of what they are, but because of what they are not. They are not gadže. Francesco sees you as a gadžo.'

I was disappointed, but prepared for the rejection. I explained that I knew from books and was sensitive to the idea of ritual pollution. It was central to Romani belief especially at times of a great ceremony, like marriage. The eleventh century Indian caste system was alive today with these travellers as it is with many of the Indian *Banjara* people. Members of the same *jati*, sub-caste, for instance, may eat together without risk of contamination, but the food will become polluted if they eat with members of other *jatis*; and because the *jatis* of one's associates might not always be known, contact between the mouth and the various utensils shared with others at a meal is avoided, just to be on the safe side. In conservative Romani culture, liquids are poured into the mouth from a container held away from the lips, so that the rim of the vessel, the *kerlo*, is not touched; smoke from a shared tobacco pipe is drawn through the fist clenched around the stem. The surest way not to touch utensils used by others is to eat with the fingers.

I ordered some more beers and tried another argument. I asked Ilia to keep translating.

'I understand that there is anger at the *gadžo* academics who have obtained their higher education as a matter of ease and who are now making their professional reputations by studying the Romani. This anger is about the things they have written in their books. Most of what I know comes from books like these, I admit.'

There was a short burst of dialect. 'He says that books do not impress him.'

I ploughed on. 'I understand that Romani children know of the clear division that exists between people who are Romani and people who are not. Children are taught that it is a good thing to be a Romani and that *gadži* are not their betters. Your people go to great lengths to protect your identity. I understand that this is so serious that if time is spent in the non-Romani world then spiritual energy, *dji*, is drained away; this involves emotions, heart, soul, and mood. Spiritual batteries can best be recharged by spending time in an all-Romani environment. This is reinforced by cleanliness, eating habits, the handling of animals, sexual behaviour. So, I understand that the *gadžo* and their customs are distrusted by the Roma. I want you to know that I respect all this and do not want to do anything that would upset anyone.'

Francesco had no time for lecture, promises and *gadžo* waffle. Feet shuffled and he looked at me full in the face. 'To know Romani customs is not to be Roma,' he said.

'You are looking into my eyes,' I replied. 'They are black, like yours.'

It was the first chink. He hesitated and said, 'Perhaps you have some

Roma blood from many years ago, but I do not know this? I do not think that you know this.'

I shrugged with a touch of resignation. 'If your mind is made up, then I thank you for your time and your courtesy.' I smiled. 'Can I see your horses before you go?'

Each of the wagons had its animals tethered to each other and strung out. They had all drifted to the road edge and were pulling away at the scant grass and budding bushes or pushing over the low walls trying to reach the young grapes. Some were draught replacements for pulling the *vardi*, but others were of greater value and a few were spirited when approached.

'Which are the most difficult,' I asked?

There was a brief conversation and Ilia explained that the Arab mare, black and almost fifteen hands, had not been ridden. She was bought cheaply because the previous owner could not train her, but she was expected to be fast if she could be mastered. I went to the mare's head, we nuzzled and I spoke soft words. Before anyone realised, I slipped her leading knot, and led her to the other side of the road and through a half-hanging gate into an open field. I was not so sprightly but, by placing a foot on a jutting stone half-way up the field wall, I managed in one movement to mount bare-backed. We trotted off and I made a fifty-yard circle. As we approached the group, I nudged her into a canter and then let her run. She was like the wind and free. I was impressed by her control and gait and had no difficulty staying on. I let her slow when she had had enough and we walked back. I dismounted and handed the rope to Francesco.

'You are most welcome to my wedding,' he said. 'In return, I ask that you do me a favour. We will talk later.'

Ilia and I went back to Perpignan where I bought a small tent, chose a few clothes, and placed the remainder in a bag in a station locker. We left by bus for Tarérach. The site would have been difficult to find were it not for the converging vehicles, carts, wagons, cars and lorries. This was not a formal place, but an excellent piece of flat land down the lane from the priory at Mercévol and butting on the west bank of the fast-flowing river. Gitano weddings can last up to three days. By the time the authorities realised what was going on and sent someone to check, then called a meeting to decide what to do, then sent the police around to double check, it would be time to go anyway. Men were already at work building a small platform, *caseta*, for a boxing tournament, but also to showcase a revered flamenco artiste from Seville.

Ilia and I put up our tent on the outskirts of the encampment and wandered around meeting people, making casual friends, sharing drinks, unleavened bread, and meals, of which just the fatty white meat of a hedgehog, a bit like 'rabbit light', was new to me. Traditional Spanish and Italian Romani place a high value on the extended family; everyone was a relation of somebody, but as expected, there was a separation into the two main wedding groups. I had lots of questions which were handled with patience and amusement.

Today, Preciosa's family lived near Barcelona, but they were from Andalusia and rooted in its culture. Their history was of a one-hundred-strong group that entered the peninsula in the fifteenth century pretending to be Christian pilgrims and who sought safe conduct from nobles. Their language developed into *Caló*, 'black', their own name for themselves, and, at heart, Andalusian Spanish with a large number of Romani loan-words. During the Muslim rule in southern Spain, referred to as Al-Andalus, Sephardic Jews, Muslims, Christians and Gitanos lived a short period of peaceful coexistence and prosperity, *La Convivencia*. Yet, decades later, the lingering repercussions of post-Inquisition Spain's political and economic upheaval spawned an illiterate and poverty-stricken population, including persecuted and oppressed Gitanos. Families at the wedding, *el yeli*, asserted that flamenco emerged from these anguished human conditions. It was their music.

The engagement party, the *pedimento*, began with much conviviality, alcohol, guitar playing and swirling around the small fires used for cooking and as a meeting point rather than comfort as the weather stayed warm. I was impressed by the storytellers who gathered enthusiastic audiences that listened in silence, loosed a collective groan at a sad event, whooped when a dramatic victory was won. Ilia was not able to help much with translation, but the general drift was always clear. This tradition was similar to the *kathakas* who used mimetic gesture, song and recitation to propagate Hindu ideology in village and temple courtyards. I liked to believe that what I witnessed was a throwback to the two-thousand-year-old tribal tales and dances of Rajasthan.

Through the night, *bulerías* were danced to their dramatic rhythm and some sung with fervour. Favourites from Jerez were mixed with more modern *rumba gitana* and *rumba flamenca*.

The first morning saw the ritual of the *pañuelo*. Virginity is essential in unmarried women, although not among unmarried men. Watched by the whole community, a group consisting of an *ajuntaora*, a well-respected elder woman, along with aunts and senior women of the families, took the bride into a separate room. There, I was told, Preciosa laid down on a *pañuelo*, a cloth with three rose petals on it. The *ajuntaora* conducted a physical examination while the other women held witness. After a successful inspection, the women came out of the room and sang to the couple and to the crowd. The men, took up the singing, ripped their shirts and lifted the bride and groom onto their shoulders. This was the time for me to return the favour requested by Francesco. I rode the black mare through the crowd and up to the couple. For extra flair, I brought the horse to kneel, slipped off the bare back, and handed the red silk rein to the groom who, in turn, passed it to the bride's father as his wedding gift. This small performance was applauded with excitement. As I moved to the back of the gathering, I received many pats on the back and head.

At the *casamiento*, the formal ceremony that followed, the bride was lauded with the *alboreá*, the wedding song, for giving her honour to her husband as proven by the *pañuelo*. This was the only occasion when the *alboreá* was sung; a performance at any other time would bring bad luck.

Boxing was common among Romani because at school the boys were taunted and made to feel different. The natural response was to lash out. Gypsy boys trained hard and became known as fighters. When people are subjected to unremitting humiliation and often unmerited attack, they lose their sense of self-restraint, even self-respect, and their behaviour creeps towards their stereotyped image.

The afternoon was set aside for the tournament and eight young men stepped forward, two of them swaying as they tried to focus. It became a tribal affair fuelled by drink; calls to glory and insults, not always in jest, added spice to the din. Young, rival supporters were forced to restrain each other as umbrage was taken, but damaged egos seemed soon forgotten. It was, of course, a knock-out contest. The final was brutal. The popular victor was one of Preciosa's brothers and he was carried to his tent and I saw no more of him during my stay. The loser took his defeat with bad grace. He might have suffered permanent damage by his obstinate refusal to submit, but with impressive reserves of stamina kept dragging himself to his feet to be knocked down again. His face was drawn with anger and, I felt, hatred. He was a *Quinqui*, a *merchero*, and from the band I had met at Baixas. As he was dragged away he looked at me with vicious eyes and spat blood in my direction as if his humiliation was made worse by my presence.

I was shaken by the young man's complete and instinctive dislike of me. I sat down on a tree trunk and found myself involved in a debate, in truth more of an historical rant, about the persecution of the Romani. I was proclaimed English and blamed for a decision in 2001 by the UK Government to give their immigration officers special powers to discriminate against certain groups of non-UK citizens attempting to enter Britain. The irony was that this was as a result of an amendment to the Race Relations Act outlawing racial discrimination by public authorities. In a flagrant violation of commitments under international law, the UK immigration service was allowed to exclude Kurds, Albanians, Tamils, Somalis, Afghans and, crucially for my interrogators, Roma. Dozens of Roma had been banned from cheap flights to Luton and Stansted from the new EU accessions in eastern Europe. This was a hot topic and I was taken to task. I suggested that blaming a citizen – me – which brought an inner smile, for the actions of their government, was like blaming all Roma for the crimes of a few. For this group, the English action meant that Roma were not seen as European, but being something else.

What was a European anyway? I took both sides. I suggested that many Gypsies didn't see themselves as Roma or European, didn't engage in politics, and swapped countries like other people swapped socks. However, being European didn't mean being from a part of Europe. If that were true, the Saami and Hungarians and Finns and Estonians would not be Europeans. Neither was having a country a necessary qualification because if that were so then the Basques, Catalans, Cornish, Frisians and Shetlanders wouldn't qualify.

These arguments always get back to the Nazis and I was, at least, able to reclaim some moral ground. I was reminded that, in the 1930s, Roma were stripped of German citizenship, in response to what Hitler called the

'Gypsy Question'. What followed was genocide and I recounted my visits to the Gypsy and Ravensbrück memorials in Amsterdam. The complaints moved on to the Communist governments that required Roma to speak the national language, to settle in towns and to work in factories. These policies eroded time-honoured Roma values and shattered the cohesiveness of their traditional communities. It left the new Roma generation prone to sexual, alcohol and drug abuse, and filled state-run orphanages with Roma toddlers. Obstetricians in the Czech Republic were accused of sterilising Roma patients without their consent.

In 1996, the European Union facilitated the European Roma Rights Centre (ERRC), a Roma-led international public interest law organisation 'working to combat anti-Romani racism and human rights abuses'. On the one hand, the ERRC secured two million euro in compensation for its adherents, but it also led to the EU's normal practice of assuming moral ownership. The EU's social scientists produce 'definitive' reports on the state of the Roma and then enforced these interpretations on their member countries. The technique in Brussels, as always, was to undermine local attitudes and customs and to attack local words, like *Gitano*, or generics, like Gypsy, and to make them beyond the pale, unacceptable on social media, declare them racist. In turn, this placed the EU as the arbiter for the Roma, their chosen generic, and for the broader debate.

I decided to go to bed for a few hours before the flamenco and the party lurched towards its finale.

Some English might say that flamenco is like *Marmite*: you either love it or you hate it. Unlike *Marmite*, flamenco is best appreciated with some sense of its tradition. With half a chance, Romani will argue into the night about their origins. Some see a transition from the deserts of Rajasthan; another that it is a derivation from the Arabic, *felah-mengus*, the wandering peasant; others that it is a much more modern phenomena, an ideological resistance and carries the cruel burden of marginalisation and nomadism. It needs *Gitano* artists who hold it in the bosom of the family to bring it to light. Spanish *Gitano* say that the stamping feet, flashing eyes and violent gestures of flamenco are a silent 'stylised aggression', an outlet which in the past reflected resentment at being offered protection against racism by wealthy *patrones*, but having to pay for it by providing entertainment.

The truth lies in the *cante jondo*, the deep flamenco song, with more serious flamenco forms such as *seguiriyas* or *soleá*. These *cante* are cherished by a dozen Gypsy families living between Triana, the *Gitano* neighbourhood of Seville, and Cadiz; long-standing networks and trade routes along the Guadalquivir River basin, the Royal Road linking urban centres with Cadiz and neighbouring agricultural communities like Jerez de la Frontera.

While Romani formed orchestras in Hungary, their flamenco artists became a part of Spanish culture, which, in the nineteenth century, became romanticised for early tourists. Since then, there has always been a search for the true heart of the dance, but reality is that performances followed the audiences more than the other way around, and that meant following the money. From the English author Richard Ford came rapturous accounts of the ladies of Cádiz, which inspired Merimées's *Carmen*.

Two other important travellers chronicled their experiences in Spain. Baron Jean-Charles Davillier, a French art scholar who travelled with Gustave Doré, a prolific artist who by the early 1860s 'was unchallenged as the foremost illustrator in France'. Like Ford, Davillier and Doré were also escorted across Seville's Guadalquivir River into the Gitano *barrio* of Triana to witness an 'authentic' evening of local dance. Davillier conjured an ultimate Romantic scene by describing being led by Colirón, a local resident, through dirty, dark streets to a *botilleria*. There, a performance was held in a patio built in Arab times, intoxicating with its sea of fragrant flowers. Doré's sketches emphasised qualities that were of value to a paying public.

The romantic, dangerous Gypsy has been ever present in Western art for over a hundred years. As well as Carmen and the music of Liszt, we have had Borrow with *The Zincali*; Hugo, *Hunchback of Notre Dame*; Bronte, *Wuthering Heights*; the second Strauss, *Der Zigeunerbaron*. Flamenco, unlike folk music, has been performed for money since the start. It took uncommon talent that commanded respect and could earn more money than picking olives. It is important to recognise *gitanismo*, the fashion for 'pretend Gypsy' and 'put-on' Spain where jobbing performers do a few moves that have been practised in order to appear spontaneous.

The split-second sinuous and subversive gesticulation encapsulates the essence of Spanish flamenco dance and like many stereotypical images there is some truth in it – even if it is not the whole truth. While dances from countries other than one's own may seem hard to understand, as if they were a foreign language, there is something about flamenco's combination of power and grace, intense rhythms, and unabashed expression of human emotion that has far-reaching appeal. Flamenco invented a modern body language for itself analogous to American jazz.[52]

At the start of the *fiesta*, it was a flamenco party or jam session, a *juergas*, an intimate gathering among friends. After a number of enthusiastic rather than skilled family members, *bailaora*, dancers, and *cantaora*, singers, and with the night just drawing over, torches reaching higher and drink cascading, we came to the main event. The tension was thick and smelled of testosterone and fruit perfume. The artiste, *La Capitana*, was named for and mentioned in the same breath as Carmen Amaya, the Romani from Barcelona – the greatest of her generation. She was the first female to master footwork that had been reserved for the best male dancers due to its speed and intensity. Jean Cocteau's tribute was legendary:

Carmen Amaya is the sound of hail on the windowpane, the cry of the swallow, a thin, black cigar between the lips of a pensive woman, a thunderstorm of applause. When she and her family come to town, they consume the ugly, the torpid, and the dull the way a swarm of insects consumes the leaves on the trees. Not since Serge Diaghilev's Ballets Russes have we been able to experience this kind of lovers' tryst in a theatre.

Wrapped in a rich embroidered shawl, emblem of wealth and empire, with a red rose in her dark hair, Carmen's corset-defying bends, lascivious hips, and sinuous arms and hands seduce the viewer ... then rejects this invading gaze with a stamp of defiance ... She is present throughout the centuries, transmogrifying yet hewing to her sensuous and rebellious nature ... part human, part panther, part mystic abstraction.

And then La Capitana was there. She did not disappoint. No tight trousers here but a full *bata de cola*, a dress with a long train. This Gypsy girl danced. Indescribable. Soul. Pure soul. Feeling made flesh. The floorboards vibrated with unprecedented brutality and scarce credible precision. La

Capitana was a gross product of nature. Like all Gypsies, she must have been born dancing. What she emitted must have been sensed from birth. Her fierce *chaflan*, a sounded hop on one foot followed by a stamp on the other, the two sounds so close together; the aggression of her *golpe*, full-footed stamps; finger snaps, *pitos*, used to mark the rhythm; the bravery of her pirouettes; the force of her broken turns: an animal ardour ran parallel with the astonishing accuracy of her execution.

There was a moment when *duende*, the spirit, flooded the amphitheatre, and gripped everyone. The skin itched, hair bristled and breathing stopped. It was *cañí*, pure-blooded, authentic, angry and graceful. It was flamenco.

I don't remember going to bed and, in truth, I don't remember getting up either. The sun was high. I strolled back from the makeshift toilets, which had become smelly and unappetising without disinfectant in the heat. I stopped to look at the rushing river pushing over rounded stones. Small fish whipped in and out of the steady shade from the alder and hornbeam. Cigarette stubs and packets dotted the bank. There was an unexpected quiet, no one bathing, no women going about domestic chores. It was post-*duende* when the world seemed satiated and needed rest.

Was I surprised to see him stand in front of me, the vanquished *merchero*, face still bloodied, the same hatred in his eyes? People without self-respect are dangerous, both to themselves and to others. It was whispered to me after yesterday's confrontation that he was unstable and had spent time in prison. This, on its own, was not unusual. In some areas where Gypsies make up, say, fifteen per cent of the population, they also make up eighty per cent of the people in jail. The great shadow comes from *Gitano* involvement in drug trafficking. In Spain, Romani women represent twenty-five per cent of the female prison population, and over ninety per cent of these were involved with drugs.

For this *merchero*, whose life was inherited from hundreds of years of slavery where every single thing – food, clothing and even one's spouse – was provided at the discretion of the owner, he might be forgiven an assumption that this was how one survived in the world. Historic crimes majored on trespassing, lighting camp-fires, poaching, grazing horses on private property and stealing fruit and vegetables from farms and orchards. Today, the offences were similar: theft, public nuisance, trespassing, but seldom embezzlement, murder, rape or extortion. Perhaps these *gadže* crimes were minimised within a tight community, perhaps there was less opportunity. What marked out my *merchero*, I was told, was that his crimes had been violent and drug-related, unwarranted and little planned.

'Do you know of *El Lute*,' he asked in French?

'Everyone knows Eleuterio Sánchez,' I replied, waiting for him to get to the point.

'What do you know of *El Lute*?'

'He was poor, illiterate, and he went to prison for armed robbery of a jewellery store in Madrid. A security guard was killed. He escaped several times from prison and headed the 'most wanted' list. He was pardoned and I know him because he became a lawyer and a good writer. His stories of his life are most interesting.'

My recalling this much made him angrier. '*El Lute* was my grandfather and, today, I am *El Lute*. He wrote *Camina o revienta*, Forge on or Die. This is my belief.'

I was losing patience and feeling a little reckless. The blows were coming. There was nothing I could do to stop them. My best chance against this young, experienced, but tired and battered, fighter was to make him mad and reckless.

'Have you read his book,' I asked? 'Can you read?'

'You,' he spat, 'are a *gadžo*. You are also a *cabrón*', although why he thought me a cuckold is hard to say. He was winding himself up. He drew an unpleasant knife from inside his jacket.

'Mierda. Jodor. Coño.' These were a crescendo of insults, but I had been insulted by experts and his words had less point than his knife.

'And you,' I said, 'are ugly and cannot satisfy a woman.'

'Ya está!,' he screamed and rushed me.

I took one step inside the swinging blade as he stumbled on the uneven ground. My plan was to grab his arm as it went past, turn him with my body weight and use his speed to throw him to the river-bank. Then, I would run as fast as I could, which was not so fast these days. The first part went better than expected, but there was a bonus as he slid down the slope to the water's edge. I made to flee, but noticed he wasn't lifting his head from the water. Then I saw a whisper of red that gathered pace. I waited for a moment then, against my better judgement, went down to him and rolled him over. The knife, to my satisfaction, was deep in his neck. He was dead.

I realised I was being watched. Ilia stood above me, his flies undone.

'I was waiting to see what would happen. I thought you were finished.'

He indicated the body. 'This is not good. *Mercheros* are unforgiving like the Albanians.'

'Ilia, I need your help. For all sorts of reasons I do not want to talk to the police, even though I have done nothing wrong. There were no witnesses except you. I guess you feel the same way?'

He nodded.

I used a large leaf to pull out the knife and threw it far out into the river. I then dragged the body until the racing water caught it and rushed it away, perhaps far from the camp and immediate discovery. There was no blood on the shore that I could see and nothing that said fight or murder. I washed my hands as I often did after a disagreeable episode.

'Find us a car to Perpignan. Now.'

Ilia ran off and came to me ten minutes later at our tent where I was packing. I exchanged greetings with sleepy neighbours, and said we were on our way. Our lift was a couple returning home to Marseilles. We spent the short journey in a mixture of silence and brief awed statements about La Capitana and the wonder we had witnessed.

Ilia and I shared a last coffee in the palm-filled main square. He went to the hole-in-the-wall for me for the last time and I gave him a bundle of euros. I thanked him for his friendship.

'I will take a plane today and leave France,' I told him. 'I am sad, but we will not meet again. It is best this way. You did not see the fight and the money will help you to stop having any memories.'

He agreed, stood up, shook my hand and walked off into the lunchtime crowds. I swear there was a little tear in the corner of his eye. I waited until he was out of sight, walked around for a while to make sure he wasn't watching and made my way to the station and my luggage. There was a train to Barcelona just after three o'clock and I paid cash for a second-class ticket for the eighty-minute trip. There was no incident. At Barcelona, I left the station, found a toilet in a café, changed my shirt and trousers, bought a baseball cap from a stall outside, and went back to the ticket office by another door. The high-speed trains to Madrid were every half an hour and this time I travelled first class. I thought of Bashō again:

> *As firmly cemented clam-shells*
> *Fall apart in autumn,*
> *So I must take to the road again,*
> *Farewell, my friends.*[53]

Every mistake in my life has been met by an attitude, either right or wrong. What was tragedy for one man was not always so for another if he could assume the right attitude. I did not think I had done anything wrong except to run. I never felt guilt, never let what had happened trouble me. Madrid and its museums were always on my list of places to go and the inconvenience of a quick departure had been slight. I realised some people might see this as odd. Most people would have experienced insomnia, bad dreams, after being involved in a violent death, but I did not. He was a *coño*. The world was best rid of that self-appointed *El Luce*. His body might never be found and, if it were spotted soon, then perhaps it would be far away from where he died. After being bumped around and picked by crabs and carrion birds the knife wound might not be spotted. I did not imagine that the chief of police for Tarérach would seek unnecessary work. Knife crime would be rare, just about unheard of except that once in a while a fight might take place among the Gypsies who sometimes camped out of town, made a living from their horses, and enjoyed flamenco.

12. RUN TO FREEDOM

'That corpse you planted last year in your garden,
'Has it begun to sprout? Will it bloom this year?
'Or has the sudden frost disturbed its bed?
'Oh keep the Dog far hence, that's friend to men,
'Or with his nails he'll dig it up again!'[54]

The death of the *merchero* was a message, writ clear. If I had stayed in a comfortable hotel in Perpignan, it would have been bad luck to get involved in some unpleasant incident. What I had done was a world away. I had sought out a band of travellers in the company of an Albanian with a questionable background and gone with him to a remote woodland and crashed a party of Gypsies, people who lived on the edge. Why? Because I was curious about tribal habits and customs. Because I had a thing about nomads from when I was a boy and their lives always fascinated me? And . . . because I loved flamenco.

When I was young, I used to think that life was a thing that got richer and deeper each year. At the beginning, it often does when you explore boundaries, learn more and gain insights. Today, I know it's not like that for me. I don't get any wiser, just more wary. I enter new situations, appreciate them for what they are, but I compare with what I have done before, make connections and build houses of thoughts like playing cards. I let them stack how they will and because there are so many cards to use I can end with stacks which are unusual or, at least, I think they are. Somewhere, somehow, in conversation, or painting or music or books, someone has probably been there before. It's just me that hasn't got to that experience yet. When I do, my small discoveries might add a little value or, if not, look sadly tawdry and second-hand. And collapse at the slightest push.

I wanted to spend time in Madrid, enjoy the city and surrounding area, as I had done over winter in Perpignan. I decided to take a week in a central hotel, test the idea, and then find an apartment, one where I could pay cash and not have to register. My approach in each new town was to use one passport for hotel registration, when it was necessary, and to pay cash for the deposit and to settle up. For all other activities, I used a credit card to get money, and used the same card for payments only when necessary. My logic was that, if I had to leave in a hurry, only one card might be compromised. This, I believed, had not happened yet.

I chose the Hotel Mediodia in the Plaza Emperador, close to the Atocha railway station and within walking distance of the main museums. The receptionist was most helpful over their security procedure. My passport was slid into a machine reader that automatically populated the hotel registration form I had to sign. The machine was not sophisticated enough to copy the passport picture, nor did it connect to the police reporting system. Like most European countries, a daily list of guests with identification details had to be sent to a central police record. In Madrid, that meant that the receptionist had to re-enter the information. If the receptionist had a busy evening and then went for a sleep, or felt lazy, the data may not be forwarded until after the morning check-out rush. The police could not start checking the city's visitors until well into the following day. It was all good to know.

I spent my first day at the Sabatini Building of the Reina Sofia Museum, part of the city's dedication to modern art and which, I suspect, will leave most visitors with mixed feelings. It was chilly and, as I was early, it was coffee, croissant and orange juice in a corner café of the large square fronting the entrance. Sabatini was an architect from Palermo loaned by the bad Bourbons from their court of the Two Sicilies in Naples. At the death of King Carlos, the building was unfinished, but became the Hospital de San Carlos which functioned until 1960. It was then abandoned until rescued at the turn of the century to become a museum. I mention all this because from my coffee table this home of examples of the best of what today's world can produce is viewed across a soulless concrete graffiti-filled space. Its eighteenth-century neoclassical façade, best described as 'sombre', supports two monumental towers in steel and glass containing the public lifts. Even the museum's own publicity can't raise much enthusiasm for these monstrosities, designed by 'rationalist architects'. The operation to facilitate tourism whilst maintaining architectural integrity has killed the patient. As to the public square, intended as a second courtyard for the hospital, the combination is a call to stay away.

As I shuddered, an elderly gentleman in an overcoat, scarf and panama hat, despite the heat to come, sat at the table next to me.

'A piece of excrement,' he offered.

'What a waste of an important space,' I replied.

'To my mind,' he said, ordering an espresso, 'it must be kept as it is and the architectural students of Madrid should be made to enter an annual competition to turn this abomination into a vibrant place that people might seek to visit.'

'There are not many trees,' I thought out loud, 'but the orange juice is good.' A small gang of screeching skateboarders rattled past.

We went into the Sabatini and spent the next hour together. Not far from security and the information desk there are some portentous statements on plaques introducing various works. Our favourite claimed that culture was a way of making up for 'interactive pleasures', or even taking their place if we cannot 'reach' them. There is a lot of 'reaching' going on these days. A helpful list suggested pleasures that might be 'reached' including personal relationships, touch, physical contact and the wind. I confessed I was always confused by this type of statement, not so much for what they say, or try to say, but that behind them there is an intelligence, and one assumes a selection committee, that thinks in these terms and finds them valuable.

'I often consider this plaque,' said my comrade. 'It is for me depressing because it speaks of art as a substitute and it is aimed, I fear, at people who are not comfortable with their lives, who do not seek to experience the world. They will be happy to be told that art is for them to use to reduce their loneliness.'

'It is the perfect internal companion to the square outside,' I offered.

I said that I had come first to see *Carmen* and I was led to the inner garden that defines the Sabatini. We circled the sculpture three times. It stood motionless as there was no wind, and we settled onto a green slatted garden bench for a longer view. Parties of small schoolchildren with notebooks came with harassed teachers, stood for less than a minute, then moved on.

A mobile that is not moving has its limits.

The courtyard was a pleasure with trees grown through the grass in contrast to the surrounding galleries, all supported by broad stone pilasters. Some, not enough, were open to natural light as originally intended.

The Reina Sofia is not renowned for its celebration of Spanish Gypsy art, but in *Carmen* it makes small amends. Designed by American Alexander Calder out of aluminium and iron sheet it is large and confident. It has four flared skirts painted black that narrow well above head height to support eight riveted blades in orange and yellow which move in the air.

'I do not think this is a great work,' said my new friend, 'but I find it interesting and relaxing.'

'I have just come from a *juergas*, a Gypsy gathering in the north,' I said and wondered whether I had made an error with my free sharing of information. 'A young woman from Barcelona danced there. She was compared with Carmen Ayala. She was electric. The *duende* was tangible.'

I knew that, for Calder, *Carmen* was not meant as a tribute, but as an independent work. It was finished in the year before his death. I didn't agree with his protestation; I had seen the real thing. This was a black-gowned metal Carmen stamping her foot.

'You have experienced La Capitana. I have not and I envy you,' said my companion. 'I should remind you that Jean-Paul Sartre said that Calder does not "suggest" anything, but captures what he called "living moments". He said that mobiles have no meaning, but make you think of nothing but themselves. "They *are*, that is all; they are *absolutes*." However, I feel the strength of your *duende*. I award you the argument against Monsieur Sartre.'

I nodded in acceptance.

'Now', he said, 'I have a class to give. I hope I have your permission to mention our thoughts to my spotty inmates. In that way, I shall find out if we have been right or mistaken due to a combination of age and capitalist intransigence. And, by the way, my great-grandfather was the architect Ricardo Velazquez Bosco who was part-builder of the Palacio de Velázquez in the city's Parque del Buen Retiro, an annexe of this museum. Please visit. I do believe that an Englishman will find the structure convivial although I cannot vouch for the artistic content.'

A pleasure. One of those delightful ships in the night.

I found Pataut's exhibition from Saint-Denis on the third floor. His photographs were conspicuous because of the length of their display along one white-washed wall. I don't know what I expected, but I immediately recognised some of the faces in the small prints. I was back in 1993 and it was easy to contrast the bad, which had been done because of my visit the previous year to France's glittering sporting monument.

I started to cry, sobbing the while, and had to find a piece of wall to lean on. Was this to do with Tarérach a few days ago or Paris long past? There were two other viewers, so embarrassed by my tears that they left. I stayed for an hour and thought of my small personal and ultimately useless rebellion against the god of football. I wondered what had become of all these proud, hard-working people?

I made my way by the efficient external lift to the fourth floor and a collection speciously titled, 'Is the War Over? Art in a Divided World'. I was clucking my way at speed though works which claimed to 'recuperate the avant-garde in the early years of Francoism' when a small woman, perhaps in her forties, covered in layers of multi-coloured silks that seemed to give off their own light, approached and stood close by.

'It's a mistake to start at the top,' she opined. 'One ends up by being depressed. And for what purpose? Only to end up on the first floor paying homage to *Guernica* and realising that everything that is being said up here has already been said much better down there by Picasso in one painting.'

'There was I thinking that we were going to have a disagreement,' I replied. 'Which do you find the more depressing up here, the subject or the quality of work?'

'Most of it, how would you comment, is intellectual shit. But, as to war, what can a woman say? My grandparents were killed by the Republicans. It was an irony as they were both against Franco, but they were in the wrong place. The Communist diehards were careless with their bullets and keen to make examples.

'So, while the subject is awful, it is real. It is what men like to do from time to time. Manipulated they may be by the landowners, the rich, the catholic church, and the big companies, but they always turn up in their eager battalions to follow some flag or other and to kill each other.'

I told her I had just published a history book on the First World War, and thought again how easily I was giving identity information away to strangers. I said that I was appalled even at the distance of one hundred years at how much Prussian militarism had been embedded in the German leadership.

'You can see the residue even today,' I ventured.

She turned and looked at me full in the face. 'What is the smell of it, do you think?'

If you have researched at length the Great War, this is not such a wrong-footing question.

'Every time I opened a box of original records, rarely viewed, there was a disconcerting scent that is all its own. It was acrid, fragile, but persistent. There are hints of blood and pain and chlorine. There is a longing. It is pervasive and frightening.'

'You have been there,' she said. 'I would add lonely, but then I am not a man and have not experienced the comradeship that I read comes with killing. I think, also, that you have had first-hand experience of violent death and not just once. It is in the back of your black eyes.'

Now, may I suggest, we escape from this floor that reeks of a lack of experience and that I buy you a coffee, you tell me about your book, and that we share our moment with Signor Picasso.'

To find *Guernica* you follow the crowds. One tip, said my guide, was to stand at both sides in turn rather than only in front, which we did. The blues, blacks and greys give an interesting perspective of the horror of the Nazi's casual bombing of the Basque town. The bull remains dominant, signifying, said Picasso, brutality and darkness; the hard-working and terrified horse standing for the people. Some critics call the painting the *Mona Lisa* of our age, which seems a little far-fetched. I was intrigued, given the subject of the paintings and pottery, that in early photographs showing him at work, Picasso is dressed in collar and tie. There were some other Picassos about, second-rate, I thought. Thank God for Miró who was abundant.

'Have you noticed how much more space is given on walls and in rooms for modern art?' she said as she left me. 'Some of them are like an oasis in a giant white wall of desert. When a work becomes accepted, venerated, and then an old master, it is crammed together with other masterpieces so that there is no room to breathe.'

'Except in Japan,' I ventured.

For a few seconds, I visited the attached Nouvel Building, modern, administrative, uninspiring and walked to the park. Bosco's Palacio was a delight, the main pavilion for an industrial exhibition in the 1880s. It was all spacious floors, vaulted ceilings, iron structure and natural lighting. I was sitting on the Ganges-style steps at the front that led to the lake when a group of Spanish schoolchildren came and scattered nearby away from their teachers. Crisps and fizzy-drink cans appeared. I was captured in conversation as they asked if they could practise their English. I told them that their palace followed the example of a famous Crystal Palace in London that had been a successful exhibition centre thirty years before this one. I had that morning met the great-grandson of its architect called Bosco.

'Is your palace still there?'

'No. It was moved and then it burned down in a great fire that started in an office.'

'How big was it?'

'Three times larger than London's biggest cathedral.'

'Is any of it still there?'

'The best bit remaining is a dinosaur park. The models are quite old and many of them are inaccurate because we know much more about dinosaurs now, but it is still a remarkable place.'

'Did you see the fire yourself?'

'No, I wasn't born in 1936, but Winston Churchill was there.' I was not sure that they had heard of him.

And then they were gone, disappearing like burbling water.

I felt that in my contacts that morning, I was the classic case of the person who tries to swim away from the mainstream, to go far away, perhaps not to be anonymous, but to be free – no phone, no name on the house, no taxes – and then to discover that the world beats a path to his door, making him conspicuous. I thought of B. Traven in Mexico and J. D. Salinger in New Hampshire in the USA. Wherever one goes, the past is always all around.

I took my evening meal alone in *La Andaluza*, a restaurant in Calle Atocha, which leads up the hill from the station and the hotel. It had a garden growing from its ceiling. Amid the *tabla Ibericos*, *calamares* and *cervesa*, I fell to musing about organic traces from the *merchero* and other bodies I had come across. Central to the little I knew about police investigations were the forensic theories of Edmond Locard, a pioneer criminologist who began his career in the Lyon police department in 1910. I came across him during my research into the First World War. He worked for the French secret service attempting to identify causes and locations of death by examining stains and damage to soldiers' and prisoners' uniforms. He was a godfather to the study of fingerprint pores and stated that if twelve specific points were identical it would be sufficient for positive identification.

Locard's 'Exchange Principle' is still taught in police colleges around the world. This theory relates to the transfer of trace evidence and dictates that when two objects come into contact each will take something from the other or leave something behind. Unless an incriminating object had been found, like the knife in the river at Tarérach, touched by me with a leaf, or a wiped gun on the battlefield at Waterloo, then it all came down to these damned body parts. My security lay in that I believed no one was looking for me because no one knew my name or who I was.

However, I did leave the trace of a name every time I went to a cash machine or used a passport which contained my photograph. I worked through the options.

For photographs, I employed casual acquaintances like Ilia, the Albanian. Sometimes I pulled a cap down low over my face, although twice machines had failed to work when I did this. I deduced that some terminal cameras need to see a full face so I took to wearing large dark glasses and padding out my cheeks, probably like the assassin of Juncker and Selmayr. Should I buy a wig? I had destroyed all of the photographs of me as a child at home. But, there were bound to be others connected with my flying training, pilots' union card, marriages, as a journalist, as a driver, passports, as an author, pictures taken by people I had met on holiday. Perhaps I was in the background of collections of airmen in and around Biafra? My saving grace was that if I was identified on any of these, I was now none of these people nor used any of those names.

The two exceptions were the passports using my original name and my adoptive name, the latter attached to school photographs in which I would surely not be recognisable? Who would know of these now, as they were never used? There would have to be some exhaustive digging and some impressive lateral thinking.

Fingerprints? I wore gloves whenever I thought it necessary, always with cash machines. I wiped down hotel rooms with antiseptic wipes, but pound to a dollar, some greasy, single impressions had been missed. I relied on restaurants and bars to do their cleaning for me.

DNA? Hairs in bed? Faeces or urine? Sperm? Skin flakes? Sweat? Clothes, shoes and toiletries: these last items I changed every time I left a country. Nothing stayed with me. Microscopic evidence from the debris and dust of my life. Where would it end? Was this way of life, its relentlessness, getting to me? It was impossible to organise complete protection.

Blood? I had left the RAF before any unique records had been collected, I thought. They knew my height, weight, eye colour, but all in another name. I had missed one blood test that captured most of the North American and European population, including all of these in the UK, and constituted a hidden national database. Each new-born child since the 1960s receives a pinprick in a heel at five to eight days to gather a sample. Devised by Robert Guthrie in 1962, the blood was entered into pre-printed collection cards. It was intended as a test for bacteria, but newer techniques allowed it to be used to spot a variety of congenital diseases like sickle cell disorders and cystic fibrosis. The Irish realised in 1984 that hospitals were retaining the test cards without consent and had amassed a database of over a million people. In the UK, the requirement to destroy cards after five years is routinely sidestepped with parents unwittingly signing agreements that records can be kept for 'public health research' for lengthy and inconsistent periods. The UK's law enforcement agencies have been eyeing this treasure trove, but I knew because of my age, that whatever use was being made of the database, I wasn't in it. But, who knows what medical and dental records have been stored in some deep NHS basement and can be accessed by anyone with sufficient knowledge and a warrant?

And, finally, voice? Since early in 2017, the British tax office has been trying to force callers using its helplines to allow voiceprint recordings in order, ostensibly, to identify future contacts and to save identification time. In law, explicit consent is required to do this, but this is not requested in an honest or open way. The recordings are made with and without permission, and then analysed for voice patterns and rhythms, checking more than one hundred behavioural and physical vocal traits. The illegal database now stands at over five million individuals, the largest held by any state in the world. Despite a refusal to delete it, citing cost, HMRC has just been forced by law to do so by the UK Information Commissioner.

Banks have now started to use this process for telephone customers and all are powerless to reject instructions for assistance from government security services.

I try not to use my throw-away country-specific phones except for occasional checks for contacts from my UK credit card holders or the hawala bankers.

Dwelling on possibilities like these might make for better planning of my movements, but it does make you nervous and take away from the enjoyment of life.

My plan for the next day was to make an extensive revisit to the Prado, one of the jewels in Europe's crown. However, reacting to my restlessness, I resolved to take an unusual precaution. The next morning, I checked out of the Hotel Mediodia while at the same time making a reservation to return that evening, explaining that my travel plans were fluid and I needed to be flexible. I also bought a pre-paid ticket for the Prado from the concierge to avoid the queues. I took my case down to Atocha railway station and left it in a luggage locker by the tropical garden.

It was a casual stroll in the morning sunshine among the plane trees, trimmed box hedges and ornamental iron fences of the grass plots of the Paseo del Prado. After the security gate on the right of the Jerónimos entrance, I made my way upstairs to Caravaggio's *David with the Head of Goliath* with its exhilarating lighting, but cramped by other works.

After a fill of Greco, Tintoretto, Rembrandt, Goya and Tiepolo, I went back down to take a look at a work of Lucas Cranach the Elder, *Hunt at the Castle of Torgau*, painted in oil on a large panel in 1544. Cranach, a close friend of Martin Luther, delivered several similar works. They became his trademark with the Elector of Saxony, John Frederick the Magnanimous, showing himself off with his esteemed guests, this time Emperor Charles V, at a well-organised stag hunt in the extensive grounds. Lots of hounds with bared teeth dealt agonising bites to the beasts while driving them into an ambush of crossbows. The beautifully attired ladies are safely cordoned at bottom right taking turns at firing a dainty crossbow of their own, but aimed dangerously close to the Elector's wife, Sibylla of Cleves, seated in a punt on the lake. These fictional hunts were laden with political and allegorical meaning and symbolised good governance and the legitimacy and power of John Frederick. It was this emphasis on governance that I wanted to compare with a work on the same subject, an idyllic townscape completed two hundred years before, one of three fresco panels by Lorenzetti on display at the Palazzo Pubblico in Siena.

I was having a general muse about my own situation, the Cranach hunt and the Spanish enthusiasm for dramatic executions: Goya's *Third of May, 1808*, showing Napoleon's firing squad at work dealing with Spanish resistance to the army of occupation in the Peninsular War; and Gisbert Pérez's *Execution of Torrijos and his Companions on the Beach at Malaga*. Torrijos was returning from exile in England by way of Gibraltar in 1831 with supporters, members of the Liberal constitutional regime quashed by Ferdinand VII. The whole party was ambushed and captured. The huge painting is a cry for freedom dampened by the expressions of the captured men as they face their death: resignation, pride, defiance and fear of the end. The compositional and dramatic similarities between these two paintings interested me.

Out of the corner of my left eye, I noticed the *Mona Lisa* silently mocking. She was at the other end of a large rectangular room with a spacious wooden central bench. I had given up on the da Vinci sister painting in the Louvre in Paris because of the crowds just a few months before and seen Picasso's supposed comparison that morning. Here was a reinstated copy, realised for what it was a few years ago. There are dozens of replicas of the *Mona Lisa*, but this one modern radiography disclosed was likely painted by a student standing at the same time and alongside the great man and was thus drawn from a slightly different perspective. Da Vinci also suffered from nerve damage from a fall at this time, which turned his painting hand into a claw and forced him into the role of tutor which may explain why the version in the Louvres seems unfinished.

I turned back across the room thinking of a beer and sandwich and paused at a large vibrant-coloured triptych filling a wall. It was three of four tempura panels by Botticelli showing scenes from the story of *Nastigio degli Oresti* from Boccaccio's *Decameron*. It is a gory tale of a young woman who rejected her suitor and was unmoved by his suicide. She also died and was condemned to hell for her indifference: every Friday, she was chased and her heart ripped out and fed to mastiffs. Another hunt. Another punishment. I reflected on the irony of this work that was commissioned by a father for the marriage of his son. What message was being passed to the bridal pair?

I was distracted by a noisy disagreement coming from behind Botticelli's wall where the Cranach was on display. A severe lady guard, hair gripped in a bun, tight uniform skirt stretched over a large bottom, rose from her seat at the connection of the two rooms and sailed to reprimand. A woman came into sight, walking backwards, gesticulating and loudly arguing her defence. An unseen man was barking at her in Spanish. I went cold and backed into a corner near where a dog was ripping into a young lady's bare buttock.

I knew that Morningside precision very well: Morag, my companion from Waterloo and Paris. How on earth …?

I heard more words, muffled though concrete, and interrupted by shrill interventions from the security warden. Despite the sense being unclear, it was evident that the man and Morag were known to each other and were at the Prado together. Was there any way their and my visits could be co-incidence? Perhaps Morag was acting as a guide to a group of English or Spanish tourists? But the pair appeared to be alone.

The man said 'Geoff', clear as a ship's bell, and Morag was shaking her head and moving back out of sight. I had used this name just once and that was while with her. It did not appear on any of my cards or passports. Was I mistaken? Did she fleetingly catch my eye?

Two armed *madera*, members of the anti-terror squad in black combat uniform, approached the couple. I hunched my shoulders, pulled a cap from my bag, made by way into the next room, passing Raphael's *Cardinal* and his oddly named *Madonna of the Fish*. This was not a time to think, but a time to go. I walked firmly down a long corridor and through the inner courtyard of the Villanueva Building, brushing past a protesting doorkeeper and out into the blinding sunlight through the tall open door of the Murillo exit.

I paid no respect to the bronze statue of the great painter that blocked my path and cut straight across the hedges and marigold fillers to the gate of the *Real Jardín Botánico*. I decided that a walk through trees and shrubs was preferable to a return in plain view along the *Paseo del Prado*. The queue was short, but the teller seemed intent on having a conversation with each customer. I slapped down my fifty-cent charge for *personas mayores*, ignored the shouts to wait for my ticket, and set off down the central path that led towards Atocha railway station. Ignoring the monumental *Puerta del Rey*, built to allow King Carlos access to his hunting park, because it was padlocked and dangerous to climb, I kept going at a fast walk. My heart sank when I found there was no back gate but, faced with retracing my steps, I climbed a palm tree, stepping up trimmed leaf stems. I fell rather than slipped over the garden's rear wall and dropped heavily but unnoticed into the *Calle Claudio Moyano*. After a patient wait for lights at the pedestrian crossing, I was in Atocha.

Was it time to stop and reason? To be honest, it didn't cross my mind. It was half past two and I had choices – Pamplona, Malaga, Barcelona, Toledo, Seville ... and Renfe's all-year daily service to Algeciras at just after three o'clock. I realised that, despite an intention to visit the classic Spanish cities, especially in the south, the coast around Gibraltar was always my final European destination. I collected my bag, bought a first class ticket for cash for Cordoba and listened for the dual-language announcements. At Cordoba, I planned to buy another ticket to complete my journey to Algeciras, hopefully free of any cameras.

I was exposed on the upper platform waiting area so made for a café and a beer and jambon sandwich. Where would you be without jambon in Spain and a beer to quench the thirst that the salt brings? When the platform number was called there was a dash to form the queue, but with first class I could hold back, my comfortable reclining seat reserved and waiting. To the second, as in Japan, my express pulled out and I settled back for the over five-hour journey. I watched the grimier parts of graffiti-covered Madrid slide past and give way to the everlasting central plain, with its soft, rolling mounds, parched red earth, gorse bushes and olive groves.

Had I got away with it? What had Morag and her aggressive acquaintance got to do with each other? Perhaps it was chance meeting? I found this difficult to swallow. Was the man directing Morag? She had no skills, no knowledge, to enable her to seek me out. Was she even looking for me? The man's 'Geoff', the argument, the arrival of the police, all suggested she was. Or that someone had asked or told her to search? There seemed no connection between now and my meeting with her in Waterloo and that was a year ago.

Morag did not know that I might visit Madrid, I thought, although she could well have guessed. Certainly she did not know when, because neither did I. Had she been persuaded to help an investigation? For whom? Why? For money? I didn't believe she would willingly admit to her part in my travels. Did I imagine that she had caught my eye and protected me?

Was the connection to do with credit cards, visual recognition? And why go looking at the Prado? Had my hotel been found and the concierge interrogated? Was one of my credits cards and passport compromised?

Here, at least, I could fathom some logic: an expert profiler might be at work, a skill that was available to national agencies. If elements of my travels had been picked up, would they suggest a pattern? Well, yes, I was going south. I was travelling under assumed names. And I visited national museums, looking at famous art. And, if pieces of this were gathered together, wouldn't it make sense that sooner or later I would arrive at the Prado? Had my hotel reservation been forwarded too promptly to the police?

The trouble and expense of getting Morag to the Prado on the off-chance would be significant. That suggested my 'mistake', if there had been one, had been recent. If a loose profile had been built, it meant that my face might not be known. Why else would it be necessary for a civilian who had seen me to be coerced into joining the hunt? This smacked of a large organisation, one that had power, time and money. If someone had been made resolute by something that I had done; they were not about to give up any time soon. The situation was disturbing and the more so because I was no closer to identifying my actual pursuer.

No one bothered me at Cordoba although I sat ready to buy my ticket extension. While the city is most of the way to Algeciras, it is the next section of the journey as the train winds off the Castilian plateau and up and through the Andalusian hills and down to the sea that takes most of the time. It is also by far the most attractive. The track doesn't follow the road, but wet and dry river-beds, winding through narrow gaps and tunnels until it reaches the coastal plain. Here there is much in common with the south of England – gentle hills, fields, copses, a few sheep and the occasional pig, terracotta roofs, white-walled farms and ubiquitous eucalyptus, olive and cherry trees. The railway line was built in the 1890s by the British to provide recreational breaks for their officers garrisoned at Gibraltar. At its peak, six trains a day travelled the 110 miles passing twenty-two stations and costing six pence for a first class seat. Algeciras, a dust-heap of a town, needed suitable accommodation to greet its important passengers and the splendid Hotel Reina Cristina was built with its twenty acres of sub-tropical gardens overlooking a sandy beach. It was where I planned to stay.

As the express reduced to a crawl down the single track, I spent time approaching my dilemma from another direction. What did I know of the surveillance activities of government secret services, like those operating from the UK or the EU? Not very much.

Personal data should belong to individuals, not to governments that will use it to compile your every move. Since the General Data Protection Regulations of 2016 every person and their dog has been hounded by agreements to click this and that to allow recording of actions taken. The law is vague, badly written and a feeding trough for lawyers. In one sense little has changed. In another real sense, a lot has altered because now the terms and conditions must relate to the service being provided, for instance, a mapping service which had implicit agreement to access a phone's location cannot use the same 'ap' (or 'app' if you are Google looking to rebrand the abbreviation as its own) to download phone data and photographs.

That's all well and good for the technology companies. Governments in the UK and the EU are keen to legislate for commercial business, but do not wish to see any constraints on themselves and their ability to store any and all information about its citizens without permission. London's Metropolitan Police decided to ignore upcoming court cases and to deploy facial recognition on the city's streets in the middle of December. The UK government has been rebutted in its attempt to introduce a single standard ID card and so has been driven to many other devices to identify its citizens. Many might now view that ID card as much less intrusive than having to take a council tax bill, a driving licence and a passport into a bank manager before being able to open a bank account.

But the bulk personal data sets trawled by government are kept secret: they might well include telephone directories, the electoral roll, driving and vehicle licences, credit reference agency databases, national insurance numbers, tax and customs returns, welfare recipients, criminal records, passports, passenger flight records, Oyster card data ... Automated programmes are used to sift through billions of phone, mobile, internet and postal communications from the entire population every day. There is a growing ability to use sophisticated algorithms to collect information from street cameras, vehicle number plate cameras, phone records, medical records, financial transaction so as to anticipate an individual's next moves or, more directly, to use it to decide whether to offer a new job.

You think this is all pie in the sky? Never going to happen? You're safe because you never do anything wrong? Mistakes will easily be cleared up without real personal cost? Government can be trusted to get it right and not to misuse its powers?

Don't look over your shoulder. It's here. The foothills are inhabited. The peaks are being climbed. Algorithms are mathematical nightmares, based on abbreviated and often flawed logic and wishful assumptions, which more often target society's helpless, exacerbating inequality. They are opaque, unquestioned and unaccountable and operate at scale to optimise millions of people. The more privileged you are the more likely you will be processed by people rather than by machines.[55] Not so the poor. The human victims of algorithms are held to far higher standards of evidence than the algorithms themselves.

Any rules, agreements or laws can be overturned in secret in the name of national security. The Single Intelligence Account is the funding vehicle for the main security and intelligence agencies in the UK. In 2014–15, it spent over £2½ billion; that's a four-year-old figure. Counter-terrorism police have recently been given the finances to employ an extra thousand counter-terrorist spies, which, of course, I applaud. However, who knows how wide the definition of counter-terrorism may be allowed to spread? UK police treat legitimate campaigners and complainers in a similar way to their response to organised crime networks. They build profiles of the campaign groups, single out organisers for particular attention, visit them at home, film meetings and protests, and routinely monitor social media.

Would I, or any British citizen, stand a chance against this level of potential scrutiny? If a government was determined to find someone, they would likely succeed, but with someone who was trying hard to hide they would need to be knowledgeable, clever, well-funded and lucky.

Algeciras's new train station is bright enough, but the town is ramshackle. I had thoroughly upset myself by the time I arrived, ticket waived through and I decided on the third lower-level hotel I saw. I said that my passport was packed away and that I would bring it down later. By the time I left the next morning, I had forgotten to do so.

That evening, I decided to reminisce and walked up the road leading out of town to Seville. I came, a little out of breath, to the *Meson Las Duelas* where I had last been about fifty years before, a repeat visit and may be symptomatic of carelessness and danger. There were tapas at the bar again, friendly, cod and hot aubergine salad, sausage flamed in a terracotta pig, plates of acorn-fed ham and sausage, cheese, wine and a brandy; it was a perfect antidote to the day's distress. Even the music was to taste. The manager, part of the same family as my last visit, had put together a compilation of old gravel voice, Joaquim Sabina. After a final glass with the barman, I strolled down the hill at midnight. The town was empty, but with the occasional corner shop still open and discarded fast-food wrappers blowing in the wind and chased by rats and gulls.

During the walk, I finally agreed with myself on what I was going to do. The next morning, I would seek a favoured city with a comfortable apartment and try to write down what had been going on and what I had set out to do. If I could write my story well enough and get it published perhaps I could take the heat off. Everything would be in the open and there would be nothing more for anyone to attempt to cover up. If I had done the State some disservice, or they thought I had, I would write my words, then go. If I arranged it right, I would disappear once and for all. The hunt and the desire for my chastisement might diminish over time.

I would go back to Morocco.

13. FREEDOM TO WRITE

Who is the third who walks always beside you?
When I count, there are only you and I together
But when I look ahead up the white road
There is always another one walking beside you
Gliding wrapped in a brown mantle, hooded …[56]

PART 1 (MARRAKECH, AUGUST 2019)

Perhaps it would be wiser when I reached Morocco not to draw too distinct a line between dream and reality. I now understood that there is a lot more to being free than packing a suitcase.

Last year had been a retreat from the waste land of my life, beset by memories and petty intrusions, in which I enjoyed tilting at windmills. My delight in breaking bureaucratic chains often led the desire for personal freedom; what should have been aids had sometimes become aims. As I now felt I was a 'nobody', I hoped that my preoccupation with vulnerable identity would wane.

The Greeks had a word, autopsy, which embraced independence, the right to make up one's own mind based on what one's own eyes have seen. By the Middle Ages, autopsy was at war as authoritarians laid down their version of the natural world for all time; all further enquiry was seen as frivolous and often dangerous.[57] If discovery and reasoning revealed new worlds to the curious, these might be a blasphemy to be rooted out and their exponents punished. Today's rulers in government and commerce are little different. They seek to direct new knowledge in their own interests. They have a fear of the active individual because he may promote unruly competition, an attractive call for freedom; not dismissed today as blasphemous, but populist. Far better if the masses accept the enjoyment and comfort that is on offer.

In the South of France, I had been more alive. Clearly, there was a chase, from whom or why I did not know. But, despite the shock at the Prado, I felt that my sour preparations were working. It is a pleasant thing to be in a place where one can have at least an illusion that the individual is in charge. There is spiritual healthiness in the absence of patriotic emotion, indifference to tribal loyalties, and even rampant opportunism. I needed to concentrate on tomorrow, my mind calm, choices spontaneous, looking forwards, not backwards. I wanted a life based on a quest for knowledge and enjoyment, for challenge and comfort.

It was a fifteen-minute walk from my hotel to the ferry terminal. Algeciras is the second port in Spain and the third of the Mediterranean. From the time of the Muslim presence, *La Convivencia*, this was the crossing point to Tangier and North Africa. Despite it being May, the passenger areas early in the morning were all but empty, the few tourist cars queuing elsewhere. Before leaving the huge bay, all ships sail past the Rock of Gibraltar, not as dramatic as overflight, but well worth going out on deck. Passports are checked on board. A long snake formed to reach the two officers, bored but efficient, sitting at a table armed with a laptop to check online for undesirables. For the first time, I used my Bulgarian passport. The new port of Tangier is half an hour from the city and I was warned in the passport queue that after the short bus ride to the customs shed where baggage was scanned I should get Moroccan dirham at a cash machine in the terminal. If you had no lift arranged, be ready to bargain hard with the taxi drivers who would share the impending death of their starving children rather than accept the statutory 250 dirham fare. The tariff board can be found hidden under hanging jackets.

An urbane Frenchman behind me in the snake asked if I had a room booked. He saw me hesitate and explained that he managed an empty hotel. It was the lunar month of Ramadan and there was no need to pre-book in Morocco.

'No tourists,' he said. 'I'll give you an upgrade and free breakfast. If you don't like it, I promise you a taxi. You won't be disappointed.'

Two middle-aged Australian ladies standing behind him looked interested.

'Want to join us,' I asked. They checked with each other and nodded. 'Looks like I should get a bigger discount,' I suggested.

The hotelier's car and driver were outside. The worst of the sun was held at bay by the steady, all-day, sea breeze across the peninsular. Riad Mokhtard was down an uninspiring alley above the kasbah and through a large locked wooden door. It had a delightful fountain leading to a first room, highly decorated in the Islamic tradition, studded with modern art, and open to the air on one side. My refurbished room was of a high quality.

That evening, the two ladies and I walked in the dusty heat down the well-lit, busy hill of the rue de la kasbah to the Restaurant Hamadi, one of the few places to serve alcohol during Ramadan. We had to wait fifteen minutes while the staff ate their meal and broke their fast. Eating habits are turned upside down during the dedication to God through rejection of earthly needs: meals must finish before dawn which was recognised when black and white thread could be distinguished in the creeping half-light; no eating or smoking or water in the burning summer days; and, later, sitting with your loved ones and guests, meals prepared, waiting for the mosques, and the TV, to announce that the sun has fallen. Towards the end of the cycle, increasingly hungry and tetchy adherents gave up work and retired to bed with fatigue. Until the new moon was glimpsed and the fast ended, this was not a good time to be among dozing drivers in a country that has nine times more road deaths than the UK.

My new Australian friends, sisters, were introduced to harissa-flavoured harira soup and seven-vegetable couscous. Four septuagenarian musicians trooped out and the evening went well. As we climbed home, the ladies suggested that we continue the evening in their room and it was a delightful way to spend the late hours. It was a sexual relationship that broke at least three Moroccan laws.

Over breakfast at a table overhung by a lemon tree from which a fruit was picked for the pancake, I told the ladies that I was leaving that day. As my phone had been 'stolen' in Spain, they gave me their schedule and a phone number and we agreed that if our paths crossed while they were in Morocco, I would make contact. The hotel manager who joined us for coffee said that, for him, Casablanca had lost much of its charm. It was now a business centre for head offices of Moroccan companies and multi-nationals with a large building programme and apartment prices to match. I thought of Arabic Fez, but plumped for Berber Marrakech. This was emotion ruling the heart. I also thought that it would be easier to lose myself among the sizeable ex-pat community and thousands of tourists, and to find an amenable hawala banker.

With a bit of bustling, I got a taxi to the station, skirted the unfinished entrance hall, and caught the slow day train to Marrakech, changing at an all but deserted Sidi Kacem. I was soon involved in a discussion about French imperialism and was pressed to share some delightful snacks. I arrived mid-evening and walked to a small hotel where I was left to my own devices.

Marrakech is 'the Great Babylon of carnal lust, magic, tourism and beautiful sights'.[58] Later that evening, I went back to *Djemaa el Fna* for the first time for almost fifty years. I was not a tourist for I had come to live and work in the city. I was, I suppose, an observer. The square no longer held any secrets for me and the awe of my first night was replaced by something far more pedestrian. I was still heckled by orange juice sellers, pestered by men with Barbary apes on their backs, women trying to squeeze tubes of henna onto the back of a hand, or approached by water carriers and snake charmers who offered photo opportunities. The continual percussion is provided by Gnawa musicians, dressed in blue, wearing skull-caps decorated with tassels and cowrie shells.[59] The charmers, dancers and story-tellers were no longer beings from a different world, but hard-working people. I saw their efforts to attract audiences, the counting of sad takings, their efforts between performances to snatch sleep wrapped in a burnouse. I had changed, but the relentless influx of tourists had done its work as well. I watched the skimpily dressed amateurs haggle as they flirted with the ritual of bargaining, saving the price of a coffee and still paying twice the value.

The next morning, I hired a taxi with a driver who could speak French and told him that I needed an apartment to stay for a few months and asked him to drive around outside of the walls of the Medina. It took me a while to calm him down as he suggested luxurious hotels and guest-houses run by his many cousins. I told him I wanted somewhere self-contained, anonymous, no paperwork, no questions, with accepting neighbours. I found an area that I thought might provide what I wanted between the Ville Nouvelle and Guéliz, a corruption of 'Les Églises'. On the Avenue Mohamed V, one of the wide French-colonial boulevards book-ended by roundabouts, near a Royal Air Maroc office, the driver pulled over to check with a man who sat on a chair by the entrance to a block of offices and flats. The man made a phone call and I was told that Kamal would find me at *Le Grand Café de la Poste* in thirty minutes. Morocco is a land of connections. People pass you on with your requirements until your needs are met or you tire of the search.

The café, with its 1950's renovation, exuded colonial decadence at its best. I found a seat outside among the shrubs. Kamal was only ten minutes late, a modern suit, logos everywhere about his accessories. He was a young man on the move for whom a week was always too short. He told me that his mother had been a Muslim refugee from Srebrenica, a great beauty, quickly snapped up by his father, a Berber tribesman who owned many date palms in a distant oasis. Kamal checked first that I wasn't American.

'Three thousand Americans die,' he said, 'and it changes history. Eight and a half thousand Muslims are murdered at Srebrenica and it's forgotten.'

'I'm sorry for what was done at Srebrenica,' I offered. 'Did your family suffer any personal loss apart from having to flee?'

'No, we all got out, but we lost our house and our land. Many cousins died. I carry resentment in the family's honour.' We ordered some very sweet mint tea poured from a great height for aeration and infusion.

'Death from war is in decline,' I mused. 'I read that in 2012, war and the like killed 120,000 people, many fewer than I thought, especially when compared to the half a million who died due to violent crime. Both those pale beside the 800,000 who committed suicide in the same year. If you add all of those together, you get to one and half million, the number who died from diabetes. Sugar is now more dangerous that an AK-47. For the American, *Coca Cola* poses a far deadlier threat than al-Qaeda.'[60]

We ordered another tea and began business. Illegality was assumed. Kamal let out his black-market flats to couples seeking a quiet few days away from people who might report their pre- and post-marital affairs. He also managed a good trade with small business offices and migrant and international workers looking for a short-term stop-over away from the tourist hotels.

Kamal and I nodded to the man in his chair as we made our way past him, the forty locked letter boxes, and up to the third floor, 'lift fixed tomorrow': two bedrooms, living room, Wi-Fi, shower, bathroom, small balcony overlooking the main street. Kamal wanted 1,500 euro a month in advance in cash, no receipts, no taxes. Building maintenance was included and so was Aisha who would come one morning a week to fly about the house in her baggy drawers, her arms full of washing or buckets and brooms. She seemed honest, clean and willing. Everything was nearby, but with none of the *souq*: small business shops, car hire, laundry, restaurants, banks, vegetable, meat, fruit, date and nut stalls, café tables with idling men, more locals than foreigners, sitting inside colonnaded street-side tiled passageways. And, of course, always men on chairs guarding entrances, watching, noticing, looking for deals. The area was unkempt, but it suited me. There was even a Credit du Maroc cash machine by the front door and across the nose-to-tail avenue was Carre Eden, a newish tourist department store with an expensive Carrefour food supermarket on the ground floor.

Only birth can unshackle the chains of an old identity, not the rebirth of the old identity, but the birth of something not immediately apparent. One must find comfort in a place that is embraced for what it is, not inspected for what it is not. I needed to look within myself for an inner peace that allows curiosity and friendships.

First, I needed to write that book. Which small part of my writing might be important enough to stop the pursuit? I bought a laptop and borrowed the son of the shop's owner to install what I wanted and to connect to the internet. I used this internet connection for research and to jog my memory and make encrypted contacts against official interference.

It was best to assume that the Moroccan authorities mirrored the UK police and intelligence agencies in their ability to hack into any part of any system, including home computers, to watch, to change or to destroy data without the user knowing. This includes cameras, microphones, data and passwords. Internet companies are legally required to store the who, what and when of all communications. When a security organisation is not sure who it is targeting, international bulk warrants are issued for six months.

I established some email addresses at three local internet cafés and used two of them to set up cloud storage with different host companies. I invented complex passwords that were easy to remember. Four random common words, for instance, '*correct horse battery staple*', give a high level of uncertainness. While being easy to remember, they are difficult for another computer to guess, compared to, say, '*Troub4dor &3*', which is difficult to remember but is easy to guess. The four-word example needs up to 550 years at one thousand guesses a second to break while the password '*Troub4dor &3*', which would receive high on-line approval ratings with its capital letter, punctuation, space and numerals, can be broken in just three days at the same rate. I also invested in a memory stick that was set up with a paper-clip-like device that with a strong push in an emergency made it unreadable. Each day, I loaded my work on the stick while deleting it from the computer and took it to a café and uploaded the content to the clouds. At the same time, if necessary, I sent my rare coded financial emails. A pay-as-you-go phone cost just pennies from a market stall. Mine looked like it had a number of previous owners, some of whom may have mourned its loss.

Feeling in need of company, I broke one of my firm rules and called the number left me by the Australian sisters. They had arrived in Marrakech yesterday afternoon by train from Casablanca, disappointed by the stage-set *Rick's Café*. There was a brief private discussion before they agreed they would be delighted to have dinner with me that evening. I arranged to meet them at *Le Tanjia*, an up-market restaurant near the Bahia Palace serving slightly westernised Moroccan dishes. I thought they might enjoy the belly dancing, inauthentic, but erotic none-the-less and, hopefully, suggestive.

It was a delightful meal if slightly marred by the revelation that one sister was a sergeant in the Australian major crimes squad in Sydney, the other a senior tax inspector. Both were recently divorced and had decided to catch up on some of the life they thought their marriages had denied them. I made up stories of my life and my small family back-street riad. I thought they knew these were false, but seemed happy to go along. They were great fun and it was the evening of laughter that I had hoped. Mid-way through the dancing gyrations between the tables, I felt a hand on each of my legs and knew that the enjoyment of Tangier would be repeated. There was one incident as the bill came which gave pause. I reached for my wallet and began to count out the cash. With police-like curiosity, I was asked why I had no credit cards.

'It suits my life-style,' I confessed.

She gave me a hard look. 'With my job, you have to be careful who you mix with. Is there anything I should know?'

'You're safe with me,' I countered. 'I have secrets, but I don't have a guilty bone in my body.'

'We'll have to check that out closely,' she grinned and I took her to mean later in their bedroom.

In the morning, I squired them around the city sites, and could not avoid my photograph being taken several times. I broke another rule that evening, although they didn't know it, when I took them to a restaurant below the L'Eaudyssée spa, not far from my home. The place has a high reputation because it receives its fish fresh each morning from Essaouira, the old port city of Mogador. Over grilled sole, I told them that I intended to visit Essaouira for the fish and because it was the centre for modern Moroccan painters who sold their canvasses in numbers of collectives in the Medina. They insisted that we three went together for a short visit.

Later the following day, in a small adventure, we went to the central station for the four-hour local *Trans Intissar* bus. I bought the tickets at the window from which the driver received a five-dirham cut, but there was a much greater sales activity at the vehicle. The Arab crew, driver and mate, shouted their destination, competing with the other buses. People got on even as the bus backed and twisted through the crowded yard and into the street. Visiting relatives and friends delivered last-minute packages and wishes; hawkers pushed through with food, water, cakes, cigarettes and live chickens. As we squeezed out of the gates, the mate leant out of the always open door, shouting, 'Essaouira'. Pick-ups were made anywhere and everywhere. Once outside the city gates, the fares and drop-offs became negotiable. There were now no tickets and the income was divided between the crew with the mate holding different value notes folded lengthways between his fingers. Goats and sheep went below in the luggage space.

It was a good visit with less pressure in the sea-side *souqs*, a cooling breeze, many good restaurants and a lively arts scene. We took an express coach back to Marrakech and arranged to meet again for an aperitif before a final dinner. Sometimes it is best to follow your instincts. Mine was not to go and I didn't, but retreated to my apartment. I never saw or spoke to them again. I treated my home as a walled fortress for secrecy, privacy and tranquillity.

Finding a UK publisher was much easier than I expected. The deal was simple. I pre-paid the company £5,000 which was theirs to keep whatever the outcome. I gave them access to one cloud storage and I would send a brief comfort email at the end of each month. They agreed to open the file only in two circumstances: one, by specific instruction, or, two, if they had not heard from me for over two months. In both cases, they could then read the book and decide whether they just wished to publish it on my behalf or, if they wished, a fifty/fifty deal in which case they would invest equivalent money to promote the book and to share the profits. They were to handle all editing, design, legal approvals and marketing on my behalf.

For the first week, I arranged my work-table with the obsessive neatness that goes with the start of a project. I stared at the blank screen and sank into lonely forgetfulness. I daydreamed that I was on the bank of the River Lethe in the Greek underworld waiting to enter Elysium. The virtuous dead had to drink from the river until their memories were erased and they could be reincarnated.

Without expectation one ordinary morning, I began typing at speed. With each page, I felt another piece of worry lift. When I read the day's effort and made corrections, it was like I was reading someone else's story. The evening walk to the internet café enabled me to call in at *Le Grand Café de la Poste* for a relaxed aperitif which, like all alcohol, had to be drunk indoors and off the street. I began to make acquaintances, local people, more professional than artisan, who could afford the café's prices. My early impression was that Moors have three kinds of face, Arab, Berber and Negroid, which was accurate so far as it went, but I soon recognised infinite varieties within these types. Most negroes were descended from slaves brought north for sale by the Tuareg. Favourite and freed slaves often rose to positions of great power, and the interbreeding was so constant and continuous that there are few Moroccan families who can be certain of their bloodline. A hundred years ago, a rich man would have, say, a hundred children by his concubines and of these a full half would probably be part black.[61]

I began a nodding friendship with Moha, the security guard who sat each day on his chair at the entrance to the apartments. He checked people in and out and dreamed of his youth. He had been in the Morocco Border Force and, aged sixty, had retired. I took to slipping him a packet of cigarettes and asked him to let me know of anything unusual or if anyone made enquiries about me.

On a mercilessly hot day I came out for food and as I leant forward to shake Moha's hand my neck pendants dropped out of my T-shirt. The horsehair string carried two silver memories, the Berber *aza* and the *Hand of Fatima*, given to me by another Moha fifty years before. The mementoes were one of two pairs of remnants of my past life that I could not bear to leave behind; the other was from Nairobi, two furry animals, an elephant and a pig. Achilles' heels perhaps? What harm could pendants do? They had become so much a part of me that I thought little of it as I began to push them back out of sight. But Moha noticed and took hold of them and gazed at them with his brown eyes set deep in the folds of his desert-creased face. He said nothing and I went on my way.

At the end of the first month, the *sharqi*, a hot and dry wind blew in from the Sahara for three days. The temperature soared to almost fifty degrees. My skin had a film over it and someone called it 'an eddying whirligig of heat laden with grit'. Everyone hid their faces in the hoods of their djellabas if they moved outside so I bought some and, anonymity apart, approved of their comfort and partial protection. The *sharqi*, lungs filled with desert sand, attacked without respite. It was appalling. People from the coast said that anyone who came to Marrakech in the summer was mad.

I slept badly and I turned my sleeplessness to account by starting to learn Arabic.[62] I learned the triliteral root and that the consonants, k, t, b, for example, represent the basic idea of writing. I know that by sprinkling vowels here and there, long ones that you must take the trouble to write and short ones which are indicated by little flicks, stops and flying commas, and by the addition of certain consonants, the various parts of speech are formed. It is neat and complicated, like the laying of mosaics of which the Moors and I are so fond. One night, when I was in bed battling with all this verbal geometry, my attention was distracted by the strangest of sounds. They were not alarming, not even loud, but they troubled the air, and I could neither sleep nor write.

The heat lifted and I re-established my routine. As I came out towards sunset, Moha gave me a wave and called out a polite, *'La bes?'* How's everything? The storks had stopped circling and making their rachet-like calls as I walked to the *Café de la Poste*, where the small ceremony of the mint tea was performed. It was time to relax. I waited for old and new friends to begin conversation. When I got home, I asked Moha if he would care to take tea with me tomorrow and it became a weekly affair. I found that he lived in the Medina with his wife and a last daughter, aged thirty-five, who worked at a riad close to their home and who was finally to be married.

'A great blessing and a relief,' I was told. 'Perhaps there will be grandchildren?'

Moha's last posting was in the desert, a sergeant leading a five-man patrol on the border with Algeria. For several years, he took his Jeep out from an oasis in the Drãa Valley, loaded with food, water and bivouacs, and used his binoculars, radio and satellite connections with Rabat, watching by night for smugglers, terrorists and West Africans who hoped to enter Europe illegally. Up to twenty people cram into the back of a pickup truck with a water ration of just five gallons each and pit their trust in well-paid, but unskilled, guides. They drive across the desert away from well-trodden routes. Sometimes they stray too far and never return.[63]

Moha's team slept in the shade of the rocks while the sun was up. After a week, they drove to their military base at Errachidia and hit the cafés for another seven days. He knew the trails of the desert borderland and the men who used them.

As our *atay*, 'Whisky Bèrbere' was poured from on high in respect at Moha's favourite café, he asked me if I would care to have dinner with him at his home. He said that he wanted me, a nomad of the heart, to meet a son of a second cousin, a doctor, who would be visiting Marrakech from the country. I felt this was a great honour and was humbled to accept.

The following Friday, I went home to the Medina with him. The front door was typical, wooden with no outward signs of wealth which would be rude to neighbours, insulting even, while spending on the inside of a home was seen as a proper and good investment. The downstairs apartment, looking out onto a small, shared fountain courtyard, was cushion-filled and comfortable. Moha brought forward his distant relation, Aderfi, a vigorous man in his late fifties of wide education, dressed in Berber clothes. Moha's wife, briefly introduced, served yoghurt and then couscous with seven vegetables and hard-boiled eggs in one great bowl of food which we pinched with our thumbs and two forefingers. The sauce was a strong and thick harissa which brought tears to my eyes. The daughter played on a lute in the background, 'to make the stomach happier'.

After the meal was cleared, a large samovar was brought and the women retired to eat. I was offered some hashish from a little tin box. I scooped out a ball of the black paste, cannabis jam, *majoun*, and sucked with reverence. I asked if the two men had visited the mosque that day. Aderfi explained with a dry smile that Berbers belonged, as did all Morocco in name, to the religion of Islam, though among the remoter tribespeople there had always been those who clung secretly to an older, polytheistic worship with its blood sacrifices to sacred trees, streams and stones.[64] A simplified version of the laws of the *Qur'an, El H'aoudh*, was written for country Berbers in Morocco a few centuries ago, and it still made perfect sense today,

One may be excused from Friday prayers and from praying with the Imam if there is a great deal of mud or if it is raining very hard. One may also be excused because of elephantiasis, leprosy or old age, or if one has no clothes to put on or is waiting to be pardoned for a crime, or if one has eaten onions. These are valid excuses. A wedding feast is not an excuse, nor is blindness if one can feel one's way to the mosque.

Aderfi then came over to me and asked if he could see my necklace with its two pendants. I tugged them out for him.

'Moha was right,' he said and his face lit with a broad smile. 'You wear the gifts of my father's brother. This is an important sign to us. I think you do not remember me from a long time ago when I was a small boy leading mules piled high with crates. You are Philippe although it seems that this is no longer your name?'

It was an odd moment. I had not known Aderfi well, had talked to him as a child, but he joined together elements of my life as if the intervening fifty years had never happened. His father, Anaruz, had lived a long life and was found dead in a crevice on the mountain slopes, at peace with his carbine cradled in his arms and his black goats all around. Idir became a sought-after mountain guide among French tourists and died trying to reach an injured climber who had slipped on a rock face in a sudden blizzard. It was not far from the site of an old plane crash. Idir never married and was determined to honour his father by sending at least one of his brothers to university and saved his money to that end. Aderfi had repaid his love by studying hard and becoming a doctor, staying away from the big city medical institutions and running remote clinics among Berber communities on the fringes of the desert.

'You will know,' continued Aderfi, 'that we have a great tradition of stories told by the older men around the campfires. Of course, new stories are added as many of our people still cannot read or write. One of these stories is of a mythical man called *Feep* who came to Morocco in the night in a blizzard. He had great wings and was a friend of Atlas, another god who 3,000 years ago placed the mountains where the earth meets the sky to hold it up. *Feep* landed on those mountains and brought riches to the Berber people making their lives easier and safer. At least, that is the story told in *Djemaa el Fna* by the sightless old men. I tell it myself when I visit the oases. And the men show me their French guns, the ones that are still carried and used by the farmers, goat-herders and nomads in the Atlas mountains and the Sahara. And they shout the name, *Feep*, one who disappeared never to be seen again. I have a French carbine myself that I keep in my 4x4. It used to belong to my father. Moha has one, too.'

It was quite a story and I had to close my slackened jaw.

'I agree that Philippe has long disappeared,' I said, 'but I have heard of him and am pleased that *Feep* still brings comfort to your people. As Moha knows, I am here to write a book. I am being sought by enemies. I don't know who they are, but I think there are people who would be happy to see me dead. I hope the book may persuade these enemies to let me go. So, I am living carefully in my apartment in Marrakech, working hard, and Moha is the lion who guards the door.'

Everyone agreed that Moha was a true lion, even though he was missing some teeth. I felt emboldened to ask Aderfi if he would join me in a day's pilgrimage to the village of Imlil and then a hike up towards the summit of Tibherine. He smiled and agreed, adding that there was a cave he would like to visit, for old time's sake.

By the third glass of tea there was no doubt that the hashish had begun to take effect. I laughed at one response, perhaps a little strangely, since the others also laughed. I felt the distancing, but I also felt an old sensation, lost since Nairobi, of an inner peace, of family. All at once the room, the seated figures, the shoes ranged by the door, the fountain beyond, were remote and unlikely, although I remained aware of each word being spoken. I lay back on the cushions.

'What will you do when you have finished your book? Where will you go?'

'I have become a nomad. I have no home, but I know a place far away that I want to visit again before I die. To get there, I want to go first to Timbuktu. I want to go by caravan. I want to go with friends who will guide me; people of the desert who also wish to experience the old ways again before they are forgotten. I want to become a 'wanderer in the scorching and barren wilderness of this world'.[65] I would like to try to rediscover my humanity while I disappear, leave nothing behind, no trail for others to follow.'

Aderfi and Moha exchanged a long look. 'I think we can help you. It will be our duty and our pleasure. It will take a little while which is good because you can finish your book. We will arrange another meeting, *Insha' Allah.*' *Insha' Allah* is important, if God wills, but, of course, anything can happen to make it not happen. Other obligations intrude. 'When we introduce you we will call you *Amkssa*, the person who looks after the sheep. It is our nearest word for a true nomad.' They both thought this hilarious and fell back onto the cushions with laughter.

I decided it was time to go to my own bed. My head was like waves lapping and I did not know how many months it would take me to navigate the two miles of passageway to my home. I wanted to be alone when the visions started. The protests were endless, but I went out into the night and a boy, about Aderfi's age it seemed and with the same name, was sent with me. Thoughts began to project themselves on the moonlit walls as I stumbled along.[66]

Aderfi picked me up early two days later from outside my apartment. It was a simple two hours' drive to Imlil where we drank tea and Aderfi found a guide who knew the site of the graves and could take us to accommodation in the mountains. It was a six-hour hike, along well-trodden paths, always upward and I had to insist on a ten-minute break every hour. After two hours, we passed the site where the beheading of two Scandinavian tourists, Louisa Jespersen from Denmark and Maren Ueland from Norway, was filmed by Islamic State terrorists in revenge from the fall of Hajin, the last ISIS stronghold in Syria.

Several times I thought of giving up on the climb as my heart pounded. Mid-afternoon, we reached Anaruz's caves with the sign of freedom at the entrance. Aderfi sank to his knees and prayed while I sat and watched. Half an hour later, we came across a low pile of grey rocks; we had reached the graves. I was more affected than I anticipated. They were in a line, touching side by side, each with two small upright stones in the corners in the way of Islam. There were no other markers, no names and, in truth, a casual passer-by could easily have missed them altogether as they blended with the landscape. The guide said no-one had attended the interment; no family had ever come. The shock came when I went close and realised that with mud and foliage moved by recent rains, I could see the white of the bones. Aderfi came up behind me and laid an arm across my shoulders. 'You did not die then and you will not die now. It is not your time. *Insha' Allah.'*

We made our way to the *Toubkal Refuge* to spend the night. Along the path, we saw many scattered pieces of metal wreckage glinting in the late sun. After goat stew, I lay awake for many hours with my memories. Aderfi let me sleep in till seven in the morning and woke me with coffee.

Late afternoon, a few days after our return, committed and deep into this book, I strolled to the internet café to upload my latest material. On the way, I gave Moha a pack of cigarettes which included, by arrangement, a memory stick with my latest work. We had decided that this was the safest back-up possible.

Across the road, there was a flash of a face and I went cold and my legs shook. I leant against a door pillar as I forced myself to look again. I was sure. This was not a person who would know me. Indeed, he glanced up and down the street, passing over me as if I did not exist. But he existed for me. It was a face I thought forgotten, but there was no forgetting that dismissive glance. He got into a black limousine, the door held open by a chauffeur, an ageing bodyguard, likely sloppy and slow of reflex because he was a little tired. I remembered the man was Moroccan, but the last time we met he travelled on a Maltese passport. He was sought by security forces the world over, but none knew his identity for sure. It was Qaddura Mohammed Abd Al-Hamid, aged thirty-four in 1981 in Nairobi, now aged seventy-two and free and well-to-do.

A crazy emotion of hate, of impatience and frustration welled inside me, hampering my breathing. I wanted to kill Al-Hamid as I had wanted to most days for almost forty years. The impulse had come with anger before long-carried impotence took over. I felt ashamed that I had not protected my family. Now, I could repay them.

I hailed a passing empty *petit taxi* and passed the delighted driver a one hundred dirham note. I waved another and told him that if he followed Al-Hamid's vehicle to its destination without being spotted he could have it. The villa was ten minutes' drive away in a quiet back street of a newish development in the Targa area. The taxi pulled into the shade of sour orange and bougainvillea trees. The two-storey house had low dirty terracotta and white walls topped with a small hedge and set with a blue studded metal door. I could see through the ironwork car gates. There was no discernible external security, not even lighting, just customary satellite dishes, air-conditioning units, and a well-kept, low-maintenance lawn, cacti and stubby palm trees. The gates were unlocked and Al-Hamid's car pulled into the driveway. The gate was left open and the two men went inside. A sprinkler played listlessly to and fro. It all went quiet.

I had the driver go round the block twice and then take me to the Café Elite down the road from my apartment where I gave him his bonus. The babble of French and Arabic from its upmarket clientele and thick black coffee helped slow my heart.

Making a simple bomb is an easy enough thing to do. I had seen several variations made in Biafra although my memory was sketchy. There are many manuals on the internet for those with a little skill and determination.[67] One danger is that algorithms are set to capture nominated search words and combination of words, like 'How do you make a bomb?' These are recorded by security services and allocated against their individual IP addresses even though their location was not known. If the number and combination of enquiries became serious, tracking procedures could be brought into play.

At first, I decided to make a pipe bomb and attach it to the car. I bought a length of pipe and had it milled at both ends to take screw caps. A small amount of gunpowder was easy to get from a building site for a handful of notes. Shrapnel was available at any ironmongers. It was when I came to the timer that I started to worry. I didn't want a timer, as I didn't know for sure when the limousine would be in use. And, then, I didn't want a vibration device, of which I knew little, because I couldn't be sure that Al-Hamid would be in the car. I also didn't want the car blowing up in the middle of a crowded street. I thought about a weapon, but I had no handgun and I had to assume that either or both of my targets did. I could get a rifle, but that would disclose my hand to my Berber family and I didn't want them to know or to be endangered by an investigation. When I faced up to it, I recognised my real problem. I wanted it to happen up close and personal. I wanted to watch Al-Hamid die. It involved risk, but I decided on something easy, but nasty: a Molotov cocktail.

The next evening I scouted Al-Hamid's garden. The car was out, the iron gate locked, but not the door, and I settled down in the bushes to await its return. It swung in at dusk and the occupants went through their simple routine: chauffeur out first, not checking anywhere, unlock the house door, walk to the car back door, open it, and walk behind Al-Hamid as cover as he went straight inside. Then I realised that the back garden had a plunge pool. Al-Hamid came out five minutes later in his trunks, clutching a towel, a book and an iced drink. He was alone. After fifteen minutes in the water, he settled in a lounger, picked up the book and his drink and relaxed. When he went inside, I trialled a satisfactory escape route through the garden over the wall and across waste ground to a main boulevard where I easily picked up a *petit taxi*.

I owed my knowledge of fire-bombs to the Biafran army which had been regular makers and users. I put on some gloves, filled four half-litre glass bottles with petrol with some motor oil added which would cause the flames to flare, and importantly, to stick to whatever they touched. I screwed tops to the bottles and wrapped the necks with some old curtain material and tied them tight with string, leaving one end hanging down a few inches. An internal wick is dangerous and not needed because as the bottle breaks the petrol splashes and ignites from the burning cloth. I topped a plastic bottle with kerosene and bought and tested a cigarette lighter. Then I filled an old bag with my materials and made my way to Al-Hamid's home. I found a safe place behind a thick bush near his sun chair and waited. He was on schedule.

In one sense, it was a non-event. I let him settle. Went cold inside. Spaced out my bottles on the ground and doused the wicks in kerosene. I was just five yards away. I lit one and threw it on the tiles by the side of his chair and followed it with another two. I didn't need the fourth as the flames flew upwards, oil sticking to his body, and folded him in a fiery blanket up to his chest. I stepped out and looked into his shocked eyes as his thin hair caught and he began screaming.

He did not see my son crumpled at the foot of the staircase of the Norfolk Hotel, but I did. He did not see the heads of my wife and daughter lying on the café counter, but I did. In his final moments, he just saw me. I threw the fourth bottle for good measure and followed it with the kerosene, carry bag and gloves. He seemed to melt into fat; his pupils popped and he saw no more. I stood for two or three seconds as he melted and his bones showed and I felt a great weight lift.

There was no sign of the chauffeur, but the patio door slid back and two large Alsatian dogs rushed at me, snarling. I raised my hand, caught their eyes, and they whimpered to the ground, panting, with tongues lolling. With all of the evidence burning well, I moved along my escape route. Within fifteen minutes, I was at my regular seat in the café waiting for a mint tea. Above the table I was normal; below, my legs were shaking. I felt I had done something good and would finally be forgiven.

I heard no sirens. Nothing was out of the ordinary. I talked with a few acquaintances and had a simple dinner on my own in my apartment watching the TV news. No atrocity was mentioned. There was nothing in the newspapers the following day. I chatted with Moha and he invited me for a second meal at his home to meet Aderfi who was bringing with him a friend from the desert edge, Lahcen. Moha had no other gossip for me, no special news from the neighbourhood. Why? It was one of life's mysteries and suited me well.

Lahcen worked for a small tourist outfit called Sahara Oases Tours. He had a much-extended mud house and supplemented his income with a little farm east of Zagora, near where the road ends. As well as dates from his palm trees, he grew some seasonal vegetables and alfalfa as feed for his goats, cows and camels. He was descended from real nomads, one of the forty-four branches of the grandsons of Mohammed Atta, a sub-tribe of Kabbalah, the 'tough people'. He had limited interest in possessions that were not useful enough to warrant a place on the back of an animal; everything that was not a necessity was an encumbrance. Lahcen was on a regular trip to Marrakech for family shopping in his clapped-out Land Rover.

Moha introduced me as Amkssa who wanted to go to Timbuktu by the old way. Lahcen was about sixty years, dressed in a well-faded blue jellaba and black turban, his eyes were brown, and his face creased and sand-scoured. There was an intelligence and humour about him. He raised his eyebrows, whether this was aimed at me, my name, where I wanted to go or how I wanted to travel, was not clear. Aderfi said that of all the Berber of that area, Lahcen had the greatest nostalgia for the old way and he was interested in making a last trip before he died.

'I should warn you,' said Aderfi, 'that this man is a master at bargaining. He speaks good English and French from his guiding. It is a black day for him when he has to pay the asking price for anything. He never knows what is printed on a sign because he is illiterate; besides, even if he did know he would pay no attention, for he is deficient in respect of law. If you mention that a thing is forbidden, he is contemptuous, and calls it "a decree from the wind".'

'You are an old man, Amkssa,' said Lahcen. 'Why do you want to go maybe a long month into the desert where you have never been? You may well not survive.

'It may be beautiful, but it is not a friendly place for a European with a Berber name. It is barely five years since *Al-Qaeda in the Islamic Maghreb* captured Timbuktu and imposed the worst kind of sharia law. People like you were just unbelievers, pawns in games of ransom. After a year, the French came with their helicopter gunships, Mirage and Rafale fighter jets, and Chadian soldiers and legionnaires and chased the zealots from the Niger to the valleys of the *Adrar des Ifoghas* and slaughtered the *jihadi* in their caves. But the Tuaregs seeking Azawad are still kings of their desert. The fighters for *Ansar Dine*, the Defenders of the Faith, remnants of the mad men Mokhtar Belmokhtar and Abou Zeid, are in the oases of northern Mali and also in Timbuktu, leaning against the wooden doors, looking like local people.'

Lahcen paused and gave me a wry smile. 'Of course,' he said, 'the weapons of the Tuareg have improved since your day, Amkssa. When Qaddafi fell in 2011, Tuareg mercenaries pulled down the double gates of a 'Schoolbook

Printing and Storage' warehouse on the outskirts of Tripoli. Inside they found anti-aircraft missiles, machine guns, rockets, mortars and so gorged their pick-up trucks and headed home.'

'You are right, of course, Lahcen. But travel is already much easier. We would be a small group of Berber, devout Moslems, at home and no harm to the *jihadi*. I want to disappear, no papers, no record, no word. Disappear. There are men from Europe who wish me harm. I want to disappoint them. I may be older than you, but I still have a life to lead. There is much that I wish to do.'

'Are you a criminal?'

'Probably,' I said, 'but I have done what I had to do and I can live with my conscience. I have not harmed anyone who was innocent. Like you, I am a misunderstood man.'

This last comment pleased him. 'I understand why you wish to go into the burning sun, but why should I take you?'

'I think that you are not a man of this time. I think that sometimes you think you are less of a man than you used to be. You are fed up with taking foreign girls on simple two-day rides on your camels. You are a nomad, a man of the desert, who has ancestors to honour. You feel a longing to be a whole man again. Perhaps you wish to pass on some of the old ways, maybe to a son who needs to understand. You have a pride in your freedom. I understand that search for freedom.'

I pulled out my silver pendants and showed him my *aza*. 'From a business point of view you will not lose and I believe that by trade in Timbuktu you will return a rich man.' There was a glint in Lahcen's eyes and he nodded to himself.

'There is another reason,' I said. 'It is because you have come here today and *I* have asked you.' I put a slight accent on the '*I*' and saw that my words had struck home.

Lahcen sat down for a full two minutes and thought things through. He had a deep understanding of the hardships of the wandering journey. Then he stood up and looked me in the eye.

'I will take you,' he said. 'We will leave in the middle of September after the worst of the heat. That will give me time to get everything together. You are right, I will take my son, Asso, and I will talk to him about taking by grandson, Icho, who is sixteen and not yet a man. We will take eight camels, enough to carry food, water, wood and fodder. You will give me six thousand euro when you arrive at my farm with just one bag and will spend a week with me before we leave. You will give me another ten thousand euro when we arrive in Timbuktu. My word is law when we travel.'

'Your terms are not acceptable,' I replied, and his eyes flashed. 'When I arrive in Timbuktu, I will not give you ten thousand euro, but fourteen. The extra money is so that you tell me the old stories at night by the campfire.' There was a crash of laughter and we embraced.

PART 2 (TAMEGROUTE, SEPTEMBER 2019)

They hunted till darkness came on, but they found
Not a button, or feather, or mark,
By which they could tell that they stood on the ground
Where the Baker had met with the Snark

In the midst of the word he was trying to say,
In the midst of his laughter and glee,
He had softly and suddenly vanished away -
For the Snark was a *Berber, you see.*[68]

Two days later, I was walking home full of tajine, dressed in my jellaba, when a dirty white Mercedes saloon slid alongside. The driver wound down the window and leaned out as if to ask a question. I had drunk a few beers and was relaxed and unsuspecting. I was hit from behind and there was the stab of a needle in my neck. I remember falling, but not hitting the ground.

I came to in a warm dark. It seemed my right eye was closed because I could not feel the eyelid move. There was no shadow, no sense of movement around me and no sound of people, traffic or insects. My brain stumbled to make sense. My mouth tasted cloyed and salty, my tongue misshapen and torn. I counted my teeth, but could not remember how many I had before. I was sitting in a seat that was hard and had a slatted back. My arms were tied behind so that my hands were without feeling; my legs numb and cold as if they were missing. The pain was not intense or throbbing, it was just everywhere as if it was a natural state. I tried to call, but managed only a whimper. I could not remember how I got here, where here was, or who had done this to me. My memory outside of my close surroundings was empty and unhelpful. Was this everything? Where was my past? Was this my present and my future?

Close to my ear someone spoke in an encouraging tone. It was a man, a mature man. I heard, *'shoo iśmak'*? It was repeated while my tongue filled my mouth and I could not answer. And then again, *'shoo iśmak, What is your name?'* This man has my body, but he does not know my name. He tried again in thickly accented French, guttural as if from Marseilles. *'Quel est ton nom?'* I tried once more and shook my head slowly, instantly woozy.

'Attendez, monsieur.' A slight pause and water trickled into my mouth from a plastic bottle. It tasted of heaven. As I tilted my head, the two silver amulets around my neck slipped from beneath my shirt, the 'Hand of Fatima' and the *'Aza'*, symbolising protection and freedom. I heard quick gasps. Two people. Local.

The water cleared my throat. *'Soyez prudent,'* I offered. *'Vous ne me connaissez pas. Vous ne connaissez pas mes amis, ma famille des montagnes.'* Then, *'Pourquoi voulez-vous savoir mon nom?'* Some more water. *'Pourquoi est-il important pour vous?'*

'Parce que je veux être ton ami. Je veux t'aider.'

He decided that I was a native French speaker, but his voice now held a note of wariness. *'Tu as cinq minutes avant notre retour. Penses bien à ton histoire.'*

What is five minutes? The length of a prayer. If people with power have your body they can restrain you, hurt you, even kill you. If they don't have your body, all they have left is your name. With your name, they can harass your friends, control your property and wealth, and chase you until they have your body. If you don't have a name, are you free? I fell asleep. The two men came back. The same questions. More time alone. More questions.

I woke to Moha's whisper in my ear. 'Can you move? It is time to go.'

My ropes were cut and I was led by the hand. My legs screamed as the blood circulated. Through the door, Aderfi stood with a French carbine, a body at his feet. I bent to look at the dead man's face. It was the driver of the Mercedes. He had a thin long knife pointing through his ribs, which I removed and wiped on his darkened shirt.

'In case of fingerprints,' I said. Aderfi led the way through a well-furnished lounge and out on to the patio. It was night, but the moon blazed and the sky was awash with stars. Bats and moths flitted and cicadas sang with their legs. Supported by Moha, I made the back door when a man carrying a pistol passed between us and Aderfi. He was followed by two Alsatian dogs. For a moment, my mind flashed to another patio, two other Alsatians. The man grunted a command and Aderfi put down his carbine and raised his hands. The dogs growled, just holding their discipline. Moha moved immediately and knocked sideways the arm holding the pistol, which fired.

I stepped forward, knife in hand, and slid it with confidence into the man's throat behind his windpipe and ripped it forward. I owed a Biafran corporal called John for that manoeuvre learned in an evening's practice. The man dropped the gun, fell to his knees clutching his neck, then splashed forward into a pool, not yet dead, but unable to make a sound. The dogs came from the cover of the pink and yellow walls and I reached out a flat hand and spoke to them and they stopped and began licking at the blood spreading across the tiles. I enjoyed my companions' expressions and thought that Aderfi was, perhaps, thinking of his angry mule fifty years before.

'No witnesses,' I said. 'Only two of them, do you think?'

I started to buckle from pain and tension and was supported to a car parked behind bushes in a rough parking area outside the walls. We drove past the luxury hotels, spas and the mansions of rich men to Moha's home.

The rescue was easily explained. From his seat outside the apartments, Moha had seen the abduction, recognised the men as two local thugs for hire, and called Aderfi who drove overnight to Marrakech. For two days, they toured the larger and more secluded properties on the outskirts of the town checking driveways for the Mercedes. They found it tucked away down a dirt track deep in *Le Palmeraie*, a largely artificial oasis of several hundred thousand trees to the north of the city where the Berbers recall the Sahara and sell camel rides to tourists while the wealthy inhabit high-security resorts. The villa with its annexes was surrounded by a nondescript mud wall. The owners were away and my kidnappers had made an arrangement with the guard to use some of the garden rooms which looked out onto the large swimming pool. More money changed hands, an improved offer. Moha packed my bag and cleared my room. As

Kamal kept my deposit, he agreed to forget the let had ever happened. I thought it a fair arrangement.

Aderfi was ready to leave immediately on the eleven hours' drive into the desert to Tamegroute, Lahcen's village. Moha and I embraced, holding back the tears. After four hours in the car, the pain from the bruising became uncomfortable. Aderfi turned doctor and decided that we would stop in Ouarzazate for two nights. It was well away from trouble. I slept for thirty-six hours and woke feeling awful, but well enough to finish the journey.

We started early to stay ahead of the stifling mid-day heat. The road wound over an unforgiving lunar landscape that glinted with greenish metals. Few people lived here and each mile slipped us further from civilisation and back in time. The presence of man was no more significant than that of a tree or a rock – all were shrunk by the vastness of the landscape. The sliver of road cut through the burnished Djbel Sarhro range until, from high above the solitary market settlement of Agdz, the lush valley of the River Drãa appeared far below. To the east of the oasis and the wide brown river, the grey Kissane Mountains rose up in soft vertical ridges like folded velvet. We meandered the hundred miles to Zagora beside the green forest of palms amid increasing numbers of tillers in emerald plots of rye and wheat. There were kasbahs, the mud-castles of extended families, and ksours, fortified tribal enclaves, some still intact and inhabited, marked with primitive tribal motifs, triangles and barley stalks, others deserted, collapsing from aridity and wind like sandcastles washed away with the tide.[69]

'It was good that you did not admit anything,' said Lahcen as we sat on a bench outside his door in the late sun with Icho, his grandson, mint teas in hand. Scrawny chickens pecked about our feet. Palm leaves flickered in a slight breeze from the desert which then moved up the valley towards the mountains. For him, it was a matter of pride that I had not given what he knew to be my false Berber name and that I had kept intact what he thought was my real identity.

'What is not seen, not heard, has not happened,' he said, uttering a belief I had by then encountered too often for my liking. I wondered whether I believed Oscar Wilde or Leonardo da Vinci? Is man at least himself when he talks in his own person? 'Give him a mask, and he will tell you the truth.'

Or does fire represent truth 'because it destroys all sophistry and lies; and the mask is for the lying and falsehoods which conceal truth'.

Aderfi left the next morning. I asked him for more favours. He agreed to act as an incognito conduit for further additions to the book. I gave him a letter for my hawala banker in Marrakech, which included instructions for a package deposited with him. I had been invited to the wedding of Moha's daughter, the lute player, and now I would not be going. I wanted Aderfi to buy a suitable present and pressed money upon him suggesting a large carpet of high quality decorated with the *aza* symbol. Aderfi smiled and said he knew just the thing. He parted with a Berber aphorism, 'Only he who travels knows the value of men.'

It was another goodbye.

14. FREEDOM OF THE SAND

Here one can neither stand nor lie nor sit
There is not even silence in the mountains
But dry sterile thunder without rain
There is not even solitude in the mountains
But red sullen faces sneer and snarl
From doors of mudcracked houses.[70]

PART 1: NEAR TIMEMOUN, THE SAHARA (SEPTEMBER 2019)

As I waited for Lahcen's arrangements to come together, I caught a bus into Zagora with Icho as a guide. I wanted a change of scene and some quiet to speculate on who was behind my assailants in Marrakech.

Zagora was a warren of cool, dank darkness. Covered passageways about ten feet wide led towards haphazard junctions each offering a glint of daylight. Doors set in mud and straw walls opened into a honeycomb of homes.[71] Small boys demanded sweets, money and pens. Dozens of hands fought over pieces of chewing gum. An old man side-saddle on a donkey, head down as if sleeping, clopped past. Catching sight of a stranger, a woman in black, who darted indoors.

I told Icho that I wanted to sit with a mint tea and do some thinking and he led me to a dingy café with a sand dirt floor and smelling of days-old goat stew. A wood fire was coaxed to heat water and my jellaba ran damp with perspiration.

Fiction must ring true, but here in a real life there was a lot which made no easy sense. The two corpses – peace be upon them – only seemed interested in my name and did not know what language to use to ask me. Did they want to check they had the right man? They were thugs, claimed Moha, who were known to work on the French coast. They had kept me in reasonable condition even though a closed eye and split lips did not bother them.

The questions crowded in. If someone wanted me dead, why wait? Had I been pointed out to them in some partial way and they sought corroboration while waiting for their paymaster? The string puller was likely not part of an official organisation, not Moroccan; in both cases more proficient men would have been used. A rogue operation? A kidnap and blackmail gone wrong? Pathetic mistaken identity? Was I not the target at all? Or was there somewhere, among money, passport, internet, cameras, habits, a mistake of mine that triggered an alert far away? Was I on an Interpol 'red notice', requested by some unseen hand, and wanted for political extradition? Were my hunters part of an organisation with technological reach that needed time to get a principal to Marrakech? Did they know Morag? Had the Australian sisters played a part? The bodyguard of Al-Hamid? Had one of my Berber family been garrulous about the return of *Feep*. Had I got clean away, thanks to Moha and Aderfi?

While in Zagora, Lahcen instructed me to buy a made-to-measure pair of 'Michelin sandals', cut to fit from old tyres, and considered to be the best way to stop scalding sands shredding your feet. While we waited for the leather thongs to be attached, I found yesterday's English-language Moroccan newspaper. There was still no mention of Al-Hamid's death so someone had cleaned-up. Perhaps the authorities had been embarrassed by the presence of the ageing terrorist and were quietly pleased that the problem had been resolved at arm's length? There had been a night-time gas explosion and kitchen fire at a detached locked villa in La Palmeraie. Careless maintenance was suspected. The bodies of two unidentified men had been found in their beds with two charred dogs. I suspected Moha's efficient hand at work.

The paper always carried a part-column of news from Morocco's close neighbours in Europe, the more gruesome the better. A decomposing fish-nibbled body had been taken from a reservoir near Perpignan. Foul play was not suspected. The hunt for the assassins of Juncker and Selmayr had come to life again as positive identification was made of two GRU officers leaving Brussels airport within hours of the crime. Vladimir Putin described the accusation as typical western hysterical propaganda. In any event, what advantage was there for the Russians from the death of two unelected politicians whose actions every day made the EU's demise more likely? Britain was also thought, in private, to have some responsibility and, far from bringing any sense to Brexit negotiations, collapse was all around.

The 'Punishment of Britain' had entered official language for daring to suggest outright competition in the event of a 'no-deal'. Ironically, in view of the UK's military history, especially in the last century against Germany, France and, most recently, Biafra and Yemen, the EU committed an act of all-but war in trying to semi-blockade the British islands through slowing down port operations. French and Spanish fishing fleets were sent far into territorial waters backed by European warships, which the British were powerless to repel. One in four passenger aircraft was turned back from European airspace without warning. Queues at the ferries and Chunnel were so long that many operators had given up trying. Special arrangements were made with the Americans and Scandinavians to bring in food and medical supplies. The border in Ireland was closed to all traffic, manned by Dutch and German peace-keeping troops, and Irish dairy herds were being destroyed because the pasteurising plants in the north were denied to southern farmers. Spanish troops massed at Gibraltar. It seemed the remnants of British pride and resolve were about to collapse.

It was all a long way away and I planned to make it even further.

As we left Zagora on the late afternoon bus, we passed the famous naïve painted sign of a Berber in a blue turban with his camel, a mixed desert landscape in the background, the whole overlaid with an arrow and the caption, 'Tombouctou 52 jours'. Fifty-two days is the span of a fully laden, regularly trading caravan. Fourteen days is the minimum for a small, fast-moving group. Lahcen hoped for three weeks for the outward leg, but arrival was more important than speed. Whatever the time taken, there was a lot of scope for error and mishap.

Including sufficient time for profitable trade, Lahcen planned up to three months for the whole trip. Dromedaries in Morocco on the sea-side of the Atlas range are for tourists. They cannot cross the mountains for which the Berbers use horse, mule and truck. Those beasts kept in the south near to the Sahara were for the desert, but were declining in numbers with the advent of 4x4s and satellite navigation. Experienced camels, aged about twenty-one, would carry the four riders, another four of about sixteen years would travel for training and to carry supplies. If Lahcen's bargaining was successful, he would increase the number of camels for the return and they would be laden with gold, ivory, African hardwood and diamonds. He would offer three Berber rugs, saffron from high-altitude Taliouine, silver jewellery, and dates to be sold at the early oases before they spoiled.

I woke late one morning and saw that our camels had gone. I sought Asso and found him indoors taking mint tea with his wife, Kahina. Sensing it was an intimate moment, I sat down on a bench outside and waited. Asso came out ten minutes later. He was tall for a Berber with a dry harsh, desert face and beautiful, clear brown eyes that I thought came from looking far into the distance rather than trapped into electronic devices and the close confines of rooms. He was thin, tough and looked quick to react. Like many, he spoke acceptable English and French from leading tour groups into the fringes of the desert.

'My father and my son have taken the camels ahead,' he announced. 'They have gone on to Mhamid at the end of the road and we will drive down early in the morning in two days and meet them and leave at once. My father thought it best that you are seen as little as possible before we start.' These were sensible precautions.

'My wife does not want me to make this trip,' he explained, 'but my father wishes it, and wishes my eldest son to come with us, and so I have no choice. I have never been out into the far desert and, of course, nor has my son. We all need to look after my father because without him we will be in trouble. He has insisted that we take no phones. If anything goes wrong we must look to ourselves, like the old times. This is what you have requested?'

I nodded, but stayed silent.

'I have two questions for you, Amkssa,' said Asso after a full minute. 'First, please explain how important it is for you not to be seen, to disappear? If I know, then, if there is trouble, I can act in keeping with your wishes and my father's honour. Second, my father and Dr Aderfi and Moha say they owe you a debt?' He paused. 'If I know of this debt, it will be easier to tell Kahina why her husband and son are leaving against her wishes.'

'I understand,' I replied. 'I think some men, perhaps many men, are trying to kill me. I want to get away, to leave no trail, so they cannot find me. It is not my time to die. Both your father and I are old men and we want to take the old way for the last time. In your father's case, I know that he wants to pass on to you his skills and what I think he would call the "freedom of the desert". He believes that this will be a most important gift to you. As for your second question, I cannot tell you because your father has not. However, it is not a secret for me and any debt has been repaid many times. However, I can show you two things. These are one of them.'

Leaning forwards, I took out my silver pendants. Asso held them in one hand and stared at them and then at me. I then got up and went inside the door of his house and picked up Asso's MI carbine and came back and handed it to him. 'This is the second,' I said.

Asso looked at the gun, then the pendants again. 'You are *Feep*,' he exclaimed. A pause. 'We will leave the morning after tomorrow.' He got up and went into his hut to talk to his wife.

Asso and I arrived outside the small oasis town of Mhamid an hour before sunrise away from shifting eyes to find Lahcen and Icho had already loaded the camels. They must have been at it for hours; the boy looked exhausted.

Lahcen took in my jellaba, turban and Michelin walkers. 'Almost a Berber,' he said, 'so I am sure you can ride a camel? Aderfi said there was no need to give you a trial ride.'

'I've never ridden a camel,' I said, and three jaws dropped.

'How, how do you ...' stuttered Asso.

I walked over to my allotted beast. Mounting a camel requires both athletic ability and courage. My triangular saddle, *tahaweyt*, had a backrest and pommel shaped as a decorative cross, which would break if pressured. The *tahaweyt* was carved from tamarisk that grows in the desert alongside the acacia. The saddle is placed across the forward slope of the hump and is levelled by a blanket cushion, a *zarbea*. You sit cross-legged and guide with pressure on the neck from bare feet. As the beast rises it throws the rider backwards, forwards and backwards again, but first you have to get it to kneel so that you can climb aboard. I had heard the guttural cries of camel drivers as they manhandled their sneering-lipped mounts with necks rising like indignant snakes.[72] The drivers catch the beast by the long hair of the neck and clear their throat in as loud and revolting a manner as possible and drag it downwards and hit it on the shins. Camels have long memories and never forgive an unkind rider for cruelty. I walked over and stood in front, giving my beast the eye.

'No, no, the right-hand side,' shouted Asso.

My *algham* was small-brained and fought my gaze for, perhaps, fifteen seconds, then after a whispered 'Utch' sank to its knees with a heart-felt sigh and a great green spit. I climbed up and settled in, patted the neck, lent forward to murmur 'Oh, Oh' and it struggled up pitching me about, but I was ready for the movement. I tapped it a few times with my riding stick, picked up the loose cord rein, and trotted up to Lahcen.

'*Yellah*. Ready when you are,' I said with a wink.

The rest of your life starts in a moment. My companions climbed on their mounts, trying to look elegant because pride was at stake and we took the first strides at a slow walking pace. Once the journey started, there was no turning back; you are bound and drugged. For other, earlier travellers, thoughts might have turned to streets of gold. For me, it was much simpler. Freedom.

We spread out so that the animals could graze on any sparse vegetation; the pack camels tied head to tail. I had been allowed one small case and had given myself some luxuries – my laptop, into which I could tap brief notes at night until the battery gave out, and three paperbacks. After a couple of hours, we all slid off and walked to give the beasts a respite and to allow my stomach to settle.

What did surprise me was the dog, a tawny desert aidi that Asso called *Tamount*, 'accompany'. I knew that in the Arab culture dogs were seen as unclean whereas cats were accepted as house friends. The reverse was true for the Berber for whom the dog was a companion and at work was especially valued as a guard and a hunter. Tongue lolling, *Tamount*, matched our pace.

At first, the landscape was barren plateau seared flat and sand-less by the winds and covered with black desert stones, an *hamada*. In hard desert like this, prints could stay for centuries, the marks of Roman chariot wheels remain, the rubbish and lost items of thousands of years, baked by the sun, burnished by the wind, and washed by the occasional rain.[73] It was as if people who had made camps had gone away a few hours earlier when it might have been centuries. Flint arrowheads and edged scraping- and cutting-tools from thousands of years gathered in clusters. The Berbers had been told that these had dropped from the sky. Twice, Asso shouted '*Ass, ass*,' pointed, and sent *Tamount* speeding into the distance. An '*Ashtt, ashtt*' brought him back, both times proud with a dessert rabbit for Asso to take and to scratch his head in thanks.

There was no sense of navigation from Lahcen for it was a well-worn tourist trail, but we saw no one until mid-morning when two Jeeps roared past, spitting gravel, young Berber guides at the wheel with American ladies in tattered short jeans, flowery halter-neck tops and sun cream, waving and cheering from the back. At our first well, we stopped for rest and prayer in the mid-day sun. It was sweltering as we hobbled the beasts. We took it in turns to pull water and pour it into the animal trough. Camels can go four weeks without water, one week without food, but they can drink forty-four litres in one go. We tried to doze, choosing between a rough-blasted, palm-frond structure and two thin thorn bushes for shelter.

The terrain changed to high sand dunes, *ergs*. I reached too often for the bamboo taps of my 'Berber fridge' hanging from the saddle and was admonished by Lahcen. The fridge was a twenty-litre, thick goatskin that acted as a heat repellent, but still lost fluid to evaporation in a hot wind. Each man needed five litres a day even in the cool season. Skins were well suited for their work and could be repaired by using a twig or a piece of camel-dung and rolled up and packed away when empty.

I think I must have fallen asleep for I found we had stopped for prayers before unloading near the oasis of Ben Saleh. The mat comes out five times a day, early morning; midday, 'the hour of supreme monotony, the hour of blindness'; mid-afternoon; the end of journey and at the night camp and each prayer is preceded by washing using a soft clean stone, *tayamum*, without water, far too precious to dampen soap. I sat and watched with outward respect.

Lahcen and Icho took the camels to drink while I stayed with Asso as he prepared the evening meal. He mixed flour and water for a 'Berber pizza', *madfiuna*, placed it in a hole and covered it with sand and coals from the fire. Part of our small store of fresh goat meat was mixed with carrots, onions and herbs. It was the hour when light embraced the horizon and the rocks ceased to suffer. I sat on the trunk of a large acacia uprooted by a long-passed flash flood.[74] We ate with our fingers and drank strong mint tea with too much sugar from a walnut cup.

As the temperature dropped, we clustered around the embers. Lahcen estimated that we had travelled about fifty kilometres and was pleased, but the going had been easy. To get across the disputed Algerian border and the main Béchar to Tindouf desert road we had to evade army patrols and leave the beaten path. There were no helicopters, but it was best to travel the next hundred kilometres in the heat of the day when the patrols slept and the satellites gave hazy images. Lahcen had been briefed by Moha.

I asked whether there were wild camels and was told that any animals left to themselves in the desert would die. I knew the camel was not native to Africa, but imported from Asia about the time of the Roman Empire. That was the time when the last of the great elephant herds that roamed the northern reaches of the desert were captured and trained for use in the Carthaginian army. It was the Romans who annihilated the species to supply ivory for the European market.[75]

I prompted Lahcen to one of his promised stories. He spoke in an hypnotic lilt and I felt as if I was going into a trance.[76] Time and space loosened themselves from their fastenings and ceased to have meaning. The years fell away. This must have been what it was like in remote Berber villages or among desert caravanserai. Lahcen told the story of the birth of the Sahara. Long ago the earth was a huge garden with many palm trees and nightingales and perfumed jasmine. All men were honest. One day, a man told the first lie and it was the end of the age of innocence. God announced that for every lie that was told he would throw a grain of sand on the earth. Men were dismissive. And so, lie after lie, little by little, the Sahara was born. The odd oasis can still be seen, a trace of the original garden, because not all men lie.

Loading the camels in the morning was accomplished after much confusion and many invocations to Allah. The beasts moved their necks from right to left to chase away the loader and opened a large stinking maw to bawl ferociously.[77] Dust was brushed from withers, saddle-pads fitted, folds smoothed and saddles eased into place. The animals were slapped to make them raise their bellies so that the girths could be fed underneath, then knotted to an iron ring fixed on the saddle with a thong of leather. All of these operations were performed with meticulous care as a small mistake could result in a slipped saddle or a fall. When all was packed, rifles were slung and we mounted.

I was awed by the hugeness of the landscape, the brilliance of the light, the repeated patterns, the quicksilver shimmer of the heat-haze. This desert was the first full true wilderness I had seen. It was more compelling than the ocean or the mountains, more magnificent and frightening. The French philosopher Ernest Renan thought that blank horizons and a dazzling sky would clear the mind of all distractions and allow it to concentrate on the one God. The great desert explorer, Wilfred Thesiger, wrote that no man can live in the desert and emerge unchanged. He will carry, however faint, the imprint of the desert, the brand which marks the nomad; and he will have within him the yearning to return.

This cruel land can cast a spell which no temperate climate can match. I found a freedom unattainable in civilization; a life unhampered by possessions. I found, too, a comradeship and a belief in tranquillity. Chatwin was more prosaic, 'To survive at all, the Tuareg must develop a prodigious sense of orientation. He must forever be naming, sifting, comparing a thousand different signs to tell him where he is, where rain has fallen, where the next meal is coming from.'

The life of the desert has diminished to the point of extinction.[78] The great caravans that once sloughed between the Sudan and the Mediterranean with their cargoes of gold, ivory, ostrich feathers, raw leather, wax, incense, civet musk, indigo, gum and slaves have vanished. The trade in human beings was banned by the French in 1856, but some 5,000 slaves survived the desert crossing each year well into the twentieth century and about half of these ended up in Constantinople where they were sold at two and a half times the purchase price. At the same time, a single white ostrich plume fetched 500 francs in Paris. Ivory was used for billiard balls, piano keys, knife handles and jewellery. Now, only an occasional truck, army vehicle or tourist car races through a bleak and empty landscape. The Sahara is no longer one of the world's crossroads. It is like an empty theatre, its vast plains, abrupt cliffs and green oases stages for forgotten human dramas.

One evening, we pushed the camels as far as we could until sunset and the beasts shied from the cold. Lahcen had begun to use a silver pendant which he wore around his neck to navigate by the *amanar*, the shiny south star. Asso carried his own and was taught its use by his father who, in turn, instructed Icho. We were back on rocky terrain, sand making up just twenty-five per cent of the Sahara. We halted and dropped the animals' loads within arm's reach, then couched the beasts with their fodder. The fire was lit by a single carefully-protected match. Our camp was on a rocky escarpment above the bed of a *wadi* shaded with tamarisk and *tarha* trees. The smoke of our fire rose straight into the unblemished sky like fine-drawn pencil lines.[79] The high ground remained a place of terror, desolate, dark and dreary, where evil spirits lurked.

I had been given charge of making the *tagila*. When the fire burned down, I placed my bread dough in the hot sand and raked the embers back. Twenty minutes later, I fished out a warm, hard loaf which we ate with dried dates and ghee. Mint tea was poured into our bowls to make it foam and then twice back into the pot. We each had three fills, the first bitter, the second just right, and the last a little weak.

One early evening, *Tamount* began barking and then the sound of engines could be heard long before two 4X4s, Berber buggies, came into sight. First, they were a dark mirage on the distant horizon, disappearing and reappearing. The buzz grew until they burst over a low rise and were among us, skittering our camels. These young Berber meteorite hunters were two weeks out of Erfoud, had seen our fire, and came to join us for the night. I set about making more bread although they had a plethora of tins and soft drinks in cold boxes. It was a bizarre juxtaposition. They displayed a gazelle shot that afternoon and Lahcen set to work with his knife and we soon had the makings for a first-rate *shorba*, a thick soup of grilled meat, garlic, savoury grains, tomatoes, oil and spaghetti.

While we waited and the Berbers exchanged gossip, I wandered over to the vehicles and saw two French guns snapped into fixtures by the back seats. One was a pre-1940 bolt-action MAS-36, the other a well-oiled FR F1 sniper rifle. An odd moment: one of my Biafran guns had just killed my dinner fifty years later. At the back of one 4x4 was a satellite dish. I updated my notes, recharged my laptop battery, and in another clash of cultures uploaded these scribblings.

Lahcen explained that meteorites were the result of a planetary collision with the South Star. Most were intrinsically worthless, but had value to collectors and meteor scientists. Some, formed on Mars over four billion years ago and weighing less than a pound, could sell for $10,000. Others, black gold, contain silvery-white nickel or molten spherical chondrules, silicates, the oldest known substances in the solar system. Just occasionally, chondrules contain small pieces of the rarest minerals, used, for instance, in modern aircraft engines. One of these would pay for our trip with enough left to buy an apartment in Marrakech. Another hope.

In an almost casual way, the hunters told us of the recent string of political killings in Britain, now grouped as the *Brexit Murders* and believed to be linked to the assassination of Juncker and Selmayr. Perhaps half a dozen prominent politicians, many of them women, had been shot at close range, separately and alone, with a Russian 9mm pistol once to the forehead and once to the back of the neck. Each victim was seen to have played a part in a plan to reverse the Brexit referendum. Millions had marched, and marched again and again. There was thought to be a team of assassins at work, perhaps not closely linked. The young Berbers were excited at the idea of people rising against a repressive state and discussed Moroccan leaders who should meet the same fate. They remembered names like Cooper, Gove, Rudd, Hammond and Soubry. Each body was pinned with a card inscribed with a single word like 'Traitor' or 'Liar'.

Lahcen poked the embers with a tamarisk stick and to the excitement of our visitors told a story about promises and commitment. How a man is his word, a promise is a promise, and death is an important part of life. How a family should sacrifice almost everything to keep their word and, when as a result all seemed lost, they would receive Allah's blessing for their fortitude.

As we lay down wrapped in our burnooses, Lahcen extracted a promise from the hunters that our meeting would never be disclosed. The young men were content to agree, their stomachs filled with gazelle and good bread. We all dozed between efforts to kindle the fire. *Tamount* rose almost every hour and circled the camp, keeping guard.

There is something about the wilderness of the Sahara that stimulates the imagination: its emptiness, its silence broken only by the droning of *barchan* dunes moving in slight winds, the top layer of singing sand travelling in a different direction to the mass underneath; the mirages which encourage men to believe in *djnoun*, the 'people of the empty places' or the 'people of the night' who might even nestle in an empty food bowl if it is not turned upside down.[80] In this stillness, one can believe that mountains move, that they converse and marry, and that an enchanted oasis remains hidden in the folds of the sand.

PART 2: NEAR ADRAR, THE SAHARA (SEPTEMBER AND OCTOBER 2019)

As I trudged beside my camel I thought of sneaking a quick sip from my fridge, but Lahcen's eyes were everywhere. Nineteenth-century travellers assumed that the Sahara had once been covered by ocean. Not true, but there had been Lake Triton, described in many ancient texts, and which was, perhaps, the world's largest fresh-water lake. Classical-era Greek writers placed it in what today is southern Tunisia and also in Libya. According to Herodotus, writing in the fifth century BC, it contained two islands, Phla and Mene. Four hundred years later, Strabo noted that horses were still common in the Sahara, but that nomads needed to carry water-skins. Pliny, shortly after the death of Jesus of Nazareth, described elephant, giraffe and carnivorous beasts in what he called 'Libya', the whole of the *Maghreb* to the west of Egypt. A large quantity of prehistoric tools has been found, similar to those discovered in Europe. Most of these have been unearthed along Quaternary Valleys, in *ergs*, and at the foot of dunes, including thousands of Neolithic arrowheads and axes. In former times, the Sahara was thickly populated with numerous broad rivers in full flood that linked the Niger River with Lake Chad, their courses teeming with fish, shellfish, crocodiles and hippopotami.

In the rocks of the main mountain masses, often in the most deserted and desolate spots, particularly at Tassili-n-Ajjer in the centre of the great desert, there are rock overhangs covered with frescoes of breath-taking beauty and complexity showing herds of hunted and domesticated animals.[81] What does *Tassili* mean in the Tuareg language, but 'plateau of the rivers'? Reservoirs of rain which fell a million years ago are trapped over 10,000 feet deep in layers of porous rock covering up to a third of a million square miles. This is almost more water than can be imagined. I wasn't sure whether I wanted the desert to bloom again, but the millions of particles of algae blown as dust all lay in wait.

In the heat of the afternoon, when all around was an oven, I set to thinking of what signs of life we had seen since we left the tourist track at Ben Saleh. Berber meteor hunters apart, there had been plenty of tyre tracks in the gravel-covered hard black rock. I saw no wisps of aircraft vapour, but we did pass a rusted military tank about forty years old with its tracks lying loose; a single white Fiat truck with its occupants long gone, presumably to die of dehydration; and, often, the stark white bones of camels. At the occasional small oasis, there were olives, pomegranates and fig trees and, of course, acacia, tamarisk and date palms. Relief came with pockets of Laperrine olive, lavender, cypresses, artemisia and sage.[82] Several desiccated resurrection plants blew past in the wind, remarkable for their ability to uncurl and bloom at the slightest rain. In the evening, I saw mole rats and lizards, and a line of silver armoured ants that can survive for just ten minutes in the midday sun before being boiled alive. In the distance, some gazelle, too far to shoot, and, once, three zebra, but that may have been a trick of the light. Icho proved a master with the sling-shot and twice we had rabbit.

I wish I was better with my birds. I recognised a royal pigeon, vultures, eagles and some small black birds with white heads, which Asso called *tablkhirt* and said they brought good luck. Darwin noted that with some birds, a mother will abandon her fledglings in the nest rather than be left behind on the long migration south.[83]

Lahcen would sense when a full sandstorm was coming; twice they lasted for three days and were relentless. The hot wind filled the space between earth and sky with whipping grit and blew our robes into weird shapes. Our trail disappeared within seconds. The dryness burned my nostrils and I was glad of my veil which reduced the glare and conserved the breath's moisture, acting like an air-conditioning plant. The veil also helped keep out evil spirits that would make the nostrils bleed. Black stone was ground into powder, damped and painted on our eyes with a thorn stick, acting as mascara to keep out the worst, yet sand filled our nostrils, ears and hair. Hot wind won't let you sleep. We ate sand, but we were more or less clean because of the abrasion to the skin. Everything was clean, even our dishes. The Sahara is the only land where you don't need to bathe, but you do need help combing out the lice. Bashō travelled with me:

> Red, red is the sun,
> Heartlessly indifferent to time,
> The wind knows, however,
> The promise of early chill.[84]

For camp, we would look for an open rocky area, perhaps with a grove of trees. Our sole imperative was to save water. The worst moments were those spent digging out the wells, an operation that once took a whole day. Suffering from thirst beside a well is a true misery. After much back-breaking work, a well might be dry, or contain just a few inches of muddy water. The hole might be deep with no bucket or rope or so full of foulness as to make one shudder. Small pools were idyllically set among golden dunes, shaded by date palms. However, the water was often covered with a thick green scum, peppered with animal droppings, and containing the bodies of dead camels which had fallen in and drowned when the sand banks collapsed. We dug holes a respectful distance from these pools. Those who drank the polluted and sulfuric water were plagued by stomach disorders and sometimes died.

Night after night, we pitch camp under a moon that rises later each time. At sunset, the precise, curved shadow of the earth rises into it swiftly from the horizon, cutting it into a light section and a dark section. Once it eventually vanishes, the sky is liberated and in the darkness becomes violent. Venus is the first to herald the deluge of lights. When all daylight is gone, and the space is thick with stars, it is still of an immense and burning blue, darkest directly overhead and paling towards the earth, so that the night never really grows dark. You stand, and stay standing, and let something very peculiar happen to you, something that everyone who lives there has undergone and which the French call le baptême de la solitude. *It is a unique sensation, and it has nothing to do with loneliness. Here every memory disappears, nothing is left but your own breathing and the sound of your heart beating. A strange and by no means pleasant process of reintegration begins inside you and you have the choice of fighting against it, and insisting on remaining the person you have always been, or letting it take its course.*[85]

Darkness was falling. I scanned the landscape for the fire of our encampment at the foot of a cliff. During a toilet excursion I had been attracted to the eerie shape of a wind-swept pillar. On my way back, I realised I was lost, everything confused among the black volcanic rock.

Spurs and gullies were traps. The Sahara is not the place for this kind of loneliness. There is no false security; panic waits at the next corner. I retraced my steps to find where I had gone wrong in the hope of evading a lonely, freezing night. It took me two hours to get back to good-natured teasing and comforting tea.

Icho reminded me that it was my turn to tell a story. For a change, I read from one of the books I carried, *The Last Storytellers* by Richard Hamilton, whom I had met briefly over mint tea at *the Café de la Poste*. Hamilton immersed himself in the disappearing old men, the *hlaykia*, at the *Djemaa* and captured the public part of their lives because 'when a storyteller dies, a whole library burns'.

One of the pleasures of storytelling amongst the Berbers is the respect and lack of interruption. There are many deep sighs, supportive cluckings, little hand claps, but these show sympathy for an argument or emotional agreement. Since the *hlaykia* had to compete for audiences, their methods of attracting listeners could be ingenious. One would lift a donkey into the air. As the animal began to complain, people came running. 'You fools,' he shouted. 'When I talk about the *Qur'an* nobody listens, but all of you rush to listen to a donkey.' Another narrator seeing the crowd diminish yelled, 'All those cursed by their parents must leave now.'

I reminded my little family of the best-known story of all, *Scheherazade*, and told them that Abdessalam el Hakouni, professor of literature in Rabat, claimed the tale was itself a parable about the power of storytelling. The moral is that one should not yield to tyranny. One should use imagination, be calm and think of love rather than hate, hope rather than despair. If *Scheherazade* could save her neck for one thousand and one nights, that would be long enough for the king to forget his vengeance. But the key was not a physical weapon. *Scheherazade* had nothing except good stories to tell and the ability to tell them well. In the end, almost everything is a story. The lesson was that, if you want to survive, you need good stories.

Another night, the three Berbers sat by the fire and tested their position using their silver pendants aligned to the South Star. They agreed that we were to the east of Adrar which itself was on a well-travelled route. Lahcen and Asso would go in alone for water. I should not be seen.

Lahcen told the story of the red lantern, a favourite. Kadour, a poor sweet seller in Marrakech ran out of money to buy honey for his wares. Rather than starve, he decided to quit the city and seek his fortune taking with him his only possession, a common small tin lantern with red glass. He crossed the snowy passes of the Atlas Mountains surviving on the hospitality of the Berber shepherds until he came to a remote town in a lush valley. He was taken to the Pasha where he was treated with great kindness for three days. As a thank-you, Kadour left his lantern. To the Pasha, this gift was above value, for the city had never seen glass. In return, the Pasha gave Kadour three camel loads of jewels and he returned to Marrakech a rich man. Kadour's brother, Said, a successful merchant, was jealous of Kadour's wealth and demanded to know how he had come by his fortune. Said decided to copy his brother's journey, amassed his merchandise, but was robbed while in the mountains. By the time Said reached the Pasha's town, all he had left was an old, damaged brass watch. In turn, the watch was given to the Pasha who valued it above all things. What gift was great enough to give Said in return? The Pasha had brought from a cabinet in the treasury his second most valued possession, the red-glass lantern.

The early hours were freezing, but there was no one to hear my complaints and take pity. I snuggled deeper into my burnoose. Was it just illusion, hope maybe, that I was trying to hang onto now? What kept me going? Soon, I would leave my new friends and have no one to share with. I knew where I wanted to go for a new beginning, a chance to read, to listen, to explore, to take up a new project, a new fascination. Of course, I was travelling in the wrong direction, but at least I was moving and would soon have control of my path. So very few people could make it alone. Inshallah.

PART 3: WRITTEN BY DR ADERFI HASNOUNI, TAMEGROUTE, MOROCCO (MAY 2019)

I'm sure I neither know nor care;
But this I know, and this I feel,
As onward to the tomb I steal,
That still as death approaches nearer,
The joys of life are sweeter, dearer;
And had I but an hour to live,
That little hour to bliss I'd give.[86]

I have always wanted to write a book about my people, the Berbers of the western Atlas. What with my studies and my medical work I never found the time or, frankly, a suitable plot. I never thought that when I found a story that I would write it in English and I have had to ask friends for help to do this. I have talked with Lahcen and Icho and members of their family and I understand what happened. I think I have the right to finish Amkssa's story and to do him justice. People from Europe will never understand what Feep meant to us, what he did for us. He changed our lives and he was a legend who will always live beside our camp-fires as we eat our sand-baked bread and cradle our guns.

The group left Algeria and entered Mali south of Taoudenni, the hottest region on the planet, just over 400 miles and a week or so from Timbuktu. Taoudenni was a feared place full of evil *djnoun* where salt was dug from the bottom of an ancient lake and cut into slabs for transportation. This unfixed place crept across the dry bed stripping wealth as it went. The managers were notorious for theft and brutality. There was no town, no shops.

Here, Amkssa fell badly ill with diarrhoea. Lahcen recognised the blackness of his discharges and was prepared for him to die as it was a meandering, burning journey to Timbuktu. Lahcen set up camp amid volcanic cones and waited for two days while the water supplies fell dangerously low. There was only cumin for medicine which Amkssa was given freely. Mostly, he was delirious and often shouted that he was running into darkness.

Lahcen knew of old wells at *Oued Teli*, perhaps a day's journey, and he gave Asso detailed instructions on how to find them. Should the first be dry, there was a second well to the north along a river-bed which had not seen water in living memory. Each would need digging out.

After two days, Asso had not returned. Amkssa was near death. A first camel slumped to the ground and Lahcen stabbed the dying beast in the jugular vein at the base of the neck and then drew the blade across its throat and went to work on the flesh – the hump, the neck, the lights and the large muscles of the thighs. They ate the jelly-like fat of the hump and the liver raw, spiced by the sour-juice from the camel's gall-bladder, the 'desert lemon'. The rest they cut into strips and hung them to dry in the shade of thorn-scrub. Amkssa sucked for a while on the hump-fat and then threw it up. Camels hold water in the tissues of three stomachs, a more efficient system than storing it in the plasma of the blood as humans do. Threatened with death by thirst, the men drank the liquid from the dead camel's stomachs. As a last resort, Lahcen showed Icho how to push a stick down a camel's throat to make it vomit so that they could drink the nauseating mess.

On the third day, Icho decided to search for his father. He ignored his grandfather's objection and set off with two camels following the trail in the sand. Icho came to the dry well that his father had dug to a depth of two metres, which, in the heat, would have drained him. Icho went on to the second small oasis along the long-dried river scour. Here, Asso's digging had been successful and Icho soaked his *shesh* in the water and sucked the moisture through the cloth. The camels were less fussy. Icho found some colocynth melons growing nearby, desert succulents of the squash family with gourds as large as oranges. The pulp was bitter and caused stomach-cramps. He then ate the flowers and chewed the water-filled roots. As he sat, he sling-shot a desert hare and then saw a fennec fox and dug it out of its burrow and strangled it. The animals had little meat on them, but he ate half, cooking it on stones baked in the sun and then hung the rest on the back of his saddle to dry.

Icho struck out across the plateau on a triangular path back to the camp. After a few hours, he saw circling eagles and an occasional rising vulture. He dismounted to give relief to his camels in the high sun, but kept going through the hottest part of the day.

Icho thought Asso had walked too close to an acacia bush and a snake had struck from its shade, without warning. His father's face was darkened with the poison and the skin had a yellow tinge. Icho felt for a pulse, held a mirror to his lips, but sensed nothing. The body was warm from the sun. To make sure, Icho found the stone black area of skin on his father's leg where the snake had struck and cut deep with his knife so that he could suck out the pus. He realised that Asso had tried to do this himself for his knife lay close to his right hand. The birds had started to peck around the eyes. It was all of no use. Asso would have taken a few hours to die with great pain towards the end.

It was then that Icho saw the torza tree, the antidote to the venom, deadly to goats. Milk-sap taken from the apple-like fruit and placed on the bite draws out the poison. Under the tree was a coiled horned viper, camouflaged by its sand-blotched skin. Icho killed it with his stick. He cut off its head to make into powder to mix with ground thunderstone and baobab pith to take home. His mother would know that his father was avenged and wear the remembrance in an amulet. Icho stripped the snake flesh to eat later and travelled back to camp.

Grandfather and son returned with *Tamount* to the body where they argued whether to wash it. This the boy wanted to do, but Lahcen was worried about their water supply. They agreed to use a little water to wash the face and hands and to dry-stone the rest. The body was stripped of all belongings, especially the gun, knife and personal items, now Icho's property. He would take his father's turban to his mother for her memory and so that, in the deep of the night, she could take it from under her pillow and smell it and bring her husband back to her. A grave was dug facing sunrise and deep enough for a half metre covering. *Tamount* sat all the while at Asso's feet and cried for his friend and protector. Pointed stones were placed over the head and the feet so that those who followed would know that a devout Berber's body lay there who was deserving of respect.

Lahcen started and pointed at three sizeable black stones on the ground. Meteorites. This was why Asso had stopped and, perhaps, trodden on the viper, a snake that would otherwise have likely left him alone.

'This is a gift from Asso and from Allah,' said Lahcen, stooping to pick up one of the shiny rocks. 'He died for his family's future.'

Asso's father and son prayed together and then silently rose and rode back. Amkssa was severely dehydrated, but lucid enough to hear the news. Icho placed his father's silver navigational pendant around Amkssa's neck where it nestled with its Berber fellows. He was also given his share of the three meteorites to hold.

'I want to give you freedom from your promise to me to take me to Timbuktu,' Amkssa said. 'I am going to die anyway with a whimper. I have told my soul to be still and to wait without hope. You have suffered a deep loss. If you feel that it is right to return then I support your decision.'

Lahcen was a broken man and sat without moving clutching a shiny meteorite, his dreams shattered. It was left to Icho to answer.

'My father is with Allah,' he replied, searching for the right words, 'and he watches over us. Inshallah, we will reach Timbuktu even though you will die on the way. My grandfather welcomes the respect in your offer. However, we have no choice but to complete my father's contract with you. And, even if I did have a choice, I would do no different. We are bound together.'

Nothing more was said. In the morning, Amkssa, a desiccated hulk, was tied to his saddle and given a piece of viper to try to chew. Just as the sun first cracked across the horizon, all were mounted, Icho leading.

That afternoon, they met a band of surly Tuareg, the blue men of the desert. They were dressed in flowing black robes, indigo smeared on the face against the sun, their heads swathed in a *litham*, four yards long, of Sudanese cloth sewn together. Only their eyes were visible. Their saddles were decorated with the cross leading some to conclude that the Tuareg were heretics driven into the wilderness by the Arabs. The Arabs sometimes called them the 'Christians of the desert'; 'Tuareg' meant 'abandoned of God' or 'lost souls'. These Tuareg called themselves the 'People of the Veil', *Kel Tagelmoust*, and the *Imochagh*, 'the free ones'. In reality, most were ruthless brigands. Their verb, *iohagh*, means both 'he is free' and 'he pillages'.

Icho had strayed into a squabble between two tribes over water rights. He rode forward, told the men his story, threatened to fight if necessary, and after handing over some money, negotiated a safe path.

Kahina, Asso's wife, as every early evening, climbed to the roof of her home on the outskirts of Tamegroute and searched slowly several kilometres up the river-bed through the rocks and gorges of the Drãa Valley for her husband's return. This time, she glimpsed a desert-weary train of moving shapes tied head to tail. There were not eight animals, but fourteen, and they were laden. *Tamount* brought up the rear, stopping from time to time to look behind him. The men had made Timbuktu and conducted satisfactory trade. Worries about money, about food, clothes, and, perhaps, the education of her four younger children were over for several years.

The foreigner was not there. Had he been delivered safely? A coldness crept over Kahina as she realised that there were only two riders. It was her son, Icho, who sat perched on the lead algham, seeming taller in the saddle, more resolute; her father-in-law, Lahcen was half-way down the line, his posture less confident, older. Asso was not there, not being carried, not walking.

The truth reached into her. She began to wail. Her cries reached the valley walls as they migrated from despair to a terrible loneliness. Sisters, mothers, daughters joined Kahina and the volume intensified, the sorrow pushing into every crevice. Women from the extended family left their tasks in the fields, potteries and mud huts and swelled the lament which pushed upwards towards the whole blue sky.

PUBLISHER'S STATEMENT, JULY 2019

A short while after we began work on Dr Heal's narrative, a statement arrived by email from Dr Aderfi Hasnouni, who plays an important part in the story. Essentially, this was a file of the only known picture of Heal, his last written words and an addendum by Hasnouni detailing his own investigations. The picture is included in this book and the written material at the end of Chapter Fourteen. Hasnouni also sent us a quote, reproduced at the end of this statement, which we have identified as from Andrew Keen's *How to Fix the Future*, a book carried into the Sahara by Heal. It may prove a suitable epitaph.

Hasnouni believes he has concluded his obligations to Heal, has refused to answer our supplementary questions, and has broken contact with us.

Under an *in camera* court order, two parcels of fifty copies each of *Disappearing* before the cover was added were despatched to confidential addresses in London and Brussels. The UK Home Office compiled a file on *Disappearing* in order for UK ministers to decide whether to try to suppress publication. Parts of the file were leaked to the *Daily Telegraph* by an undisclosed mole. The Government refused to comment. Extracts from the leak are printed on the back cover. Names of the individuals quoted have been redacted.

No censorship has been ordered, but we have received a number of enquiries, direct and indirect, from security organisations in the UK and elsewhere, and from private individuals, asking for details of Heal's whereabouts. Our reply is always the same. We believe that Heal is dead and that his body is lost in the Sahara.

Readers may like to know that under our Agreement, Heal's fifty per cent of the profits, will be donated to organisations dedicated to exposing threats to privacy and freedom.

The future, it seems, is broken. We are caught between the operating systems of two quite different civilisations. Our old twentieth-century system doesn't work anymore, but its replacement, a supposedly upgraded twenty-first-century version, isn't functioning properly either. The signs of this predicament are all around us: the withering of the industrial economy, a deepening inequality between rich and poor, persistent unemployment, a fin-de-siècle cultural malaise, the unravelling of post-Cold War international alliances, the decline of mainstream media, the dwindling of trust in traditional institutions, the redundancy of traditional political ideologies, an epistemological crisis about what constitutes 'truth', and a raging populist revolt against the establishment. And while we are all too familiar with what is broken, we don't seem to know how we can get anything to work anymore.

Chattaway & Spottiswood
Taunton
July 2019

READING LIST

Acton, Thomas, *Gypsy politics and Traveller identity*, 1999

Aeschylus, Vellacott, Philip, *Prometheus Bound and Other Plays*, c. 463 BC

Anacreon, *The Odes of Anacreon*, c. 450 BC (1846)

Ascherson, Neal, *Black Sea*, 1996

Asher, Michael, *Impossible Journey*, 1989, *Death in the Sahara*, 2008

Bartlett, Jamie, *The Dark Net*, 2013; *The People Vs Tech*, 2018

Bisseul, Captain H, *Les Touareg de L'Ouest*, 1888

Bodley, R V C, *The Soundless Sahara*, 1968

Borrow, George, *The Zincali*, 1841, *Lavengro*, 1851

Bourseiller, Philippe, *Call of the Desert*, 2004

Bowles, Paul, *The Sheltering Sky*, 1949; *The Spider's House*, 1955; *Days, a Tangier Diary*, 1991; *Travels*, 2010

Brett, Michael and Fentress, Elizabeth, *The Berbers: The Peoples of Africa*, 1997

Briggs, Lloyd Cabot, *Tribes of the Sahara*, 1960

Brown, Hamish, *The Mountains Look on Marrakech*, 2007

Byrne, Tony, *Airlift to Biafra*, 1970

Campbell, Joseph, *The Hero with a Thousand Faces*, 2008

Carroll, Lewis, *The Hunting of the Snark*, 1874-1876

Cervantes, Miguel, *Don Quixote*, 1605-15

Chatwin, Bruce, *The Viceroy of Ouidah*, 1980; *The Songlines*, 1988; *What Am I doing Here*, 1989

Draper, Michael I, *Shadows, Airlift and Airwar in Biafra and Nigeria*, 1999

Eliot, T S, *The Waste Land and other Poems*, 1940; *Four Quartets*, 1944.

Englebert, Victor, *Wind, sand, and silence*, 1992

Fester, Uncle, *Home Workshop Explosives*, 1990

Flanagan, Richard, *The Unknown Terrorist*, 2006; *First Person*, 2017

Forsyth, Frederick, *The Biafra Story*, 1969; *The Day of the Jackal*, 1971; *The Dogs of War*, 1974; *Emeka*, 1982; *The Fourth Protocol*, 1984; *The Outsider*, 2016

Gardner, Brian, *The Quest for Timbuctoo*, 1969

Goldberg, K Meira, Bennahum, Ninotchka Devorah, and Hayes, Michelle Heffner, *Flamenco on the Global Stage*, 2015

Grossmith, George & Weedon, *Diary of a Nobody*, 1892

Haleem, M A S Abdel, *The Qur'an*, 2010

Hamilton, Richard, *The Last Storytellers*, 2013

Hancock, Ian, *We are the Romani people*, 2017

Harris, Walter, *Morocco That Was*, 1921

Harari, Yuval Noah, *Homo Deus*, 2016

Hartog, Francois, *The Mirror of Herodotus*, 1988

Herodotus, *The Histories*, c. 450 BC

Herron, Samantha, *The Djinn in the Skull*, 2015

Highsmith, Patricia, *The Talented Mr Ripley*, 1955; *Ripley Under Ground*, 1970; *Ripley's Game*, 1974; *The Boy who Followed Ripley*, 1980; *Ripley Under Water*, 1991

Hughes-Wilson, John, *On Intelligence*, 2016

International Monetary Fund, 'Remittance Senders and Receivers: Tracking the Transnational Channels', 2003

Jorre, John de St, *The Brothers' War, Biafra and Nigeria*, 1972

Kant, Immanuel, *Kant's Critiques*, 1787

Kaplan, Philip, *Legend, A Celebration of the DC-3*, 2009

Keen, Andrew, *How to Fix the Future*, 2018

Keenan, Jeremy, *The Tuareg, People of Ahaggar*, 1977

Keita, Lt Colonel Kalifa, and Henk, Colonel Dan, 'Conflict and Conflict Resolution in the Sahel: The Tuareg Insurgency in Mali', *US Army War College*, 1998

Kradin, Nikolay N, 'Nomadism, Evolution, and World-Systems', *Journal of World-Systems Research*, 2002

Kradin, Nikolay N, Bondarenko, Dmitri M, and Barfield, Thomas J, *Nomadic Pathways in Social Evolution*, Russian Academy of Sciences, 2003

Landau, Rom, *Invitation to Morocco*, 1950

Langewiesche, William, *Sahara Unveiled, A Journey Across the Desert*, 1996

Lanier, Jaron, *Ten Arguments For Deleting Your Social Media Accounts*, 2018

Leblon, Bernard, *The emergence of the art of flamenco in Andalusia*, 2003

Lhote, Henri, *The Search for the Tassili Frescoes*, 1959; *Les Touaregs du Hoggar*, 1984

Maçães, Bruno, *The Dawn of Eurasia*, 2018

McDowell, Bart, *Gypsies: Wanderers of the World*, National Geographic Society, 1970

Mandelstam, Osip, *Tristia*, 1920

Matras, Yaron, *I Met Lucky People, The Story of the Romani Gypsies*, 2014

Maxwell, Gavin, *Lords of the Atlas*, 1966

Mayne, Peter, *A Year in Marrakesh*, 1953

Millar, Peter, *Marrakech Express*, 2014

Morris, Desmond, *The Naked Ape*, 1967

O'Neil, Cathy, *Weapons of Math Destruction*, 2016

Pohren, D E, *A Way of Life*, 1980

Porch, Douglas, *The Conquest of the Sahara*, 1984; *The Conquest of Morocco*, 1982

Rolle, Renate, *The World of the Scythians*, 1980

Schwartz, Walter, *Nigeria*, 1968

Shakespeare, Nicholas, *Bruce Chatwin*, 2000

Theroux, Paul, *The Pillars of Hercules*, 1995

Toynbee, Arnold, *Mankind and Mother Earth*, 1978

US Department of the Treasury and Interpol, 'The Hawala Alternative Remittance System and its Role in Money Laundering', 1999

Vaknin, Sam, *Hawala, or the Bank that Never Was*, 2005

Varoufakis, Yanis, *Adults in the Room*, 2017

Venter, Al J, *Biafra's War 1967–1970*, 2015

Vinci, Leonardo da, *The Notebooks of Leonardo da Vinci*, 2003 & 2018

Walther, Ingo F, *Van Gogh 1853–1890, Vision and Reality*, 1993

Wharton, Edith, *In Morocco*, 1920

Windo, Pamela, *Zohra's Ladder and Other Moroccan Tales*, 2005

Yuasa, Nobuyuki, *Matsuo Bashō, The Narrow Road to the Deep North*, 1966

ENDNOTES

1 Eliot, *Waste Land*, 315–18.
2 Borrow, *Lavengro*.
3 Shakespeare, *Chatwin*.
4 Burton, *The Anatomy of Melancholy*.
5 Kipling, *Letters of Travel*.
6 *British European Airways* and the *British Overseas Airways Corporation*.
7 Eliot, *Waste Land*, 20-24.
8 Richardson, *Bristol, Africa*, Vol. 2.
9 *The Spectator*, 31/5/1968.
10 Eliot, *Waste Land*, 366–70.
11 To refresh my memory, I have quoted freely from a description of a similar flight made at that time by *Observer* journalist John de St Jorre and described in his book, *The Brothers' War*. It may even have been the same flight.
12 After the war, Forsyth's anger spilled over, particularly into three books which I have used liberally to recapture our first conversation: *Biafra Story*, 1969; *Emeka*, 1982; and *Outsider*, 2016. He also provided regular assistance to other books on the war like Draper, *Shadows*, 1999, and Venter, *Biafra's War*, 2015. Author de St Jorre noted, decades after that war, that 'you only have to spend a short while with Freddie Forsyth before he lets loose - sometimes vituperatively'. Forsyth took strong issue against the role of the supposedly neutral BBC, especially its external service, which became a powerful pro-Nigerian and anti-Biafran lobbying medium. Editorial comments were liberally infused, he insisted, into what were supposed to be factual news reports.
13 Schwarz, *Nigeria*.
14 Heal, *Sound of Hunger*.
15 Blanton, *Mental and Nervous Changes*.
16 Eliot, *Waste Land*, 307-311.
17 'Fine, fine.'
18 'Uncle, would you like tea?'
19 Landau, *Invitation to Morocco*.
20 Eliot, *Love Song of J Alfred Prufrock*.
21 Compagnies Républicaines de Sécurité (CRS) are the general reserve of the French National Police. They are primarily involved in country-wide security, but are best known for riot control. The CRS were infamous in their brutal putting down of student riots in 1968.
22 Bartlett, *Dark Web, People Vs Tech*.
23 Eliot, *Waste Land*, 52–56.
24 Heal, *Sound of Hunger*.
25 Lanier, *Ten Arguments*.
26 O'Neil, *Weapons of Math Destruction*.
27 *Daily Telegraph*, 20/8/2018.
28 Bartlett, *The People*.

29 Carlo, *Big Brother Watch*, 21/3/2018.

30 Eliot, *Waste Land*, 179–83.

31 Parking Eye v Beavis, 4/11/2015 (UKSC 67).

32 *Daily Telegraph*, 7/11/2017.

33 Child, *Jack Reacher* novels. Also, Leith interview, *Spectator*, 1/12/2018.

34 Larkin, 'Poetry of Departures'.

35 Vaknin, *Hawala, or the Bank that Never Was*; *IMF*, 'Informal Fund Transfer Systems'; *MIF*, 'Remittance Senders and Receivers'; *US Treasury & Interpol*, 'Hawala Alternative Remittance System'.

36 Eliot, *Waste Land*, 331–35.

37 Eliot, *Love Song of J Alfred Prufrock*.

38 Camellia *sasanqua* is a species native to Japan. Bashō, *The Records of a Travel-worn Satchel*.

39 Aeschylus, *Prometheus Bound*.

40 Ascherson, *Black Sea*. Also, Rolle, *World of the Scythians*; Kohl, *Reisen in Südrußland*.

41 Toynbee, *Mankind and Mother Earth*.

42 Herodotus, *Histories*.

43 What an appalling sight! They are doing this themselves! So many palaces! What extraordinary strength of mind! What men! They are Scythians!

44 Moore, *Anacreon*.

45 Mandelstam, *Tristia*.

46 'Ease their way into their new life and deliver them from their bonds of sorrow.'

47 There are other Romani and Sinti holocaust memorials including in Berlin, Buchenwald, Budapest (Hungary), Lety (Czech Republic), Munich, New York (USA) and at Ravensbrück.

48 Chatwin, *Songlines*.

49 Eliot, *Gerontion*.

50 Eliot, *Love Song of J Alfred Prufrock*.

51 *The Spectator*, 15/12/2018.

52 Acton, *Gypsy politics*; Hancock. *Romani People*; Leblon, *Gypsies and Flamenco*; Matras, *Lucky People*; McDowell, *Gypsies*; and Pohren, *Way of Life*.

53 Bashō, *The Narrow Road to the Deep North*.

54 Eliot, *Waste Land*, 71–75.

55 O'Neil, *Weapons of Math Destruction*.

56 Eliot, *Waste Land*, 359–63.

57 Ascherson, *Black Sea*.

58 Landau, *Invitation to Morocco*.

59 Hamilton, *Last Storytellers*.

60 Harari, *Homo Deus*.

61 Maxwell, *Lords of the Atlas*.

62 Mayne, *Year in Marrakesh*.

63 Bourseiller, *Call of the Desert*.

64 Maxwell, *Lords of the Atlas*.

65 Dostoevsky, 'The Grand Inquisitor', *The Brothers Karamazov*.

66 Bowles, *Travels*.

67 Fester, *Home Workshop Explosives*.

68 Carroll, 'Fit the Eighth: The Vanishing', *Hunting of the Snark*,

69 Windo, *Zohra's Ladder*.

70 Eliot, *Waste Land*, 340–45.

71 Windo, *Zohra's Ladder*.

72 Bourseiller, *Call of the Desert*.

73 Asher, *Death in the Sahara*.

74 Bourseiller, *Call of the Desert*.

75 Bowles, *Travels*.

76 Hamilton, *Last Storytellers*.

77 Porch, *Conquest*.

78 Porch, *Conquest*.

79 Asher, *Death in the Sahara*.

80 Bourseiller, *Call of the Desert*.

81 Lhote, *Tassili Frescoes*.

82 Bourseiller, *Call of the Desert*.

83 Darwin, *On the Origin of the Species*.

84 Bashō, *The Narrow Road to the Deep North*.

85 Bowles, *Travels*.

86 Moore, 'Ode VII', *Anacreon*.

ALSO BY CHRIS HEAL

978-1-911604-41-19. Hardback • 768 pages • 234 x 155 mm
100 B&W illustrations, 12 colour maps • June 2018

Just before throwing off his identity and embracing a nomadic life, Chris Heal published in 2018 an applauded social history of two brothers, u-boat commanders in WWI. He examined their lives and careers against the politics and culture of their day. Applauded that is, until the BBC encouraged him in a radio book programme to explain his views on the European Union and Germany's modern-day role in running the continent. Then the roof fell in.

Plaudits for Sound of Hunger

The depth and breadth of this book is staggering. You would have to read a dozen others to get anywhere close to what's given you. The author wants you to know that WW1 was not won by the titanic slaughters, but by the slow starvation of the civilian populations of Germany and Austria. This is mature erudition from a man of three score and five who has produced a magnum opus to which I say, 'Bravo, Sir.' This is the kind of book I love because as soon as you finish it you start reading it again to see what you missed and enjoy it all over again.

Jack V Sturiano

This handsomely produced volume will be recognised as a distinctive and valuable con-tribution to the history of the First World War. Its author has been very careful in his re-search and shows both commendable levels of objectivity combined with real imaginative sympathy for his subjects. This is gripping stuff and should not disappoint its audiences. Four years into the publishing jamboree that is the War's centenary, here is a title that stands out and deserves its place on (and one hopes frequently off) the shelf.

Dr Richard Sheldon

Chris Heal's writing is densely packed with a wide variety of subject matter that flows thick and fast, but it rewards the reader with a deeper understanding of this critical pe-riod in German and European history. It covers events that are usually recounted at the national and international geopolitical level. It is much rarer to have a social, family and personal viewpoint and that is why Sound of Hunger *makes a valuable contribution to the current literature.*

Dr John Greenacre

A major contribution to WWI military history ... excellent work ... the author writes extremely well and his style is both lucid and engaging ... such a scholarly source book is a welcome addition to my bookshelf ... an objective, dispassionate foreigner's view of German history.

Col John Hughes-Wilson